Critical Muslim 56

Journalism

Editor: Ziauddin Sardar

Deputy Editors: Robin Yassin-Kassab, C Scott Jordan, Zafar Malik,

Senior Editors: Aamer Hussein, Hassan Mahamdallie, Ebrahim Moosa

Reviews Editor: Alev Adil, Shamim Miah

Poetry and Fiction Editor: Naomi Foyle

Publisher: Michael Dwyer

Managing Editor (Hurst Publishers): Daisy Leitch

Cover Design: Rob Pinney based on an original design by Fatima Jamadar

Associate Editors: Tahir Abbas, Abdelwahab El-Affendi, Naomi Foyle, Marilyn Hacker, Nader Hashemi, Jeremy Henzell Thomas, Leyla Jagiella, Vinay Lal, Iftikhar Malik, Peter Mandaville, Boyd Tonkin, Medina Whiteman

International Advisory Board: Karen Armstrong, Christopher de Bellaigue, William Dalrymple, Syed Nomanul Haq, Anwar Ibrahim, Bruce Lawrence, Ashis Nandy, Ruth Padel, Bhikhu Parekh, Barnaby Rogerson, Malise Ruthven

Critical Muslim is published quarterly by C. Hurst & Co. (Publishers) Ltd. on behalf of and in conjunction with Critical Muslim Ltd. and the Muslim Institute, London.

All editorial correspondence to: editorial@criticalmuslim.com

The editors do not necessarily agree with the opinions expressed by the contributors. We reserve the right to make such editorial changes as may be necessary to make submissions to *Critical Muslim* suitable for publication.

© Copyright 2025 *Critical Muslim* and the individual contributors.

All rights reserved.

C. Hurst & Co (Publishers) Ltd., New Wing, Somerset House, Strand, London, WC2R 1LA

ISBN:9781805264361 ISSN: 2048-8475

To subscribe or place an order by credit/debit card or cheque (pounds sterling only) please contact Kathleen May at the Hurst address above or e-mail kathleen@hurstpub.co.uk

A one-year subscription, inclusive of postage (four issues), costs £60 (UK), £90 (Europe) and £100 (rest of the world), this includes full access to the *Critical Muslim* series and archive online. Digital only subscription is £3.30 per month.

The right of Ziauddin Sardar and the Contributors to be identified as the authors of this publication is asserted by them in accordance with the Copyright, Designs and Patents Act, 1988.

A Cataloguing-in-Publication data record for this book is available from the British Library.

EU GPSR Authorised Representative
Easy Access System Europe Oü, 16879218
Address: Mustamäe tee 50, 10621, Tallinn, Estonia
Contact Details: gpsr.requests@easproject.com, +358 40 500 3575

Critical Muslim

Subscribe to Critical Muslim

Now in its fourteenth year in print, *Critical Muslim* is also available online. Users can access the site for just £3.30 per month — or for those with a print subscription it is included as part of the package. In return, you'll get access to everything in the series (including our entire archive), and a clean, accessible reading experience for desktop computers and handheld devices — entirely free of advertising.

Full subscription

The print edition of *Critical Muslim* is published quarterly in January, April, July and October. As a subscriber to the print edition, you'll receive new issues directly to your door, as well as full access to our digital archive.

United Kingdom £60/year
Europe £90/year
Rest of the World £100/year

Digital Only

Immediate online access to *Critical Muslim*

Browse the full *Critical Muslim* archive

Cancel any time

£3.30 per month

www.criticalmuslim.io

CM56

AUTUMN 2025

CONTENTS

JOURNALISM

Al-Jazeera journalist, Mohammad Salama, killed by Israeli attacks on Nasser Hospital on 25 August 2025.
Photo: Al-Jazeera

Ziauddin Sardar	INTRODUCTION: THIS *IS* THE BBC	3
Andrew Brown	RETURN TO COCKBURN	27
Shiv Visvanathan	DEMOCRACY AND INDIAN JOURNALISM	35
Eric Walberg	MY DIGITAL MEDIA LIFE	45
Muhammad Saad	COVERING THE FLOODS	56
Josef Linnhoff	ASAD'S *UNROMANTIC ORIENT*	67
Robin Yassin-Kassab	THE SUWAYDA MASSACRES	81
Saoussen Ben Cheikh	WORKING FOR ALTERNATIVES	99

Boyd Tonkin	HRANT DINK – THE JOURNALIST AS MARTYR	109
James Brooks	SYSTEM FAILURE	122
C Scott Jordan	JOURNALISM HAS FUTURES	136

ART AND LETTERS

Abdullah Geelah	REDESIGNING MOSQUES	151
Ibrahim N Abusharif	SHORT STORY: JAMEEL'S TREE	165
Hamida Riahi	SHORT STORY: 'I MARRY YOU MYSELF'	174
Wietske Merison	FOUR POEMS	177
Saba Zahoor	THREE POEMS	183

REVIEWS

Shamim Miah	RECONSIDER, REEVALUATE, REIMAGINE	189
Zain Sardar	GOOD JOURNALISM	197
Leila Sansour	MORAL AMNESIA	206
Yahia Lababidi	SPIRITUAL JOURNALIST	213
Khuda Bushq	DEMONISING MAMDANI	219

ET CETERA

M Yaqub Mirza	LAST WORD: ON HALAL INVESTING	229
Barnaby Rogerson	OBITUARY: ROBERT IRWIN	240
The List	A DOZEN MEDIA OUTLETS TO CHECK OUT (DAILY)	258
Citations		265
Contributors		274

JOURNALISM

INTRODUCTION: THIS *IS* THE BBC *by Ziauddin Sardar*
RETURN TO COCKBURN *by Andrew Brown*
DEMOCRACY AND INDIAN JOURNALISM *by Shiv Visvanathan*
MY DIGITAL MEDIA LIFE *by Eric Walberg*
COVERING THE FLOODS *by Muhammad Saad*
ASAD'S *UNROMANTIC ORIENT by Josef Linnhoff*
THE SUWAYDA MASSACRES *by Robin Yassin-Kassab*
WORKING FOR ALTERNATIVES *by Saoussen Ben Cheikh*
HRANT DINK – THE JOURNALIST AS MARTYR *by Boyd Tonkin*
SYSTEM FAILURE *by James Brooks*
JOURNALISM HAS FUTURES *by C Scott Jordan*

Introduction
THIS *IS* THE BBC

Ziauddin Sardar

Mrs Robertson lived two doors from my humble abode in north London. She had one daughter who migrated to Australia. In her early seventies, she lived alone; and survived on her meagre pension. Every now and then, I would go and sit with her and we would talk mostly about her past, her daughter who never rang, and her late husband she missed so much. Occasionally, I would take some *biryani* with me as she loved 'Indian food'. She was a vegetarian, so it had to be a *sabzi biryani*. Every Friday morning, come rain, shine, or snow, I watched her make her way to the post office, knees wobbling and walking unsteadily, to buy BBC licence stamps. She was determined to pay her TV licence, especially after she received a threatening letter from the BBC around the time she turned seventy.

One day, I interrupted her journey. 'Morning Mrs Robertson', I said. 'Morning', she replied. 'Must rush to the post office for my stamps', she said. 'Isn't the BBC awful', I said in misguided sympathy. 'It is giving you so much bother'. 'No, no', she replied. 'No bother at all. I love the BBC. We must ensure its independence. Mustn't we?'. She paused. 'People around the world *love* the BBC', she said emphatically.

'People around the world' included me; and my father. In those days there was such a thing as 'BBC English': establishment Oxbridge accents of the upper-class variety, English heritage pronunciations, which is still recognised standard for broadcasting in English in some corners of the world. My father would urge us to speak BBC English, even though he never could. Neither could I. Having grown up in Hackney, I spoke a mixture of Pakistani and cockney with a deliberate dose of gibberish reminiscent of *Rab C Nesbitt*. My days had a fixed routine. Reading, researching, or writing till 18.55 and then rushing down from the attic, where I did most of my work, to watch the *Channel 4 News*. Then dinner, followed by BBC *Ten O'clock News*. The day ended with *Newsnight*. Then, as now, I considered *Channel 4 News* to be the best programme on terrestrial television, although the departure of Jon Snow has brought its critical level down a couple of notches. *Newsnight* has now degenerated to a superannuated chinwag. BBC News: well that's what we are here to discuss.

The BBC, my father used to say, always uses the correct word for every occasion. Solemn words for solemn occasions. Objective words for controversial issues. Given that words are the medium though which the news is conveyed, reporting truth required the use of truthful words. However, as I soon learned, words – and the news which are attached to them – can be easily weaponised.

Consider *sabzi*. The other half of the biryani that I occasionally delivered to Mrs Robertson.

I have eaten it all my life. It was a staple of my mother's cooking as it was of my late wife's cuisine. In Urdu, Farsi, and Hindi, languages of a couple of billion people, *sabzi* is vegetables. So a book called *Sabzi* would be nothing more than a tome on vegetarian cooking; and a restaurant called 'Sabzi' would be catering mostly to vegetarians. But what if the owner of a chain of delis, a member of the general set 'people', called Kate Attlee, claimed that *sabzi* was her trademark, and the family cookbook, *Sabzi*, by Yasmin Khan, was infringing her trademark? She had two supporters on her side: British law, which allows common words to be trademarked; and the Duchy of Cornwall, the private estate of Prince William, which stood up to defend Attlee, whose husband is the great nephew of the even greater former Prime Minister, Clement Attlee. Of course, the struggle over *sabzi* went online where both sides threw accusations and abuse at each other. Attlee was accused of weaponising cultural identity; Khan of stealing her brand. Bloomsbury, the publishers of *Sabzi*, who also happen to be one of my publishers, rejected any notion that any trademark was infringed. Stalemate. However, I am glad to report, the matter was resolved amicably. Attlee withdrew her claim on *sabzi*, and even wished Khan the very best for her *Sabzi*.

What about 'people'? Both Attlee and Khan are people. In common parlance, people are human beings, and include females as well as males. So, what should we make of 'pregnant *people*'? When the words appeared on the autocue, the BBC newsreader, Martine Croxall, was taken aback.

INTRODUCTION: THIS IS THE BBC

She was telling people to be careful during a heat wave. She raised an eyebrow, grimaced, and offered an alternative: women. Pregnant *women*! That upset the powerful people at the BBC. So she was disciplined. Allegedly, she had violated another word that the Corporation utters *ad infinitum*: impartiality.

'Impartiality', we are told, 'is fundamental to the BBC's purpose and is enshrined in the BBC's charter'. The BBC generously offers a definition: 'It means not favouring one side over another and reflecting all relevant sides of the debate. It means not taking sides, reflecting all relevant strands of public debate and challenging them with consistent rigour'.

Forgive me if I raise more than an eyebrow here!

The Gaza genocide is the defining event of the twenty-first century; just as the Holocaust was for the twentieth century. The Holocaust could not happen without the technology and administrative capability of modernity, as the noted sociologist Zygmunt Bauman has pointed out. The Gaza genocide is a product of our postnormal times, where truth has evaporated and lives are played out on social media. It was live streamed on digital network platforms and media outlets like Al-Jazeera and Al Araby for all the world to witness. So it is an ideal place to see just how 'impartial' the BBC is.

Let's begin with words. For the BBC, Israeli casualties are 'massacres' and Palestinian casualties, if they are actually reported, are just ordinary 'deaths'. Israel targets 'critical sites', while it is handing out collective punishment and grossly violating human rights for all to witness on their mobile phones. Israelis captured by Hamas are 'hostages' but Palestinian detainees, including children held without charge and mercilessly tortured, are 'prisoners'.

When Israel escalates its killings in Gaza, the BBC tells you they are 'pre-emptive strikes', attacks are 'targets', when a threat is made it is simply a 'warning', and it is all carried out in the name of 'Israel's right to self-defence' – repeated ad nauseam. It does not occur to the great minds at the BBC – albeit I am not sure if there are any – that it is the occupied who need defending, not the occupiers who are mercilessly butchering them.

Moreover, Israeli deaths are more significant than those of the Palestinians, because the BBC clearly sees them as lesser 'people'. Indeed, people don't die in Gaza, they die in 'Hamas controlled Gaza'! While interviewing a volunteer medical doctor with Medical Aid for Palestinians, who had just returned from Gaza, about the harrowing conditions in hospital, the cartoonish Croxall asked her about Dr Alaa, a paediatric emergency doctor at Nasser Hospital. While Alaa was treating patients at the hospital, her home was bombed killing nine of her children, their bodies charred and dismembered beyond recognition. Croxall describes this horror simply as 'children who died', as though they died mysteriously and were not brutally murdered by the IDF. In one video that shows Israeli soldiers throwing Palestinians they had murdered from the roof of a building, Croxall suggested that maybe they jumped. In other words, the dead, murdered by the Israelis, got up, went inside the building, climbed a few floors to the roof, and then threw themselves to the ground. Bravo BBC journalism!

The statistics of death and destruction coming from Gaza are cited with a warning that they are provided by the 'Hamas run health ministry' to cast doubt on their accuracy, despite the fact that they have proved to be consistently more accurate than the constant stream of lies – widely recognised as such – peddled by Israel. But how about balancing that, since the BBC is very concerned about 'balance' and 'impartiality', with 'according to the neo-fascist regime in Tel Aviv'? That, of course, would require admission that the Israeli 'regime' – a word that only applies in western journalism to non-western governments because only they can be authoritarian and nasty – has gone totally fascist. But words uttered by Israeli politicians that are clearly of fascistic nature never appear on the BBC. Say from the likes of Itamar Ben-Gvir, Security Minister, who openly admires mass murderer Baruch Goldstein and is a follower of Rabbi Meir Kahane, who the previous Israeli government (I am being generous) suggested was further right of Attila the Hun. Or, Bezalel Smotrich, former Minister of Finance, who denies the very existence of Palestine and its people, and says 'international law does not apply to Jews'. The BBC even neglected to mention the Biblical Amalek reference uttered so clearly by Benjamin Netanyahu! The Amalek were people the Jews were – allegedly, is this the right word to use here? – instructed by God to wipe from the face of the earth. Netanyahu's genocidal statement was targeted at Israeli soldiers from extremist communities who read the Bible as literal truth. It was permission to commit genocide.

INTRODUCTION: THIS IS THE BBC

Genocide is a word the BBC hates most. Its newsreaders have systematically shut down the mention of the word by interviewees hundreds of times. Sometime even taking them off the air at the very mention of the word. In an interview with a Palestinian journalist, Croxall – the very same; she is quite shameless – asked: 'you just used the word genocide?...Are you really using that *word*?' In another interview, she says I have to say that 'Israel denies that (ie genocide), they say they were in pursuit of terrorists'. Whenever the dreaded word is mentioned, the newsreaders suggest it is not widely accepted.

Yes: it is not accepted by the US administration, and the UK, France, and Germany, the chief allies of Israel. But it is universally accepted by rest of the 'people around the world'. And since, 'BBC World' is broadcasting to the world, it should, at the very least acknowledge what the rest of the world is openly, permanently, constantly, loudly, describing as genocide in Gaza. That includes the UN and its agencies. And it includes International Association of Genocide Scholars, Physicians for Human Rights, Amnesty International, Doctors Without Borders, the European Center for Constitutional and Human Rights, Human Rights Watch, the International Federation for Human Rights, the Lemkin Institute for Genocide Prevention, and B'Tselem, Israel's own human rights organisation. On the other side, the humanitarian organisations that are openly and deafeningly saying that Israel is *not* committing genocide: none, zilch, zero, nada! Oh Heck! Even the Israelis are saying they are committing genocide. Read *Haaretz*. OK, that's too left wing. Listen to the Minister of Social Equality, who said: 'I am personally proud of the holocaust of Gaza, and that eighty years from now, they will tell their grandchildren what the Jews did'. Or the debates in the Knesset where the genocide is discussed openly. One proposal is to kill everyone in Gaza by 'destroying all food, water and power sources', and then shooting them. They are willing to be kind to those who carry white flags; they will only suffer ethnic cleansing. (However, the last time Israeli soldiers came across people carrying white flags, it was a group of hostages escaping from Hamas. Guess what? They were – what's the right word – murdered – anyway). Or watch the volley of videos where Israeli pop singers, rabbis, children, and citizens are gleefully singing, dancing, announcing, that 'every child in Gaza is an enemy, we should target their offspring', 'may their village burn', or enumerating the genocidal rights of the 'chosen race'. You don't even have to go that far: turn to *Channel 4 News*, where Israeli spokesman, the repulsive British subject David Mencer, will no doubt be interviewed yet again by Matt Frei. In one interview, Frei asked Mencer if he feels 'shame' Israel is accused of genocide. Mencer replied: 'I will tell you how I feel. I feel pride'.

If you have been following the BBC, you may come to the conclusion that the horrors visited on Gaza are somehow descending from the sky and no one is really responsible for them. 'The lonely death of Gaza man from Downs Syndrome' suggests he died naturally and was not murdered by Israeli soldiers. Or, 'West Bank violence: My child's destiny is to get killed' suggests that children in Gaza are destined to die by some misfortune – not be brutally murdered by a genocidal regime. 'Gaza destruction risks lost generation of children says, UN official', not really; Israel's destruction of Gaza risks lost generation of children, says UN official'. By deliberately leaving out 'Israel', the BBC attempts to sanitise Israeli crimes.

The BBC verifies and fact-checks to confirm the truth of videos and fake news, including Russian claims in its war with Ukraine. Yet, it remained conspicuously silent in checking Israeli claims. Elsewhere, an investigation found that the Israeli army used fake 3D animations taken from video games, online assets, content creators, and a Scottish museum to claim Hamas was hiding under Gaza's hospitals. But the BBC backed Israeli claims without subjecting it the standard scrutiny of its Verify department.

Apart from impartiality, there is another word in the BBC lexicon that is frequently mentioned: context. Indeed, it even has an hour-long show on its news channel called 'Context', where mostly the American and British worldview is promoted. The BBC guidelines emphasise that context is crucial for the different aspect of a complex story to be truly appreciated. 'When considering whether content may cause harm or offence, the context in which the material will be published or broadcast should be taken into account', it declares.

To begin with, the context demands that the Jewish community is represented in all its complex diversity. As far as the BBC is concerned, the only Jews in the world are Netanyahu supporting Zionists. There are, of course, Zionists, with Israel in their veins, who do not support the

INTRODUCTION: THIS IS THE BBC

current regime and are appalled by its actions. There are liberal, left-wing Zionists who do not believe in the notion of a 'Jewish state'. (Just as there are countless Muslims who reject the idea of an 'Islamic state'). And then there are Jews who are not Zionists. And the world is full of them. Did the BBC report on the massive anti-Zionist, anti-Israeli demonstrations by Jews in New York. No! Did the BBC cover that ultra-orthodox Jews, who refuse to join the IDF, have been systematically reviled, beaten up, and denigrated. Nope. Has the BBC ever had anyone on its programmes from Jewish Voice, or Voice of Rabbis (who describe themselves as 'Jews United Against Zionism'), or any leader of the Sephardic Jewish community? Or anyone from the Bukharian Jewish community, the oldest diaspora in the world! Never!

Would it not be the right, let us say the 'impartial', thing to do, to provide the broader context of what Israel has been doing for the past seventy years. By all means describe Hamas as terrorists, if that is your position, but do point out that the founders of Israel were the ones who first introduced terrorism in the region. I am referring to the Stern gang and others of similar ilk, who started their terror campaign by murdering British soldiers. Since the BBC has repeatedly focused on the Hamas massacre on 7 October 2023, how about giving some context to Zionist and Israeli massacres? We can start with a string of massacres in Haifa, Jerusalem, Balad al-Sheikh in 1937–1938 and move on to the number of massacres committed in 1947–1948, and then to the Khan Yunus massacre of 1956, the Jerusalem massacre of 1967, the Sabra and Shatila massacre of 1982, the Al-Aqasa massacre of 1990, the Jenin refugee camp massacre of 2022, to one massacre after another in Gaza: 2008–2009, 2012, 2014, 2018–2019, 2021, arriving at the genocide that the BBC can't see.

Oh, that's too far in and too much of history. So how about providing context for the massacre that BBC does recognise: the one on 7/10. It just so happened, somewhat like Kipling stories, that the highly respected journalist, Peter Oborne, author of *Complicit: Britain's Role in the Destruction of Gaza*, came face to face with a certain Richard Burgess, a rather dim bloke said to be BBC's executive news editor. They were at a parliamentary meeting held at the launch of *BBC on Gaza-Israel: One Story, Double Standard*, a report by the Centre for Media Monitoring (CfMM). Originally established by the Muslim Council of Britain, CfMM is now independent; and have published reports that are painstakingly and extensively researched, including an earlier report: *Media Bias: Gaza 2023–24*. It also just so happened that the brilliant British journalist, Jonathan Cook, columnist for *The National*, Abu Dhabi, and *Middle East Eye*, was there to record the encounter between Oborne and Burgess.

Oborne, writes Cook, 'makes a series of important points that illustrate why the BBC's slanted, Israel-friendly news agenda amounts to genocide denial, and means executives like Burgess are directly complicit in Israeli war crimes'. The BBC never mentioned the Hannibal directive, invoked on 7 October and widely reported in the Israeli press, that permitted the IDF to kill soldiers and citizens to prevent them from being taken hostage by Hamas. In other words, the IDF murdered its own people by Apache helicopter while blaming Hamas for the killing. The BBC, Oborne went on to say, 'never mentioned Israel's Dahiya doctrine, the basis of its "mowing the lawn" approach to Gaza over the past two decades, in which the Israeli military has intermittently destroyed large swaths of the tiny enclave. The official aim has been to push the population, in the words of Israeli generals, back to the "Stone Age". The assumption is that, forced into survival mode, Palestinians will not have the energy or will to resist their brutal and illegal subjugation by Israel and that it will be easier for Israel to ethnically cleanse them from their homeland'. The BBC's refusal to acknowledge these doctrines 'leaves audiences gravely misinformed about Israel's historical abuses of Gaza, and deprived of context to interpret the campaign of destruction by Israel over the past 20 months'. Moreover, the BBC has disregarded 'Israel's campaign of murdering Palestinian journalists in Gaza. A greater number have been killed by Israel in its war on the tiny enclave than the total number of journalists killed in all other major conflicts of the past 160 years combined'.

Cook describes a revealing exchange between Declassified journalist Hamza Yusuf and Burgess. Yusuf asks Burgess why the BBC is not covering the story of British spy planes operating over Gaza from RAF base Akrotiri on Cyprus. Burgess replies: 'I don't think we should overplay the UK's contribution to what's happening in Israel'. Cook concludes:

> So the British state broadcaster has decided that its duty is not to investigate the nature of British state assistance to Israel in Gaza, even though most

INTRODUCTION: THIS IS THE BBC

experts agree what Israel is doing there amounts to genocide. Burgess thinks scrutiny of British state complicity would be 'overplaying' British collusion, even though the BBC has not actually investigated the extent or nature of that collusion to have reached a conclusion. This is the very antithesis of what journalism is there to do: monitor the centres of power, not exonerate such power-centres before they have even been scrutinised.

So, to paraphrase the well-known adage of journalism (attributed to Jeremy Paxman but originally uttered by *Times* journalist Louis Heren), why are the lying bastards at the BBC lying to us? Because that's what the BBC has always done when it comes to Palestine. As the late, great John Pilger, who knew a thing or two about journalism, noted, 'the BBC is, and has long been, the most refined propaganda service in the world'. But the refinement has now faded; BBC propaganda is now crude, lies are astonishingly obvious, the cognitive bias so bent and so visible that it can be legitimately used to put the Corporation in a strait jacket.

There are reports and there are reports. The BBC has turned a blind eye to all the reports coming from the various off shoots of the UN. A number of reports by Special Rapporteur on the situation of human rights in the Palestinian territories occupied since 1967, the Italian lawyer, Francesca Albanese, have been given the cold shoulder. The absence of one particular report, 'Gaza Genocide: a collective crime', which alleged that both UK and its Prime Minister were complicit in genocide surely deserved a headline. But the BBC did not think it newsworthy. The report states:

> The ongoing genocide in Gaza is a collective crime, sustained by the complicity of influential Third States that have enabled longstanding systemic violations of international law by Israel. Framed by colonial narratives that dehumanize the Palestinians, this live-streamed atrocity has been facilitated through Third States' direct support, material aid, diplomatic protection and, in some cases, active participation. It has exposed an unprecedented chasm between peoples and their governments, betraying the trust on which global peace and security rest. The world now stands on a knife-edge between the collapse of the international rule of law and hope for renewal. Renewal is only possible if complicity is confronted, responsibilities are met and justice is upheld.

The BBC paid no attention to the meticulously documented reports of CfMM. A 'Panorama' documentary, commissioned by the BBC itself, that looked at the work of doctors under Israeli bombardment, and examined their detention and killing, was shelved because the BBC feared it would undermine its confirmed bias for Israeli propaganda. It was later shown on Channel 4 which saw no breach of any particular guidelines, even though its mandate is not too far from that of the BBC. It pulled another documentary on Gaza from its iPlayer; and ignored its own 'Report of the Editorial Review into "Gaza: How to Survive a Warzone"' by Peter Johnston, Director of Editorial Complaints and Reviews. The documentary features fourteen-year-old Abdullah Al-Yazouri chronicling daily life in Gaza. The BBC acted after it was informed that Abdullah's father, Ayman Al-Yazouri, holds the position of deputy minister of agriculture in Gaza's Hamas-run government. This was seen as breach of impartiality. But Johnston's detailed thirty-page report emphatically stated: 'I do not consider that anything in the Narrator's scripted contribution to the Programme breached the BBC's standards on due impartiality. I have also not seen or heard any evidence to support a suggestion that the Narrator's father or family influenced the content of the Programme in any way'. The BBC also ignored an Open Letter in support of the documentary from 450 film and television professionals, actors, journalists, and broadcasters, who know something about making documentaries, including the celebrated directors Ken Loach and Mike Leigh. The letter defended the Gaza documentary as 'an essential piece of journalism, offering an all-too-rare perspective on the lived experiences of Palestinian children living in unimaginable circumstances', pointed out that Ayman Al-Yazouri was little more than a civil servant tasked with food production, and 'assumptions about Palestinians in administrative positions are rooted in "racist tropes."'. That too was ignored. Also ignored was the June 2025 letter of 400 'talents', to use a BBC term, which included Jewish actor Miriam Margolyes and the comedian Alexei Sayle, historian William Dalrymple, and 111 BBC journalists. The letter claimed that 'BBC is not reporting "without fear or favour" when it comes to Israel". The BBC journalists express concern 'over opaque editorial decisions and censorship at the BBC on the reporting of Israel/Palestine'. The BBC journalists declare:

INTRODUCTION: THIS IS THE BBC

We, the undersigned BBC staff, freelancers and industry figures are extremely concerned that the BBC's reporting on Israel and Palestine continues to fall short of the standards our audiences expect. We call on the BBC to do better for our audiences and recommit to our values of impartiality, honesty and reporting without fear or favour...For many of us, our efforts have been frustrated by opaque decisions made at senior levels of the BBC without discussion or explanation. Our failures impact audiences...As an organisation we have not offered any significant analysis of the UK government's involvement in the war on Palestinians. We have failed to report on weapons sales or their legal implications...In some instances staff have been accused of having an agenda because they have posted news articles critical of the Israeli government on their social media.

A report – rather, a 'memo' or maybe even a 'letter' – did receive serious attention from the BBC. It was written by a corporate lobbyist called Michael Prescott said to be an 'independent advisor' to the BBC's Editorial Guidelines and Standards Board for three years until June 2025. He acquired this appointment largely due to the courtesy of his friend Robbie Gibb, a 'proper Thatcherite conservative', spin doctor for Theresa May, and former owner of *Jewish Chronicle*, who was appointed to the BBC Board of Trustees by the veracious Prime Minister Boris Johnson. Under his ownership the *JC* (which I used to read avidly during the 1980s and 1990s and learned a great deal), became so rabidly pro-Israel, that five of its leading columnists, including Jonathan Freedland of the *Guardian* and my former colleague, David Aaronovitch, denounced the coverage and left. Freedland declared, 'too often, the *JC* reads like a partisan, ideological instrument, its judgements political rather than journalistic'.

The report laid four charges against the BBC. It suggested that the BBC had an anti-Trump bias. Evidence: a Panorama programme 'spliced' together two segments of his famous 6 January 2021 speech and thus made it look like he encouraged the violence that followed. It attacked the BBCs Arabic Service arguing that it had selectively covered stories critical of Israel. The report also claimed that the BBC had misrepresented the number of Palestinian women and children killed by the IDF and inaccurately portrayed the likelihood of children facing starvation under Israel's aid blockade. Furthermore, the BBC was biased in favour of transgender issues, and produced oversimplified and distorted narratives about British colonialism, slavery, and their legacy.

It was leaked to the unhinged mega-right wing *Daily Telegraph* – which is dominated by *JC* folks, which now reads like the house rag of the IDF. It pursued the story relentlessly – until the enforced resignation of the Director General, Tim Davie, and head of news, Deborah Turness, in November 2025. There is nothing in this story that says it is anything but partial. The June letter from the BBC journalists had already highlighted political interference by Gibb. It expressed disquiet at the 'inconsistent manner in which guidance is applied draws into focus the role of Gibb, on the BBC Board and BBC's editorial standards committee'; and expressed concern 'that an individual with close ties to the *Jewish Chronicle* ... has a say in the BBC's editorial decisions in any capacity, including the decision not to broadcast 'Gaza: Medics Under Fire'. This was clearly a 'conflict of interest', which 'highlights a double standard for BBC content makers who have themselves experienced censorship in the name of "impartiality"'.

What about the Prescott memo itself? Compared to the 185-page detailed data-filled CfMM report, the report is pathetic. In his analysis for the *Observer*, David Aaronovitch dismisses it as half-baked, biased, selective, and unworthy of attention: it 'flunks the impartiality test'. Aaronovitch wonders 'how the preoccupations and prejudices of "independent advisors" came to play such a major role in guiding editorial discussion'.

The answer is simple: the BBC bends to power, and always favours the establishment. It has always done so. Even the saintly Lord Reith, the first Director General of the BBC credited with establishing the principles of public broadcasting and the 'Reithian principle' of 'political neutrality', was not all that impartial. According to Mark Damazer, former controller of BBC Radio 4, he 'hemmed and hawed before finally allowing Labour leader, Hugh Gaitskell, who was bitterly opposed to Britian's involvement in the war, to address the nation. The Prime Minister, Anthony Eden, was livid and claimed that the BBC had – what else – acted against "the national interest"'. 'The truth', Damazer asserts, 'was, very, very, often not told'.

The truth was defiantly not told during the Iraq war. And it has been the case ever since I started watching BBC news on a daily basis – way back in the 1980s. I not only saw but experienced, as I was personally involved,

INTRODUCTION: THIS IS THE BBC

how the BBC manipulated and demonised Muslims during the Rushdie affair – who got on *Newsnight* and who did not. I witnessed how the BBC was systematically economical with the truth during the Iraq invasion. In 2004, Tim Llewellyn began his chapter for *Bad News From Israel*, with the words:

> Watching a peculiarly crass, inaccurate and condescending programme about the endangered historical sites of 'Israel' – that is to say, the Israeli-occupied Palestinian Territories – on BBC2 in early June 2003, I determined to try to work out, as a former BBC Middle East correspondent, why the Corporation has in the past two and a half years been failing to report fairly the most central and lasting reason for the troubles of the region: the Palestinians' struggle for freedom.

> Since the beginning of the Aqsa Uprising, or Second Intifada, in September 2000 there have been countless examples throughout the BBC's news broadcasts, discussion programmes, features, documentaries and even online of this muddying of the clear waters of the Israel-Palestine crisis.

Way back in 2004, *Bad News from Israel* showed that British television news coverage of the Israeli-Palestinian conflict lacked historical context, and unfairly favoured the Israeli perspective. Reporters relied heavily on and often cited Israeli official sources while presenting Palestinian positions as 'claims' rather than 'statements'. The book cites many examples where false claims by Isreal are presented as fact. The end result: reinforcement of the power dynamic. In other words, British television news prostrated in front of the powerful Israeli lobby and its supporters in the establishment. We can safely say that nothing much has changed. Except, as *More Bad News from Israel* revealed bias had increased by 2007. By now, in 2025, it has become blatant and all encompassing.

Just how barefaced the BBC has become is well expressed by Karishma Patel, a former BBC journalist and newsreader, who resigned because of her disgust at the Corporation's coverage of Gaza. She saw 'a shocking level of editorial inconsistency' with journalists 'actively choosing not to follow evidence' of Israeli war crimes 'out of fear' of powerful executives and presenters. 'It's important', she writes, the public understands how far editorial policy can be silently shaped by even the possibility of anger from certain groups, foreign governments, our own government, mega-corporations – any powerful actor'

Perhaps no one illustrates the degeneration of BBC journalism more than Jeremy Bowen, former BBC Middle East editor who is now dubbed 'International Editor'. Sometime in May 2025, I caught him interviewing Philippe Lazzarini, head of United Nations refugee agency UNRWA. He introduced the highly respected Lazzarini as someone 'Israel says he is a liar, and that his organisation has been infiltrated by Hamas'. Then, he goes on to justify why Lazzarini is being interviewed. 'But I felt it was important to talk to him for a number of reasons. First off, the British government deals with him, and funds his organisation. Which is the largest dealing with Palestinian refugees. They know a lot of what is going on, so therefore I think it is important to speak to people like him'. These are not just offensive and uncouth words coming out of the mouth of a BBC journalist, but totally unforgivable. Would Bowen, who looks increasingly constipated during his links to camera, introduce Netanyahu, as 'Prime Minister wanted by International Criminal Court for crimes against humanity', or 'the leader of the fascist regime in Israel'? Being interviewed because he knows a lot about using starvation as a method of warfare, mass murder, and other inhuman acts? Bowen refuses to call ethnic cleansing by its name, never fails to describe Hamas as terrorists, and was quite happy to perpetuate the myth that numerous hospitals in Gaza are Hamas 'command and control centres' – thus, indirectly justifying the bombing of medical facilities by Israeli forces. Yet, had Bowen bothered to go out of his luxurious hotel in Jerusalem and looked at Israeli society he would have seen the evidence of ethnic cleansing with his own eyes, settlers beating up and stealing from Palestinian homes, dozens of prominent Israeli rabbis giving the IDF religious approval to bomb Al Shifa Hospital, citizens uttering inhuman xenophobic chants. Israeli people have been fairly open about their position on Palestine and Gaza. Bowen only had to stop a few people in the streets of Tel Aviv or Jerusalem and they would have told him that ethnic cleansing is justified and that Palestinians are not truly 'people'. As one Tel-Aviv school principal described what they tell their pupils: 'Arabs are inferior to us. That's why we kick Palestinians and slap them. We train dogs so they will bite them strongly and tightly. That's why we shoot them. They're nothing'. He would have bumped into a posse of young men shouting, 'We will tear their mothers apart. We will fuck them in the arse'. Had he

INTRODUCTION: THIS IS THE BBC

bothered to talk to Israeli soldiers they would have openly admitted, on the record, that they raped Palestinian persons (men, women, little children), they used them as human shields, and shot and killed unarmed civilians whenever and wherever they wished. He could have cornered an Israeli prison guard who would openly confess they torture, starve, amputate, and routinely kill Palestinian prisoners; and admit that their prisons are death camps, 'grave yards', as they call them. Heck, if he had just switched the television on in his hotel room, he could have witnessed ethnic cleansing and genocidal talk twenty-four hours a day! He could have watched the drama of the Israelis cheering soldiers who gang-raped and filmed the horror unfold before his eyes. The video of the rape was leaked by the Military Advocate General, Yifat Tomer-Yerushalmi. In court, the soldiers claimed they gang-raped Palestinians prisoners 'out of duty to protect Israel'; and talking about the *trauma* they suffered! He could have switched on to Al-Jazeera where live coverage of genocide and ethnic cleansing was broadcast – day after day. Including a report on a South Africa-bound plane carrying an Israeli-Estonian national, the man behind the dubious front company 'Al-Majd Europe', involved in deportation and ethnic cleansing of Palestinians. Back in snow clad Britain, he should see the ITV documentary, 'Breaking Ranks', in which over a dozen soldiers relate how they were ordered to fire on unarmed Palestinians, use teenagers as human shields, and level districts which presented no threat, and ignore international law. But Bowen, like many other BBC journalists, has been blind to the truth, has whitewashed Israeli lies and privileged genocidal narrative, insulted and suppressed Palestinian voices, and largely ignored the suffering of the Palestinians.

I focus on the BBC because it is the oldest public service broadcaster. If the BBC has sunk to such low depths, what can one say about other western media institutions?

A good indication of where we stand with western media in general is provide by the notorious Hamas 'rape' and 'beheaded babies' story that was spread worldwide. It first emerged on the Israeli news channel i24NEWS. Journalist Nicole Zedek claimed that '40 babies/children were beheaded at the kibbutz Kfar Aza'. On 10 October 2023, Britain's *Daily Mail* carried the headline on its website: 'Hamas cut the throats of babies'. The front page the following day declared: 'This was a Holocaust pure and

Oh yeah?

simple'. On the same day, the front page of *The Times*, London, announced: 'Hamas "cut the throat of babies" in massacre'. The following day, President Joe Biden, on a Fox News alert, stated that he had *seen* evidence of beheadings. When questioned by Al-Jazeera reporters, a White House spokesperson said that 'comments were based on news reports and claims by Israeli officials'.

But the story that really spread the 'beheaded babies' and rape allegations worldwide appeared on 28 December 2023 in *The New York Times*. Under the heading, 'How Hamas Weaponized Sexual Violence on Oct. 7', described as an 'investigation', it carried the by-lines: Jeffrey Gittleman, Anat Schwartz, and Adam Sella. The debunking of the story began within a few weeks when Declassified UK pointed out reports of Hamas attack atrocities were not corroborated with evidence: 'Beheaded babies' – how UK media reported Israel's fake news as fact'. DCUK showed that exact words of the original channel i24NEWS were repeated by Biden, IDF spokespersons, and Benjamin Nathanyahu on CNN. But neither French journalists or even Israeli journalists on the ground had seen any evidence of beheaded babies or rape.

A more detailed debunking on 28 February 2028 by Intercept, 'Between the Hammer and the Anvil: The Story Behind the New York Times October 7 Exposé', completely debunked the story. While Gittleman had some journalistic credentials, Schwartz, it turned out, had no reporting experience, and was recruited just three weeks before the piece was

INTRODUCTION: THIS IS THE BBC

published. She is a filmmaker who worked for Israeli Airforce intelligence. She liked anti-Palestine social media posts, and described Palestinians in inhuman terms. On one post, she declared: 'those in front of us are human animals who do not hesitate to violate minimal rules'. Sella turned out to be a nephew of her partner. The report relied on the Israeli community emergency response alliance ZAKA, not renowned for accurate testimony, serving as witness. In short, it was 'atrocity propaganda'. Even after further investigation by the superb Israeli paper, *Haaretz*, accused Zaka personnel of negligence and spreading misinformation in their testimonies about 7 October, the NYT stood by the story: 'We remain confident in the accuracy of our reporting and stand by the team's investigation'.

So, a group of fifty American professors of journalism penned an open letter to NYT demanding that a group of experts investigate the 28

December report. The NYT podcast, 'The Daily', based on the report had to be cancelled due to the newspapers own reporters raising objection. The beheaded babies fantasy was further discredited by *Le Monde* – '40 beheaded babies: Deconstructing the rumour at the heart of the information battle between Israel and Hamas'. *Le Monde*'s correspondent in Jerusalem, Samuel Forey', actually went to the Kfar Aza on 10 October, just three days after the Hamas attack. *Le Monde* found no credible evidence for claims that 'dozens of babies beheaded' at kibbutz Kfar Aza and pointed out that the youngest recorded victim there was fourteen years old. Yet, the allegations of mass rape and beheaded babies continue.

What does the maladaptive daydreaming about beheaded babies tell us? It tells us that the major western media institutions bend to the will of power. Mainstream media journalists, like CNN's Jake Tapper and Dana Bash manufacture consent to justify, not just the destruction of Gaza, but the paranoia of those in power. Note how easily the likes of ABC, CBS, *The Wall Street Journal,* and *The New York Times* bent the knee to Trump. There is not much to say about the *Daily Mail* or *Daily Telegraph*, or *Die Welt* or *Bild*. Let us not dwell on Fox News or GB News or the foaming-in the-mouth with semi-fascist gibberish of the *Spectator* either. For the so-called legacy media, it is the propaganda, viewpoint and experience of Israel that

matters. Nothing else. Vide the systematic demonisation of Zohran Mamdani, the dazzling Mayor of New York, by the mainstream US media, analysed by Khuda Bushq in his review of Equality Labs report, *Tracing the Online Hate Against Zohran Mamdani*. When Mamdani met Trump, the BBC reported the meeting but omitted – or did the BBC 'splice' – the quote where he said: 'I have spoken about the Israeli government committing genocide and I've spoken about our government funding it'. Which most news hounds will consider to be a crucial bit of the story.

However, all this is hardly news. It has always been just so.

But the mainstream media in the non-western world is just as mediocre and becoming increasingly irrelevant. As Muhammad Saad reports, the dominant news channels in Pakistan perpetually feed a frenzy of political rivalry and cannot even be bothered to report the floods that have devastated large swathes of the country. In India, the veteran journalist Shiv Visvanathan laments, the mainstream media has sold its soul to the ruling BJP party. Much of Indian television is crowded with multiple talking heads shouting across each other. The same can be said about the main channels and newspapers throughout the South.

This does not mean that good journalism is dead. In England, there is the *Guardian* (which I started reading during my student days and still read every day), *New Statesman*, and *Prospect* magazine. Across the border in Scotland, there are the *Herald* and the truly magnificent *The National*. There are journalists like Turkey's Hrant Dink, whose life and work are so inspiringly described by Boyd Tonkin, who worked for 'warm and friendly dialogue among equals'. There are journalists devoted to truth, such as Leopold Weiss (later to be known as Muhammad Asad), who travelled to Palestine in 1922 and reported for *Frankfurter Zeitung*. Weiss, writes Josef Linnhoff, 'gives us a firsthand account of life in Palestine in the years after the Balfour Declaration, at a time of heightened tension, twenty-five years before the creation of the State of Israel' and 'presents the Palestinians as the authentic, rightful inhabitants of the land'. Journalists of this calibre have always been around and always will be.

But increasingly they are not found in the legacy media; and if there, they will soon be departing to more independent abodes. Or be asked to leave as asking probing questions is simply not the done thing by legacy media. The Italian journalist, Gabriele Nunziati, politely asked on 13

October, the European Commission's chief spokesperson a simple but relevant question: 'You've been repeating several times that Russia should pay for the reconstruction of Ukraine. Do you believe that Israel should pay for the reconstruction of Gaza since they have destroyed almost all its civilian infrastructure?'. Two weeks later, on 27 October, he was sacked by his agency, Nova. Their spokesperson acknowledged that the question was 'technically correct'. But you don't ask such questions of Israel. It was being attacked for asking probing questions that led the brilliant Mishal Husain to leave the BBC (Bowen should become her pupil and learn how to respectfully ask relevant and penetrating questions). Ditto Sangita Myska et al. Mehdi Hasan suffered the same fate at MSNBC.

Solid journalism is increasingly found in alternative media like Declassified UK, Intercept, Novara Media, Media Lens, or platforms such as Substack. Saoussen Ben Cheikh describes how alternative media in the Middle East has so bravely kept good journalism alive. 'Journalism has futures', Scott Jordan tells us. Although we ought to add the adjective 'critical' to the term 'alternative'. Not all alternatives are genuine alternatives dedicated to exposing the truth. But the futures of journalism, as Visvanathan argues, is tied up to the futures of democracy. It is those who are fighting for democracy against the rising tide of authoritarianism the world over who are really dedicated to journalistic truth in this post-truth age.

So, like a spurned lover, I return to the BBC, an institution I have occasionally worked for and contributed to. There is a general perception in Britain, rather England, that without the BBC we – the people of the UK and the world – will somehow be severely diminished. Without the BBC, says Alan Rusbridger, former editor of the *Guardian* who now edits *Prospect*, we will end up with 'an unholy alliance of Murdoch (or whoever comes after Rupert), Lord Rothermere and whoever ends up owning the *Telegraph* to mediate most of our national information and conversations?'. The *Guardian* old hand, Polly Toynbee, asks us to stand up and defend the BBC. Labour MP, Peter Prinsely, thinks 'defending the BBC is, ultimately, an act of defending democracy itself'. Pat Young of British Broadcasting Challenge suggests that the BBC needs saving from 'unprecedented dangers' posed by AI-generated deepfakes, hostile state propaganda, and algorithms that amplify divisions. 'The foundations of

This is how genocide is reported!

informed democratic debate are under attack across the globe', he writes, from 'tech platforms, through which most media and news content are distributed, discovered, consumed, and shared, are owned or controlled by six American billionaires who pursue self-interested agendas'.

Nice sentiments. Shame about the object that needs to be rescued. You cannot defend the indefensible. We are talking about an organisation that has now inverted John Birt's notion of 'bias against understanding' to become a beacon of bias towards misunderstanding. Birt, a former DG of the BBC and my boss during my days at LWT, argued that television news is normally presented in sensationalised and superficial form. Everything was geared towards 'presenting the news', rather than analysing and explaining. The BBC's alleged impartiality, to use the words of Burgess, does not 'overplay' the crimes of UK Ltd. Or 'what's happening in Israel'. Indeed, its underplaying is so transparent that young people all over the world spot it immediately. As Zain Sardar writes 'the BBC's lack of impartiality' has created a lopsided 'moral universe'. 'The disposability of Palestinian lives — invoking Stalin's chilling remark that one death is a tragedy while a million deaths are a mere statistic — and the marginalisation of their suffering underscores the grotesque lack of impartiality and balance'. This is why so many independent well-established journalists, including Peter Oborne, Jonathan Cook, Mehdi Hasan, Owen Jones, Chris Hedges, and many others have accused the BBC and its journalists of being complicit in perpetuating genocide.

John Kampfner, former editor of *New Statesman*, where once I used to be a columnist, says that the BBC is in 'a permanent nervous breakdown'. I suspect that long-standing tailspin is due to the simple fact that as an institution the BBC is a very weird place. I mean, where on earth can you have a prolific pedophile like Jimmy Saville committing abuse for decades in front of everyone and no one notices? The BBC's own *Panorama* of 26 October 2012 reported that a paedophile ring could have been operating at the BBC for twenty or even forty years! The BBC does seem to be a magnet for paedophiles and perverts. There were allegations, in *Strange Places, Questionable People* by John Simpson, then the BBC's World Affairs Editor, about a certain 'Uncle Dick' who sexually assaulted children. Uncle Dick even had a side kick; and they both carried on in the 1940s and 1950s and no one noticed nor did anything about it. Around the death of Saville in 2011, over 150 allegation of sexual abuse were made involving some eighty staff or contributors. And since then, we have had the high profile cases of Rolf Harris, Stuart Hall, DJ Tim Westwood, DJ Chris Denning, right down to the highly esteemed newsreader Huw Edwards. Then we have had *MasterChef* presenter Gregg Wallace and various chaps on *Strictly Come Dancing*. If that wasn't enough, there has been scandal after scandal since the BBC's early days, starting in 1950 with involvement in

INTRODUCTION: THIS IS THE BBC

the notorious coup d'etat in Iran; the coverage of the Troubles in Northern Ireland; the falsification of the coverage of the miners' strike; the Richard Bacon cocaine affair; the refusal to broadcast the Gaza DEC appeal in January 2009; rigged phone competitions; BNP spokespersons on *Question Time*; allegations of sexism and sexism; the gender pay gap; obscene levels of pay for the executives; and the silencing of Gary Lineker. Not forgetting the Martin Bashir interview with Diana, Princess of Wales, for *Panorama*, secured, according to a new book, *Dianarama*, through lies, forged documents, and extraordinary deception. One can just go on and on.

I am afraid the 'permanent nervous breakdown' has taken its toll on an ageing Aunt. One loved her in her younger days, when she was fully compos mentis, and one was a bit naïve and believed in objective journalism. Those were the days, my friend, when my father listened to

A meme on social media

the BBC as if it was broadcasting truth as though it was revelation. And I believed in my father as I believed in the BBC. And others like me with non-English heritage were believers too, including Yasmin Alibhai-Brown, judging from one of her recent columns. But now Aunty is getting old, she is partially blind, a bit hard of hearing, and showing clear signs of amnesia, which is an indication that dementia has set in. She needs palliative care; after that, we should allow her to, what's the word, 'pass away' quietly onto never never land.

From Kuala Lumpur to Istanbul, Karachi to Cape Town, Almaty to Sarajevo – places where I have tuned into the BBC – the BBC looks parochial, amateur, and crude. Its propaganda stands out a mile. When its presenters insist on telling their guest, and hence the audience, that Israel denies committing genocide, the IDF denies this or that, they only generate derisory laughter. In the eyes of the world, it has zero journalistic integrity. People, pregnant or otherwise, do not love the BBC. And the world would not even notice if it disappeared.

Poor Mrs Robertson. She would be turning in her grave.

RETURN TO COCKBURN

Andrew Brown

Claud Cockburn, one of the finest hacks there has ever been, wrote that journalism is very simple: it is a mixture of advertising and entertainment and to succeed you need only decide who you want to entertain and what cause, as it were, you wish to advertise. He had no time for journalism as the pursuit of abstract truth, and – as a member in good standing of the British imperial class and an intermittent Stalinist – he would have laughed at the idea that journalists had a sacred duty to democracy until tears of neat whisky streamed down his cheeks.

Cockburn wished to lose his illusions without losing hope, as he wrote admiringly of a Stalinist friend. His energy, optimism, and courage are still inspiring; he was also an excellent stylist, whose plain and forceful manner concealed a great deal of art. He cared more for the English language than for all of his causes and most of his wives. So, if there is any guide who can lead us, like Virgil, through the descent into dreadful clickbait hell, Cockburn is the man.

He must have inspired many people into journalism with his autobiographies, but I don't think he ever set out to be a journalist. What he wanted was a way to travel and to savour the variety of the world, and when he was a young man working for *The Times* offered the least constrained way to do this that was still respectable. 'The press, sir, and the gentleman from the Times' as a Victorian flunkey is said to have introduced journalists to the prime minister.

So he started off respectable, and at his least respectable, invented a form of journalism that did not depend on advertising and was aimed squarely at an elite audience. To put it another way, he invented Substack eighty years before Substack did. This matters, because everything bad that has happened to journalism in the last thirty years or so can be blamed on changes in the advertising industry and the way that the internet has destroyed the economic basis of mass market journalism. This is a catastrophe for journalism as a trade, of course; but it is also tangled with a political catastrophe.

Most of the stories in the national news and almost all the stories in the tabloids might as well be about life on Mars for all the influence the readers can have on them, or they will have on the readers. This means there is no immediate penalty for most readers if they prefer to believe whatever they would like to be true. There is no market pressure on the media to prefer truth over entertainment. In fact when the press is ad-subsidised there is a considerable incentive to be studiously agnostic about all truth claims about anything. This is carried to an extreme on social media: there, partly under the influence of the American law known as Section 230, the owners and publishers take no view and no responsibility for anything that appears. Google, Facebook, and so on are really giant advertising companies. They are not in the business of delivering information to their audience, but delivering their audience to their advertisers. That is why Google pays Apple $20 billion a year to remain the default search engine on Mac and iPhone.

This was also the business that traditional newspapers were in, but that was something they did not acknowledge even to themselves, still less to their readers. When *The Independent* started, the journalists there would say 'we want to be what *The Times* would be if it were still a proper paper', but the medical correspondent was known as Oliver Willy for his ability to find sex stories in the most unlikely science, and the advertising department made much of our coverage of Formula One, which was meant to attract young men with more money than sense. That was how things worked for about a hundred years until the internet produced a much more efficient way to deliver an audience to advertisers. It was much more precisely targeted, reached far more people because it cost them nothing, and could use all kinds of media more immediately attention grabbing than print.

This is all very shocking but the more shocking question that worries me, after more than forty years in the trade, is why anyone should care at all whether a given story is true or not. Most people do not and most journalism gives them no special reason to care either. The less powerful reason for this is that we journalists get a lot wrong, usually through haste and ignorance: the kind of shameless overconfidence which causes AI to hallucinate is an occupational disease of journalism done by humans too. That's inevitable so long as speed is important. There is much we don't know when we write and, more dangerously, there is always a reliance on the errors of earlier stories, whether these are factual or the more insidious and more serious errors of interpretation – the ones where true facts are placed in the context of a false narrative.

Cockburn himself got a great many stories wrong, sometimes quite deliberately: in his memoirs he describes inventing from the whole cloth a mutiny among the Francoist forces during the Spanish Civil War. This wasn't pure naughtiness or cynicism: the French government was about to make a decision about a shipment of arms which the Nationalist side desperately needed, and Cockburn and his fellow Communists wanted to give the impression that to let the guns through would mean the government was supporting the winning side. For most readers that story raises ethical issues which permanently stain Cockburn's reputation – a journalist who will deliberately lie for his cause loses most of his credibility. But there is another important aspect to the story: it was aimed at people who would actually take decisions. It mattered whether they believed him or not.

Although his son Patrick has written a moving biography paying tribute to his father as the voice of the powerless, what gave the voice power was the people who heard it. His newsletter, *The Week*, was read by the elite and about them too. This is as it must be: the elite are the only people who might be stirred into decisive action by what they read or hear. The powerlessness of the readers of mass market journalism to affect the things they read about is both an effect and a cause of the decay of truth in the media.

The other secret of Cockburn's success in the Thirties was that he made a great parade of being too poor to be worth suing. This was not an affectation on his part. His memoirs are full of hair's breadth escapes from his creditors. Even in the Sixties, when Cockburn guest edited *Private Eye*, the novelist Henry Reed warned Emma Tennant, who had married one of Cockburn's sons, that if she went out for a drink with her father-in-law she would always find herself landed with the bill.

More prosperous news operations are well worth suing, though. They more they rely on advertising, and the more successfully they do so, the weaker they must become in political terms. Donald Trump shaking down American television networks for millions of dollars is only the latest and most vivid illustration of this. A news organisation that has a single very rich owner can resist political pressure almost as well as one that has no money at all. But once they become businesses owned and controlled by anonymous shareholders, they will always choose profit over probity. All of these factors were working to make journalism less fun and less effective even thirty or forty years ago, in what now seems the golden age before the internet.

There are two jaws to the vice that has squeezed the old media businesses and the journalism they supported. One is the destruction of the advertising market, and the other – which is what I have discussed up till now – is the destruction of an elite coherent audience, one which is neither Corbynist nor conspiracist but has a fairly accurate picture of the ways that power works and of the real, difficult choices involved in government.

There is still a market for hard facts of the sort that audience needs but it's no longer served by news organisations: trying to check my belief that there are now five times as many journalists employed in PR than in the news media in the US, I just stumbled on a site that provides apparently reliable and properly researched statistics at prices ranging from £160 to £480 a month, billed yearly – and that's for individual accounts. Corporate ones are more expensive.

AI will squeeze the vice from both sides but the real damage will be done to the economics of the business, not to journalistic standards. I am a paradoxical optimist here, because I believe that the media landscape is already so awful that the most powerful computer programs in history cannot make it very much worse. Nothing could. Humans are already doing badly the bad jobs that AI will automate. This is hardly an original insight. The earliest work I know on the impact of computers on journalism comes in Michael Frayn's satirical novel, *The Tin Men*, in which a research institute is trying to build intelligent computers. What makes the book so wonderfully prescient is that Frayn is interested in algorithms, not in the blinking lights.

> The soporific quiet which filled Goldwasser's laboratory in the Newspaper Department was disturbed only by the soft rustle of tired newsprint. Assistants

bent over the component parts of the Department's united experiment, the demonstration that in theory a digital computer could be programmed to produce a perfectly satisfactory daily newspaper with all the variety and news sense of the old hand-made article. With silent, infinite tedium, they worked their way through stacks of newspaper cuttings, identifying the pattern of stories, and analysing the stories into standard variables and invariables. At other benches other assistants copied the variables and invariables down on to cards, and sorted the cards into filing cabinets, coded so that in theory a computer could pick its way from card to card in logical order and assemble a news item from them. Once Goldwasser and his colleagues had proved the theory, commercial interests would no doubt swiftly put it into practice. The stylisation of the modern newspaper would be complete. Its last residual connection with the raw, messy, offendable real world would have been broken.

This was published in 1965, but it describes exactly the process by which today's AIs produce news. The following section, in which Goldwasser follows the computer's instructions to produce a leader on a royal wedding, is even funnier, especially if you have ever been a leader writer, but it's too long to quote. Read the whole book.

The point that Frayn has grasped is that humans can work to an algorithm quite as faithfully as any computer, if just more slowly and expensively. Perhaps news writing has always been formulaic: the word 'stereotype' itself derives from preassembled blocks of type, but market pressures gave a new direction to the algorithm. Now what you select for is not truth – about which the algorithm is entirely neutral, so long as no legal risk in involved – but enough novelty to keep the reader half engaged without ever lapsing into thought or full attention.

The whole of the web is already set up to measure the performance of human journalists against the algorithm: Reach, the conglomerate which owns most of England's regional papers, already expects its journalists to produce eight stories a day without leaving the office. While it's possible that AI will churn out rewritten press releases even more quickly than humans can, it won't make a huge financial difference to the business.

The economics are even more attractive if you don't care where your 'journalists' are. Don't anyone tell the *Daily Telegraph* but last year it cost a *Wall Street Journal* writer all of $105 to hire a young man in Pakistan to build him a fully automated website that churned out politically slanted stories rewritten from real news sites all day and night: they were supposed to shift the vote in a US Senate election. Presumably it would be even cheaper today. James Ball, a British technology writer, has knocked up a site which automatically generates podcasts in which two voices discuss the last five minutes' headlines endlessly and it cost him even less money. But sites like those are increasingly read by other bots rather than humans anyway.

What will finally crush the traditional news business is the effect of AI on the other jaw of the vice: the advertising income that keeps newspaper sites alive. About 40 percent of the traffic to US newspaper sites comes through Google. There's no reason to believe that British or other European papers are any different. And once Google starts to feed AI summaries into its search results there is no reason for many users to click through to news sites. AI gloop on Google's own site is indistinguishable in quality from the gloop on news sites, whether that is itself generated by AIs or humans imitating AI. It's hard to see how news organisations as we know them can survive another 40 percent cut in revenue.

Facebook can already deliver much more finely divided audience segments to advertisers, ensuring that they spend their money only on the people they want to reach. YouTube (which of course Google owns) delivers enormous audiences for stories which would once have gone to newspapers or conventional television.

The Nelk Boys are a couple of right-wing Canadian streamers whose breakthrough came when they told the Los Angeles Police Department that they had coke in the boot of the car, when all along it was – haha – only a case of Coca Cola. The resulting video has been watched 49 million times. Along with their fervent support for Donald Trump, this qualified them to interview Benjamin Netanyahu in the middle of the Gaza famine using questions supplied by his staff. The question, at which even their fans balked, came when they asked him what was his favourite McDonald's hamburger. How can any traditional newspaper compete with that? The Nelk Boys don't even need YouTube to make money anymore. They were 'demonetised' in 2020, meaning that Google was so disgusted by their behaviour that it decided to take all the money for the ads on their show itself rather than paying the creators a cut. They have recovered with their own brands of clothing and alcopops – the clothing brand alone is said to bring in $100 million a year. That shows what is really meant by 'relatable content'.

It also suggests the last lesson that Cockburn has to teach us. His newsletter had personality, which helped readers make judgments about its trustworthiness much as we judge the trustworthiness of other people. He had only scorn for what is known as 'the view from nowhere' in American journalism. No one, not even American journalists, really believes in that today.

Instead of the view from nowhere he offered the view from where he was and this was a very recognisable perspective. Any journalist knows of sources who are useful precisely because they are biased and passionate, driven by hatred to tell the truth. Anyone locked in bureaucratic combat will know the weak spots of their enemy and will share what they can with a journalist. And what is true of sources is increasingly true of journalists: they must be judged as individual voices. When all collective brands, like newspapers are crushed in the same economic vice, fewer and fewer can maintain their integrity.

This stress on individual voices or personalities looks like a great step backwards and perhaps it is. But I think it is inevitable. It is hastened as the skills of literacy are lost – half of all American adults did not read a single book last year; most college students, it's reported, cannot read books even if they try, because they have only been taught from extracts and commentaries. It hardly matters whether the digests that they read are produced by AI rather than human followers of the algorithms when the students never experience direct contact with the mind of a writer.

In a visual culture force of argument is replaced by force of personality, which is a quality that has nothing to do with truthfulness. Boris Johnson, former prime minister, was a successful liar as a print journalist, but he would never have been a successful politician without television. Despite the example of men like Johnson or Michael Gove, former Chancellor of Exchequer and current editor of *The Spectator*, there are still many journalists whose skills and integrity I admire a great deal but I can't imagine any of them shifting $100 million worth of branded T-shirts every year as the Nelk Boys do.

Across the Atlantic, America is now governed by a reality television star and journalism has been powerless to hinder him. *The Washington Post* claims that 'Democracy dies in Darkness' which may be true, but the Trump administration shows that democracy also dies on the screens in front of us in real time. Perhaps we should be strengthened by the reflection that Cockburn lived through times even worse and darker than our own and had to shed at least as many illusions as we must, yet still kept his hope and his style.

DEMOCRACY AND INDIAN JOURNALISM

Shiv Visvanathan

I would like to examine the failure of journalism in India in terms of the four separate myths of democracy. Democracy needs this mythical sustenance because without myth, it's difficult to sustain democracy as a local folklore or even as a general esoteric imagination. The decline of the Indian democratic imagination began with the 1975–1977 Emergency.

The Emergency was declared under Article 352 of the Constitution during a backdrop of increasing protests and high court judgement against Indira Gandhi's 1971 election victory. It provided extra-constitutional authority not just to the prime minister, but also her son, Sanjay Gandhi, and his clique who effectively ran the administration; and was an instrument for consolidating his power in the Congress party. He organised and led the forced sterilisation programme in an attempt to control population; mass sterilisation went hand-in-hand with slum demolitions. The context of Emergency, the fulcrum of this essay, is important to understand the current discourses of democracy in India, taking place in relation to political theory and political activism.

We can understand democracy in the old Greek style, in terms of the Socratic imagination, as a series of public discourses, a direct kind of politics which requires, what the Greeks called the *Agora* – a central public place for debate and discussion. In the modern context of India, it can be understood in terms of four self-sustaining myths: the myths of film, cricket, the polity, and science. All four of these myths went into the making of the democratic imagination of India. The decline of the democratic imagination, and the deterioration of journalism in India, is the weakening of these four myths.

The relationship between film and memory has hardly been explored. Film in the Indian sense, or at least Hindi films, anchors, in a deep and fundamental sense, the democratic imagination by challenging the very myth of partition – the division of the plural civilisation of India into the nation states of India and Pakistan. For Hindi film, partition is as an obstruction, a challenge to overcome. Classical Hindi films saw the partition as a breakdown of system. They argued for a new kind of conversation, a new kind of dialogue, a new kind of exchange between Hindus and Muslims, between various kinds of culture, which helps create a new kind of unity. In this sense, Hindi film has been nationalist beyond the national level; it was an attempt to create a new kind of solidarity. We can see this best in the films of Raj Kapoor such as *Ankhen* (1950), *Aag* (1948), and *Barsaat* (1949), as well as Mehboob Khan's *Mother India* (1957). Each of these represents a unity beyond culture, beyond everydayness. If film challenges the myth of the Indian nation state by challenging the violence of partition, it adds to the idea of cultural symbiosis unity between Hindu and Muslim.

To appreciate how films served as a form of cultural news, we have to look at the barber's salon – where they were hotly discussed. Film allowed the discussion of the body and the metaphor and related it to the idea of the body politic. In the barber shop, the discussion of heroines and heroes, plots and counter plots, created a mythical domain where common folks discussed politics through films. The plots of film become humanised as ordinary people explored the nature of the narrative, the understanding of the body, the mechanisms of power. Thus, film turned every person into a critic of democracy. The barber shop in India, as it has been acknowledged, is the metaphorical bedrock of democracy.

Here journalism made a powerful interjection. It combines the oral and the textual imagination. Indian democracy was always the combination of the oral and the textual. A weave one can still see as one drives across *dhabas*, the roadside eateries on the highways, as a literate person reads out the day's news and starts a discussion on oral possibilities of democracy. Journalism is not mere text. It is the gossip of orality (digitality comes later). The classic Hindi films also challenge the duality of modernity; and attempted to create a non-dualistic society. The other level at which journalism operates is at the level of discourse. It challenges a non-dualistic sociology. The opposition between tradition and modernity, urban and rural, male and female, dissolves to create a cultural unity. Hindi film was a reconciliation of opposites. And news reports the ways of reconciling conflict within a certain normative framework. Journalism in that sense is a narrative that sustains norms. Deep down democracy becomes a way of sustaining political democracy.

If film is one way, cricket is the other source.

When cricket was introduced in Tobago Islands, the local tribes tended to force a draw. The draw, they felt, was the perfect result of a cricket match. It established the equivalences of cultures and it denied the idea of the superiority inherent in any one of them. The idea of the draw proved to be distant. But to a certain extent, this same source has now become a possibility for Indian democracy because Indian democracy sees cricket as a game which is played only by gentlemen. It tries to show that the normative idea of cricket pervades the entire society. Cricket in that sense is a normative discourse.

I understood this beautifully when I first met S. K. Gurnathan, the celebrated correspondent of *The Hindu*. He had come to Jamshedpur to review a cricket match between India and the West Indies. I had an enthusiastic discussion with him about Rohan Kanhai, the adventurous Guyanese cricketer, considered one of the best batsmen of the 1960s. Gurnathan, a fascinating character, was my uncle and also a physicist who always tended to treat cricket as a kind of science. For him, cricket and the commentaries of cricket, constituted an authoritative way of creating the norms of democracy. The rights of cricket, good cricket, was good democracy and the Emergency was just not cricket. It's in this context that I want to suggest that cricket emphasised not only equality but a sense of playful competition.

As a narrative, as a collection of parables, as a list of stories, cricket generally emphasised the normative dimension of democracy. As play, cricket stresses the importance of playfulness for democracy. Democracy can be full of rule games, but eventually it is the playfulness, the surprise of cricket, that adds to the imagination of democracy. It is the destruction of play that in fact first of all signals the death of democracy in many cultures.

We tend to take the norms of democracy, from citizenship to equality, as a purely legal, frozen, reified framework. In contrast, cricket as play, as one of the major discourses of modern democracy, opens up the democratic imagination. In such works as *Beyond the Boundary* (1963) by C L R James, *Batting From Memory* (1981) by Jack Fingleton, and *The Tao of*

Cricket (1989) by Ashis Nandy, we discover, again and again, that cricket is not just a colonial, anti-colonial game; it is an attempt to create a new vision of democracy and a post-colonial imagination.

I still remember as a child, when my father was talking about the Lala Amarnath century against England. Lala Ji was from a poor family in Lahore. His test debut was at India's first test match in Bombay in 1934. India faced a massive defeat of an innings. Lala Ji, to use his own words, batted 'as if possessed by a mysterious power', and made a century in just 117 minutes. The way my father talked about the Amarnath century, one felt that he was the Tom Paine of cricket. A century against England was a blow against injustice. For my father, cricket and democracy were just two manifestations of what would be called the new imagination.

If cricket constitutes the second bulwark of democracy, the third imagination comes from modern science. We have to look at modern science differently from the rigid methodological treatises that one is exposed to, or the textbooks of the tutorial colleges that emerged later, which tended to reify and ossify science. Science like cricket was something playful, something normative. Science and cricket, in fact, added to the culture of democracy by creating, as it were, a new way of constructing rules. Rules are not rigid, rules are playful, rules are inventive, rules attempt to extend the democratic imagination.

We can see how the power and force of the Indian personality permeates Indian science through Sir Chandrasekhara Venkata Raman. He won the Noble Prize for Physics in 1930 for his work on the scattering of light and the discovery named after him: the Raman. But he did not go to the ceremony in 1930. He announced that he would be receiving the Nobel Prize in 1932 and bought his tickets two months before the journey. There was a confidence here, a cultural confidence that Indian science was on par with anything happening elsewhere. In fact, often when he was travelling and discussing light, Raman believed that the British did not understand spectroscopy.

In India then, science was not just a standardised imagination, it sought both equality and plurality. And in this diversity created the kind of basis that the cognitive theory of democracy requires.

The final aspect that I must emphasise is polity. The Indian idea of equality was more that of a carnival or a festival. The Indian sense of politics was not a reified political system. It was not a routine or a timetable. I think one of the great disasters of modern democracy is that we have reduced politics to a timetable, to a discipline, to a panoptic way of looking at reality. But the Indian idea of politics was an eruption of ideas and the possibility of alternatives. The Indian idea of democracy was not the Greek idea of politics; it was not the British idea of parliamentary systems. All that came later. All that was a part of the addenda that modern democracy added to strengthen itself. Indian politics thought of alternatives as a part of the paradigm. It saw democracy as a carnival.

I still remember in childhood, reading the *Hindu* as a ritualistic act. The *Hindu* self-styled itself as 'the Indian national newspaper'. In most South Indian houses, the *Hindu* and vintage coffee were presented as ritual acts quality. Deep down inside, the very idea of reading a newspaper became a ritual act of faith in constitutionalism. When India became free, the very idea of India as a nation-state was seen as the big news. It's in this context that one must emphasise that the general feeling in reading *Hindu* or any newspaper was the idea that India had arrived, that Gandhi was in heaven, and Nehru was in control, and it was ready for the world. A newspaper was a reportage of that idea, of its career, and its continuity.

News in that sense was a sustaining figment of democracy. News sustained the democratic imagination. News developed the democratic imagination. It is around news that the whole idea of democracy was built. The gossip of news was the theory of democracy. In that sense, the Indian imagination was not theoretical at a level of an abstract thing. Journalism, news in everyday sense, provided the everyday news of democracy.

So what happened? How was the democratic imagination desiccated? Where did the emptiness of news, the disappearance of good journalism, come from? This brings us to the Emergency, which was an attempt to completely control news, to enforce censorship, to turn Indian society into a monolith, and to domesticate and destroy the very idea of the Indian body in its plurality.

Most people realise that the country emerged out of two genocides. The Bengal famine, which eliminated 3.5 million people, and partition, which eliminated 1.7 million people, and displaced 2 million more. How does journalism and governance cope with such events? And it was in coping with such issues and the ideas around them that, in the beginning, one was caught in a celebration of democracy. But Emergency imposed a different kind of reality – the reality of censorship. It was the beginning of the end of the Indian democratic imagination. And, we need to appreciate that in a deep and fundamental way the emergency has not been revoked. India, in fact, faces the continuity of the impositions of Emergency across the country, especially in the Northeast. The Emergency was the banalisation of violence in India. It began with the destruction of the concept of the body.

The enforced mass sterilisation and the vasectomy incidents, all over India were reported in a different way. They were reported purely as a productivity index, when it was a deep and fundamental assault on the very idea of freedom. Freedom's decline became a productive index and journalism and reportage, became a lost cause. Moreover, the Emergency showed the cowardice of the Indian professional class. As Ramnath Goenka, the noted journalist who established the *Indian Express*, put it, at a time when we were asked to bow, we crawled. Emergency reflected the crawling of Indian democracy, a crawling which continues to this day.

And yet, the Emergency also indicated possibilities of resistance and revival. I am not talking only of the individual courage of journalists like Ramnath Goenka or Kuldip Nayar, the editor of *The Statesman*, the founder of the Editors Guild of India, who was arrested towards the end of the Emergency. But also how the Emergency triggered the reappearance of social science in a systematic way in Indian journalism. One outstanding example of such collaboration is the work between the Centre for the Study of Developing Societies (CSDS) led by Rajni Kothari and Ashis Nandy, and various newspapers. There was also the possibility that the very idea of journalism acquired a new dimension. For example, with the work of photojournalist, Raghu Rai, the emergency moved from text to visuality. Rai's work on the emergency and later on the Bhopal gas disaster showed to a certain extent that the body had returned as an imagination, that the body was no longer the mechanical body of the emergency. His work captured along with those of Kishore Parekh, the chief photographer of *Hindustan Times*, the power of the body as a metaphor for the return of Indian democracy.

But what Indian journalism failed to capture was the deadening of Indian democracy. Short of the Shah Commission report, which heavily criticised the 'extra-constitutional authority' exercised by Sanjay Gandhi and his coterie, very few commentators attempted to capture the way in which Indian democracy as an imagination was destroyed. One thing in particular, or what we call the sheer literalness of Indian democracy, India changed from a democratic system to an electoral system, and from an electoral system to a system of routine rigid rules. As a result, electoralism replaced pluralism in the Indian democratic imagination.

It is in this context that we have to realise that majoritarianism as a so-called democratic system arose within the context of the Emergency. There's a straight continuity between the Emergency as a panopticon and the making of the majoritarian system today. The flattening of Indian democracy comes from the flattening of Indian journalism. Deep down, Indian democracy broke down as a result of a failure of journalism and storytelling, and the majoritarian democracy is a direct consequence of this. One aspect that journalism failed to captured is the importance of riots in the making of Indian democracy. Riots became an integral part of majoritarian democracy. The anti-Sikh riots of 1984 and the Gujarat riots of 2002 revealed that riots, far from being a spontaneous act of defiance, became well planned genocidal methods. Thus the Emergency, moved on from being a mere system of forced vasectomy to become a deeply genocidal system.

Indian journalism has played its part in the totalitarian emergence of India, the transformation from a democratic to an authoritarian system. The Emergency killed the democratic imagination, and it is this phenomena that continues in Narendra Modi's idea of majoritarian politics.

The democracy as an imagination was a source of resilience and invention and I think one of the most remarkable ideas of resilience was that displayed by civil society. The emergence of civil society, of the NGO movement, of civil rights groups like the Peoples Union of Civil Liberties (PUCL) and People's Union of Democratic Rights (PUDR) added to the democratic imagination. They supplemented the sheer vitality and virility of democracy as an idea, as a source of resistance, as a possibility of resilience, as a theory of courage, as a narrator for a different kind of plurality.

I think the sadness of Indian democracy is the slow decline of all these movements as we confront the flat land of majority terrorism that is being imposed on India. Narendra Modi has to be seen as an institutionalised Sanjay Gandhi. What haunts the Emergency is not so much authoritarianism but the sheer mediocrity of the system. Democracy was an idea that allowed for imagination and invention. The majoritarian systems of Narendra Modi with their attempt to force erasure and to consume violence in fact have created the reverse system.

One can see it today in the very way in which we react to violence. Violence is no longer pathological. Violence is seen as a part of the new consumption paradigm. Violence is seen as something one consumes and in fact one can see this in the very fact that many people now indulging in rape, replay and replicate the rape on social media as a vindication of history. Such an attitude could not emerge until a majoritarian mentality made violence an act of normalcy. The riots normalised violence, rape, and genocide.

The transformation of India from Emergency to majoritarianism is something that sociology has failed to capture and journalism has not been able to narrate convincingly. Amongst the victims is the language of narrative. Many of the words that we once gave a certain passion to, which had a certain kind of poetry, have lost their ability to voice, their eloquence has dissipated. What we now see are words like security and electoralism — which have little meaning. Probably the biggest casualty in this transition from emergency to majoritarianism has been citizenship. Citizenship today is an empty word. Rather than being a guarantee of rights, citizenship today is merely a temporary solution to a problem. Here too, journalism has failed. Whether it's the narratives of Kashmir or Manipur, where ethnic violence – erupted in May 2023 between the majority Meitei people and Kuki-Zo tribal community – continues to this day, citizenship is nothing more than a fragile entity.

The reporting on institutions has also become superficial. Media reports on universities and science tends to emphasise the bureaucratic parts of science and education, rather than the idea of science and of cognitive power within imagination. As a result, the kind of debates that used to take place — the kind of resistance that was once offered by Raman and Maghnad Saha, the astrophysicist who devised the theory of thermal ionisation — is something unthought of today. At one time, Indian journalism and Indian science combined the aesthetic and the ascetic. Today, India has lost that power of faith.

Today's idea of journalism can hardly be compared to the kind of work Praful Bidwai, columnist for *Hindustan Times* and *Frontline*, did post-emergency. His investigation on the use of nuclear power, or the use of seasonal labour as triage or disposable workers — to be eradicated, erased, and forgotten — is a classic of a different kind of dissenting imagination.

The slow disappearance of that dissent has turned journalism into a flatland of the imagination. Journalism in India today has lost its sense of democracy, giving way to a certain idea of a bureaucratisation of development. Development has become the new patriotism. Development has become the goal of the nation-state. And journalism is the biggest casualty in this transition from democracy to development. What was once an act of trusteeship, of witness, of analysis, of critique, of dissent, has now become a conveyer belt of routine report of handouts from various agencies of the state. So now journalism in India has become a way of supine acceptance.

What does this mean to a person, author, columnist, to a man who is a freelance journalist? For me, the consequences of the failure of journalism, and the evaporation of the sustaining myths of pluralistic democracy, are deeply intimate and emotional.

I have witnessed how social sciences, human rights, and journalism, which at one time added to the availability of pluralist imagination, become an arid expanse. While journalism became more professionalised, it also became an entrenched bureaucratic act — more a set of sophisticated handouts run by newspaper supplements than an attempt to provide context or understand a given situation. The sense of memory, which once haunted Partition and the Emergency, has become a sense of erasure. Journalism, which has become a right to information, needs also to become a right to memory. And it is this loss of memory that shows that journalism, in the very idea of reportage, has become a failure of storytelling, the bedrock of democratic imagination.

I once rejoiced at how social science and journalism talked about the fate of the tribals, the importance of the nomads, of the question of the frontier — restoration of alternatives. Today, these issues have become non-issues. Indian democracy has become mainland democracy, mainstream democracy, middle-class democracy.

And the middle class that we talk about is not the quarrelsome middle class of NGOs or the civil rights movements. It is a middle class of aspiration. Narendra Modi, by generalising aspirational democracy, has turned even democracy and journalism into an aspirational tributary. Deep down, this creates a loss of the democratic imagination, and the failure of discourse and narrative, which once made journalism such a fascinating daily ritual — a tribute to democracy, and a celebration of life. But I am not denigrating aspiration. Aspiration is important for the middle class. What one is denying, what one is facing, is the banality of aspiration, the aspiration of development and unqualified wealth. One needs a different idea of aspiration and plurality, and a different kind of critique for journalism to stay alive.

I have observed the failure of journalism lead to the failure of the sustaining myths of Indian democracy. Film has failed to provide any answer to violence. Science has become an appendage to western Big Science and of defence-oriented contracts. Cricket has degenerated into aggressive competition with an accent on naked nationalism. And polity has become a mechanical idea of predictability, standardisation, and regularity.

The noise of democracy, which provided the music of dissent, has lost out in journalism's attempt to become more efficient and aspirational.

If you read an Indian newspaper, or watch a local television channel, you will notice that issues such as climate change and violence are completely ignored or totally neutralised. Sensationalism and government propaganda are the major themes. A plethora of talking heads shouting across each other. But deep down, we need a different understanding of Manipur today. We need a different understanding, and hence a different way of reporting and narrating, of Kashmir and the fact that we have all been waiting for peace in Kashmir for decades.

Maybe my critique of the failure of Indian journalism is outdated. Social media is changing the landscape all over India. But I am convinced that a combination of textuality and digitality is not enough. India needs to recover its self-sustaining myths for Indian journalism to thrive and itself become a catalyst for restoring the pre-Emergency democratic imagination.

Otherwise, the Emergency continues and imagination becomes a real nightmare.

MY DIGITAL MEDIA LIFE

Eric Walberg

Legacy implies truth, but that is always dicey in this turbulent, rapidly changing world. Now it is more a hoax than ever. Ideals of honesty, social and moral backbone, let alone truth, sound quaint. We must, nevertheless, look for hints, shreds of that legacy. Be brave in our Brave New World.

My favourite media gadfly is Douglas Rushkoff. His 2010 book, *Program or be Programmed*, is a worthy sequel to 1967 classic Marshall McLuhan's *The Medium is the Massage*. In the past, social change meant surrendering our agency to a new elite. Now, it is to machines. And the 'medium is message/ massage' is truer than ever. We marvel at touchpads, screens, fetishise our new toys. We are not so concerned about connectivity, integrating our new toys, optimising machines for humanity, creating them to make society a better place, not just for profit. We're just trying to keep up, to adapt to constant change. Where do bodies end? The boundaries of my cognition? Before, machines were accused of usurping labour. Now, they not only copy intellectual processes (our repeat programs) but discourage complex thought (meaning making) too. You don't need to know how to program; rather you just use programs to program other programs. Worse yet, computers are digital, everything reducible to +/-, cause-effect, deterministic, full of hidden biases. No analogue, liminal thinking.

Consumers, that's what we are in our neoliberal paradise, beware! Ideally, emerging media and technologies have the potential to enlighten, to aid grassroots movements, to offer an alternative to the traditional top-down media, to connect diverse groups and to promote the sharing of information, social currency, the degree to which certain content and media can facilitate and/or promote relationships and interactions between members of a community. Ideally!

Before the Internet, I would religiously, daily read the Toronto *Globe and Mail* and, monthly, print magazines with a liberal-socialist perspective such as *Canadian Dimension*. As someone focusing on the Middle East and ex-Soviet Union, my typical daily dose of media thirty years later begins with a hit of Arabic news. I read the headlines from *al-Quds al-Arabi,* first in English then Arabic, then listen to the Arabic courtesy of Google Translate. It includes key articles from the Israeli press which English-language news sites overlook. This is followed by a quick survey of emails and headlines in *The New York Times* (what the enemy thinks) and *The Toronto Star* for urgent and local news events, *RT* for Russia and ex-Soviet sphere. The Internet means most sources are now at your fingertips, though paywalls on almost all national mainstream media mean cut-and-pasting interesting headlines and finding articles from wherever. (I save my money for struggling bloggers). I like to vary my sources, try for local media where possible. I go to the public library to read through the week's *Star*, to reaffirm its shallow, feel-good pablum. Then, there are too many substacks/blogs/podcasts in my inbox from solid experts. For example, Larry Johnson, Douglas MacGregor, and other ex-army types analysing military and geopolitical events, often on Glenn Deisen or Judge Law's almost daily podcasts interviewing them or other experts from the US, Europe, Iran, China. *Simplicius* for details of the frontlines in the Ukraine-Russia war. Jeremy Scahill, *The Grayzone, the Misrahi Perspective,* ex-diplomat Alistair Crooke, independent researcher Roger Boyd. *Aeon* for philosophy, arts. They are even-handed and reliable, and rarely if ever get a chance to appear on mainstream media, but who cares? Especially since the start of Isreal's invasion of Gaza, the mainstream lies have meant you must create your own 'legacy media'.

I also take a weekly dose of Palestine resistance news on *Electronic Intifada*, which features interviews with key actors such as Hind Rajab (documenting IOF soldiers' atrocities for the ICC and to alert governments outside of Israel so as to arrest them) or human rights activists such as Craig Mokhiber, and wildly popular Jon Elmer's 'resistance reports' with cam footage of Hamas and al-Qassam operations targeting IOF soldiers trying to 'secure' Gaza. Weekly podcast lectures with Transnational Institute on broader in-depth issues like 'China and the World' or 'Cities beyond Growth'. And I must not forget *Yaqeen* and *Academia.edu* for Muslim perspectives.

I am called upon for commentary on nonmainstream news sites such as Iran's *Presstv* and India's *NewsXWorld*, which I can later upload and post on

YouTube and my own website ericwalberg.com. I mostly don't get paid for this and it is free to access. Colleagues who haven't squirreled away some savings lead a hand-to-mouth existence, relying on reader donations, much like struggling writers throughout history, whether they sought patrons or some access to a living wage.

Given the dead-end corporatisation and largely Zionist monopoly-control of the mainstream media, one has to keep on the lookout for honest, open-source news. Our postmodern world makes it necessary to use your own mind, life experience, to sense who you can rely on, on whatever issue. With the decline in mainstream media quality and the explosion of Internet sources, you have to plough through your own searches to find what you once accepted from a few mainstream sources on news stands.

This can sound cool or frightening, depending on your perspective, and how much time you have. Most people still rely on legacy media as a default, and also find their own niche news online, feeding into either good goals of peace and concern for the environment, or bad ones of personal prejudices and potentially stoking division and bigotry. It's hard to tell a lie from the truth at the best of times.

We are now living in an age of genocide and war, as brutish and inhuman as the twentieth century in its own way, with AI, drones, pocket nukes, bioweapons, biblical plagues, and conspiracies galore (was Covid a bioweapon?). Israel has matured as the master assassi*nation,* with the US close behind. Anyone that US-Israel doesn't like is game for murder, no questions asked, no world court with clout to bring these monsters to justice. And mainstream media earnestly repeats the official story and lies or better yet simply ignores the crimes. For example, the assassination of Iranian General Qasem Soleimani and his Iraqi colleague Abu Mahdi al-Muhandis in Baghdad by Trump in 2020, lauded by Democrat incumbent Joe Biden and Congress, now down the memory hole. There's not much mainstream media can do about the lawlessness of US leaders, from Reagan on, except report about it, condemn it, look for popular resistance and promote it in the interests of democracy and social justice. But that's never been the role of legacy media.

Popular media as we knew it till the advent of the internet was always in the first place for trade and business, maturing and mutating along with capitalism and imperialism. With the invention of the steam-powered printing press in 1810, media joined the industrial revolution. The electrical telegraph in 1847 brought globalisation of media reach, coinciding with the British empire. The radio in 1897 and TV in 1927 led the way to mass audience access virtually free of charge, which commerce immediately realised was a bonanza, and free or cheap commercial media became the accepted form of transmission, with business holding the purse strings. Britain and its colonies developed state media, which made a pretence of objectivity and at least managed to set standards for a public media culture that was not too crass. Eventually even the US did too, though its public broadcasting came late (1969) and borrows heavily from British TV, with little and always shrinking government funding. Trump cut most of its funding, forcing local affiliates to close. This despite the fact it is one of the most cherished national institutions in the US, like and loved by 40 percent of those over the age of twelve.

But then all mainstream media is in crisis with the internet. The challenges faced by old media, especially newspapers are a combination of dwindling readership and advertising funds, the inability of newspapers to monetise their online efforts, all in the context of perennial global economic crisis. Newspapers, especially in the West and the US, have lost many of their classified advertisements to the internet. As a result, closures of newspapers, bankruptcy, job cuts, and salary cuts are widespread. Given the ongoing environmental crisis, paperless news is clearly the way of the future, though this transition is fraught. What about when your sources disappear in the ether? Your own site? How do journalists make a living? Does the openness of the internet mean that there are no moral guidelines, no accountability for Trump's beloved 'fake news'?

The Canadian government, in 2023, dared to demand that the suddenly obscenely rich internet companies compensate media outlets for links to news published on their platforms, accusing it of stealing mainstream media and relying solely on US advertising. This directly means virtually all Canadian mainstream media facing bankruptcy. Meta simply blocked those links on Facebook and Instagram. The resulting information vacuum was quickly filled by unverified, right-wing content, which helped prop up the local Trumpian candidate, the alt-right Pierre Poilievre, so the Liberal government quickly backed down. Instead, the government created a system for subsidies for traditional media outlets, while coaxing Google into sharing its spoils. Mere weeks before the 2025 election was called, the Canadian Journalism Collective (CJC) began distributing the $100 million that Google is required to pay to news organisations under the Online News Act. This is in addition to the tens of millions in government subsidies the Liberal government has earmarked for news outlets in recent years. While Conservative leader Poilievre previously criticised the Liberals' news policies, it's no longer clear he would eliminate them, having recently suggested a Conservative government would fund collapsing local news media. Calls for state subsidies are even heard in the US. This has come at an enormous cost to journalistic objectivity and independence. We have arrived at the scenario many predicted, with newspapers openly advocating for preferential treatment, praising the governments that funds them, and failing to disclose their entitlements.

What a long way we have come, from Gutenberg and the promise of mass readership. Literacy blossomed in the eighteenth century in the West, contributing to the acceleration of capitalism and imperialism. Now we have been catapulted into the age of AI, where machines can do 'thinking' better and serve it to us on a platter massaged into readable soundbites. This is not proto-totalitarian, but totalitarian pure and simple. Unless we recognise it for what it is and do something about it. Or not. Are we helpless? Can we rely on everyone to find their reliable news sources themselves? I quite like the freedom though am still overwhelmed. If I miss a day of culling my emails, they can become a stressful backlog. As information flows accelerate, more and more time and energy is necessary to process them. You have to ration your usage if you want to leave time for old-fashioned reading – novels, history, social theory, science.

Mainstream media became unreliable long ago. Especially since the Russia-NATO/Ukraine war began in 2014. The only point of view is pro-Ukraine, demonising Russia. It became even more unreadable following 7 October 2023, after which it shamelessly regurgitated Israeli propaganda as objective news (Hamas beheading babies, raping). The only use in watching or reading legacy media now is to understand what our elites want us to believe.

Trump also despises conventional media. Although for the opposite reasons. It broadcast or prints facts he doesn't like. His weapon to deal with them is lawsuits to destroy both media and individuals (now, as president, at taxpayers' expense). And he has been successful, getting a $15 million 'settlement' from ABC which was in fact a bribe to get Trump's approval of a merger deal, and $24.5 million from YouTube after he was suspended by social media platforms following the 6 January 2021 insurrection. This makes Alphabet-owned YouTube the last of the three Big Tech social media companies sued by Trump — which included Meta and then Twitter, now called X — to settle over his removal from their platforms. Meta agreed to settle Trump's lawsuit in January for $25 million. X's settlement in February involved a payment of around $10 million.

If that story of intimidation and bribery isn't enough, consider the fact that the mainstream media has been strongly influenced by the Israeli lobby. It all began way back in 1949 when AIPAC's precursor, the American Zionist Council, was set up to lobby in Congress and the Senate for Israel. The CIA was soon subsidising, clandestinely, media outlets it deemed useful to US imperialism such as *Encounter* and *Partisan Review*. They paid ex-lefty journalists to spout anti-Soviet drivel, not to mention COINTELPRO, the counterintelligence program conducted by the FBA from 1856 to 1971, targeting organisations considered 'subversive', including the Communist Party USA.

The 1962-1963 Senate investigation into media control revealed Israel's clandestine programmes for 'cultivation of editors' and 'stimulation and placement of suitable articles in the major consumer magazines', as well as controlling US reporting about sensitive subjects such as the Dimona nuclear weapons facility. The Justice Department under Robert Kennedy ordered the American Zionist Council to register as a foreign agent. It transferred responsibilities to AIPAC, which was set up especially for this purpose in 1963, granted tax-exempt status in 1968, and has never been required to register as an Israeli agent. Now, AIPAC advertises itself a fine American institution. But we know that AIPAC is able to capture most mainstream outlets and all but one or two Senators and members of Congress. In retrospect, 1949 marked the beginning of the end for independent media in the America.

Now there is nostalgia for print. Books, newspapers, magazines. A recognition that many inventions and innovations are actually harmful to human mental and physical health. That we should resist, even outlaw, some new untested technology. This was the theme of Samuel Butler's *Erewhon* (1872). The Luddites were and are dismissed as wreckers, but their attacks on machines did not necessarily imply hostility to machinery as such. Machinery was just a convenient target, the only way for disenfranchised workers to protest slave-labour conditions and unemployment. Eric Hobsbawm called their machine-wrecking 'collective bargaining by riot'. But that ship has sailed. Technology is always ahead of us in the age of capitalism and we must try to catch up, even better, forestall bad innovations, watch out for potholes, suspicious *cui bonos* (who benefits?), Trump's 'fake news'.

The most infamous conspiracy around the latter is the legendary Russiagate. Russian electoral interference was supposedly responsible for Trump winning the presidency in 2016, using bots to flood social media with lies, which gullible US sheeps supposedly lapped up. Yes, Russian trolling emanated from St Petersburg, the so-called Internet Research Agency. But no, these bots were just part of the internet bilge, now an ocean with billions of bits of mostly questionable news. The 'truth' is Russia has always been the 'enemy' of the West, be it pre-Soviet, Soviet, or post-Soviet times, and doesn't have the same soft power cache in the Western media as the imperial establishment. So our black-sheep poor-cousin uses the only 'soft power' access it has, our social media.

Trolling is nasty but a drop in the social media bucket. Israel is the master troller with decades of experience. It is our 'friend', as we can see during its ongoing genocide, flooding social media with lies of babies beheaded by Hamas 'terrorists' and delicate Israel women raped by said evil Hamas. Recall CIA trolling – Operation Gladio, secret and over-the-top in the 1940s-1970s, though exposed and supposedly abandoned but for sure ongoing today through USAID and the State Department. This is far more lethal than any mini lies of Russian trollers. If we believe this heavy-handed subversion of democracy is bad, then Russia's clumsy attempts to undermine western hegemony are pathetic in comparison.

Beginning in 2004, the CIA established a network of at least 885 websites, in twenty-nine languages, targeting 36 countries directly, aimed not only at adversaries such as China, Venezuela, and Russia, but also at allied nations, including France, Italy, and Spain. Innocent-sounding sports sites are a favourite for espionage. The Iranian Intelligence Ministry arrested thirty individuals in a bust in 2010, and a further forty-two CIA operatives were identified from such websites, such as IranianGoalKicks.com, FirstNewsSource.com, and Farsi-NewsAndWeather.com. China busted a CIA network at about the same time, and executed thirty informants, one of the worst intelligence failures in the CIA's history. Beware, would-be spies: if caught, you will likely be left to your own fate, like the Iranians and Chinese. Being a spy or a stool pigeon for the CIA is as perilous as ever, unless you are Israeli.

All of this make independent voices on the internet, from all sides, all the more important. Moreover, we should be aware of 'digital settler colonialism' promoted by 'legacy media'. Coined by Herbert Schiller in *Mass Communication and American Empire* (1969), this refers to technological colonialism, a system that subjugates Third World nations to the will of the collective West via technology and then training of tens of thousands of would-be journalists in the West – all very prestigious and perfect for the imperial agenda. Half a century later, we live in the 'information era', where mining of data on consumers is now the ultimate source of wealth, both physical (DNA) and mental (purchases and beliefs). It has become normal for people to be exploited through data and other forms of technology, though resistance to this descent into totalitarianism is growing.

After a short burst of democracy in the early days of the internet, capitalism moved in. Within a decade, we got the equivalent of the Seven Sisters for the era of Big Oil (ExxonMobil, Shell, BP): namely, Microsoft, Google, Apple, Meta, and Amazon. Data is the new oil. The mind is the now the last frontier. Out with the nonprofit anarchists, in with the new Oligarchs. The internet, to use Marx's nickname for the factory owner and exploiter of labour, became Mr Moneybags II.

In this war on the 'consumer', digital platforms are weaponised. Arbitrarily shut down by 'servers', countered by Trumpian lawsuits. YouTube notoriously shuts down sites and erases archives (*RT* and thousands of legitimate podcasts), which then mutates into the creation of alternatives, a dance of death, requiring ingenuity (crowdsourcing) and stamina to keep flickers of truth alive. YouTube took Electronic Intifada off the air mid-broadcast for its use of 'Zionism', then admitted it was wrong after the broadcast was cancelled. But the damage was done. That ship sails frequently too, with no money-back guarantee, leaving hosts and viewers alike adrift in a click bait ocean of bilge. What is this but a new form of piracy, warfare, sinking your ship filled with precious cargo, putting tariffs on your intellectual offerings?

Google Search is based on hit-count, that is popularity, but that is more a result of click baiting and ad placement. It results in a fragmentation of the knowledge that people access, now produced to facilitate market manipulation by catering to pre-existing beliefs. Searching online feels like a form of active, critical thinking, but finding good information and integrating a sense of shared reality is as hard as ever. The sense of 'selfdom' sounds like the Enlightenment, but 'nothing comes from nothing' – the maze you are navigating may just be a rabbit hole.

Will generative AI counter these tendencies? Will political mobilisation now be solely governed cybernetically through algorithms? Would computers be authenticating our souls and finding our innermost truths? Already, they shape our search for meaning in an increasingly disorienting and fragmented world. They foster new forms of political communion and sectarian schism. Above it all, stands the sovereign individual – the embodiment of modern selfdom, served by the computer's ruthless logic and its power, while it lasts, to manufacture gold out of bits. As American journalist Robert Wright points out, wisdom didn't come from the top after 9/11, and it's even less likely to come from the top a quarter-century on. 'If pivotal agency is to materialize, it will probably have to emerge from the bottom up. The good news is that the current technological infrastructure for discourse is a place where, in principle, that kind of thing can happen.'

The very idea of a relatively objective, moral-based, information system, was questionable in reptilian capitalism, where oligarchic economic forces control our lives. It became laughable with the creation of Israel as a Zionist racist state under US patronage. Israel has made an art out of assassination, especially of truth-tellers. In Gaza to date, the toll is 270 journalists killed, mostly Palestinian and al-Jazeera reporters, but some of them American. Israeli lies about Hamas beheading babies are regularly repeated by august public figures and legacy media such as the *New York Times*, long after such blatant lies are exposed. Even vital public facts such as Charlie Kirk's eve-of-assassination epiphany, renouncing his love-affair with Israel and Netanyahu, resulting in his assassination a few days later, are buried in mainstream drivel, with history-shattering implications, reducing jet-age information access to something like medieval news via a town crier.

After 9/11, the American political, military, and foreign policy establishment, driven by Christian Zionists and neoconservatives, proceeded to wreck Afghanistan, Iraq, Libya, Syria, and Lebanon. Iran is a work in process. The other countries in the region have been bought off and subjugated in one way or another. Only the impecunious Houthis in tiny Yemen have somehow withstood the US-Israeli onslaught, though they have been carpet-bombed, their leaders assassinated, and their country wrecked. Many of these actions and policies are mostly hidden from the American people under a veil of propaganda dutifully maintained by legacy media and political elites.

The American people have always been kept in the dark about what our elites do in our name and with our money. In Washington, corruption investigations are usually theatre, opaque for 'national security' reasons. I won't even try to incorporate the Epstein files into my jeremiad, though it is clear to anyone who bothers to follow the stink that Trump is the star performer. Who will remain unpunished, as he controls the media spigot and has no intention of having his beans splattered all over him.

The twentieth century lurched through the most horrendous wars in human history, based on jingoism parading as legacy media. We may be laying the foundations of WWIII based on similar lies. The only truth emerging through that black century and the potentially even blacker twenty-first century is from grassroots: primarily the labour movement, less so academia, but also the peace movement, which linked truthtellers in the collective West with the (justifiably paranoid) socialist bloc peace movement, which is helping nurture disarmament and detente then and now. The aftermath of the Vietnam war and Watergate opened a window of truth telling in the West for a few years (1975– 1980), exposing past sins such as COINTELPRO and Operation Gladio. Those few years are treasured now but more as a blip in the long march to oblivion.

Now Larry Ellison, the avowedly Zionist founder of Oracle, the most 'valuable' US public company today, with a market capitalisation of $885 billion, has taken over the world's most popular social media platform TikTok. His son, David, runs Skydance Media which merged with

Paramount for $8 billion. Paramount Skydance is now reportedly aiming to buy WarnerBros' Discovery Channel. Larry is a big fan of Trump and a zealous supporter of genocide in Palestinians. He and his son will consolidate media control under Trump, giving legacy a new meaning: US-Israel hegemony forever and ever.

In the 1950s, William F Buckley was part of the oligarch-funded movement to overthrow the New Deal and travel back to the days of the 1920s and before to the Gilded Age. President Trump is doing his best to maintain this journey, gutting PBS, regulatory agencies and even taking chunks out of university research and Medicaid. What Buckley never truly understood, and Trump certainly does not, is the central role of the state in facilitating the success of advanced capitalism. The US state of the 1890s can in no way facilitate the advanced technological development of the present, but that is the kind of state that the nationalist and conservative parts of the US oligarchy now seem to want. All the king's horse and men (and legacy and social media) can't put US together again after the disasters of Trump, Ukraine, and Israel.

People of goodwill are on their own in this urban jungle of lies and disinformation. We must more and more rely on grassroots smarts, solidarity, trying to keep up with the globalist techno slalom race with its ever-shifting gates. Be unashamedly partisan; there is no such thing as objective journalism. So put yourself on the line, no hiding, no pretending.

COVERING THE FLOODS

Muhammad Saad

Talwar post, Ganda Singh Kasur Photo: Muhammad Saad

In the summer of 2025, the land of Punjab, on both sides of the India-Pakistan border, witnessed a massive flood. It damaged the livelihoods of over six million people, destroying their livestock, crops, homes, and throwing their lives into complete disarray. These devastating events were conspicuously neglected by Pakistan's mainstream media and international media outlets operating throughout the country. Not surprisingly, the government's response to the disaster left much to be desired.

Were it not for the efforts of independent, digital media organisations, and the young and eager journalists behind these endeavours, we would have never known that vast swathes of Pakistan were seriously flooded and under water. The mainstream media virtually ignored the floods. The first journalist on the scene was Adeeb Yousufzai, from the Shangla District of Kyber Pakhtunkhwa Province. He works for *Urdu News*, an Islamabad-based independent digital media organisation. As the flood waters rose in Shangla, he covered the floods and highlighted the scale of the disaster. He followed and reported on the efforts of volunteer workers from the Khidmat-e-Khalq Foundation (KKF), who rescued thousands of women from their homes, relocating them to a tent city they had set up beyond the flood's reach. Some of these women were pregnant and were forced to deliver their babies in the tent city with the help of the KKF. Throughout Yousufzai's coverage, he noted that mainstream Pakistani channels were nowhere to be found. He also reported that the locals expressed anger both with the government's and the mainstream media's apparent lack of interest in their plight.

Adeeb Yousafzai, covering the flood in Shangla, Kyber Pakhtunkhwa

The mainstream media's lack of appetite for covering the urban flooding in Khyber Pakhtunkhwa is not surprising. The north is relatively used to being ignored, as many of the major media outlets operate out of Lahore and Karachi. However, it is concerning that climate change and the disaster-wrought events that follow are unworthy of raising alarm bells within the ranks of Pakistan's mainstream media. Fixated on political news, these organisations consider climate change an unworthy 'boring' issue, and one that would not yield good audience ratings.

Pakistan is said to be the fifth most vulnerable country to climate change, although it contributes only about 0.88 percent of the world's greenhouse emissions. One would assume that the mainstream or national media of any nation state in such a precarious position would talk about little else except climate change. On the contrary, while the country's largest province in terms of population density was under water, with millions stranded without any help, with their lives destroyed before their eyes, all the primetime shows were still churning out their normal programming. They focused instead on the conflict between the two rival political parties and wheeled on pundits to predict the next release date of incarcerated opposition leader and former prime minister, Imran Khan, as if it were another slow news day and the country was not suffering an even greater crisis.

To gauge the severity of the misfocus, it helps to contextualise the landscape of mainstream media in Pakistan and its evolution over the last two decades. At the start of the new millennium, Pakistan had only one state-owned TV channel, Pakistan Television (otherwise known as PTV), though private newspapers were also published by different media outlets. That was the extent of it. Ironically, the liberalisation of the media was formalised by a military dictator, General Pervaiz Musharraf, who came to power after a coup d'état that toppled the civilian government of Prime Minister Muhammad Nawaz Sharif. As part of Musharraf's 'enlightened moderation' programme, privatisation of the economy included media outlet licensing under the 2002 PEMRA ordinance. This led to the creation of many private 24-hour news channels, which changed the Pakistani media landscape, theoretically for the better. However, in 2007, still operating under the martial law declared upon his ascent to the presidency of Pakistan, Musharraf forcibly shut down all the new private channels. This was a part of the crackdown that took place during a state emergency that Musharraf imposed to counter the lawyers' movement that was then gaining momentum against him for violating constitutional basic rights. Eventually, the lawyers' movement prevailed, leading to the demise of Musharraf's nine-year military rule. Unfortunately the executive decisions that his administration took still haunt the socio-political landscape, whether they involved privatising the national media or siding with the US during its invasion of Afghanistan and the so-called 'war on terror'.

Almost two decades since the ouster of Pervaiz Musharraf, the mainstream Pakistani media is solely focused on scandal and spectacle while half of Pakistan's population still struggles beneath the poverty line and the country faces one climate catastrophe after another. Even when massive urban flooding threatens Karachi, the nation's financial hub, and the cultural capital, Lahore, resides beneath a never-ending smog, the mainstream media based out of these two cities hardly sees anything worthy of its attention.

The gaps between trivial spectacle and what is really happening are now being filled by organisations like *Urdu News* and other independent digital media outlets. These groups are comparatively free from the bureaucratic barriers and the legacy of traditional media. They can also operate under less scrutiny from the state apparatus. This democratisation of the media allowed Adeeb Yousufzai the ability to travel with relief workers from various NGOs to the peripheral areas of Punjab and Khyber Pakhtunkhwa and document the stories that really mattered.

The journalistic void left by the mainstream media was not simply a space; it was a vacuum that was rapidly filled by independent reporting and the resilience and courage of civil society. In a disaster defined by the state's functional incompetence, the rescue and recovery operations were carried out by individuals like Muhammad Babar, known across the flood zones simply as 'Babar Bhai'. Yousufzai chronicled life and word for *Urdu News*. It provides a necessary counterpoint to the failures of the central media establishment and highlights what dedication and local knowledge can achieve.

Babar Bhai is a scuba diving instructor and the leader of the local Pakistan Water Rescue Team. These teams are operated by Rescue 1122, the primary service responsible for water and flood rescue in Pakistan. Barber acquired his reputation on 15 August 2025, when flash floods devastated the mountain regions of Buner, Shangla, and Swat. Babar jumped into action and he and his team arrived at the flood scene the very next day. They worked to evacuate people swiftly. When the water receded, the destruction remained, and Barber's team focussed on the long, unglamorous process of relief. His reputation was enhanced further in the deep waters of Jalalpur Pirwala, the confluence point of the Ravi, Chenab, and Sutlej rivers. While the mainstream media hyped the situation around

Lahore, Barber and journalists from alternative media worked tirelessly on the neglected worst-hit peripheries. Then a tragedy struck in the darkness of night. A state-operated Rescue 1122 boat capsized. 'There was no time to think,' Barber told freelance journalist Umar Daraz Gondal. 'I immediately jumped into the water and swam toward the voices'. Despite the loss of one young girl, the locals credit him and his team with rescuing nearly two thousand people in Jalalpur Pirwala. The incident was shared widely on digital and social media, and it revealed a devastating truth: competence, dedication, and rapid rescue action is the work of committed citizens, but not necessarily the state. And the mainstream media is not interested in the lives of ordinary, poor Pakistani living in remote areas.

Babar with his team on a rescue mission in Buner Photo APF

This dichotomy of individual competence and institutional failure is a central feature of Pakistani media. Karachi-based journalist Amar Guriro points out, media organisations are 'not primarily equipped for reporting on floods or any climate change catastrophe'. The resources and expertise required to cover a scuba instructor leading a large-scale rescue operation are absent from newsrooms that rely on shallow coverage of familiar political dramas. The consequence is predictable; the media narrative, already thin on technical knowledge, defaults to uncritically echoing the government's perspective. Gondal confirms this failure from the journalistic frontline. He says that reporters often viewed the floods through lens of the government. 'The journalists repeated the information that the government's PR department was providing them with, because we weren't getting real reporting from the field. Journalists uncritically accepted the official claims of work being done.'

This is where Babar's existence itself becomes a form of critique of Pakistani journalism. His team of 300 professionals systematically securing both lives and possessions represent the organised, disciplined effort, that the state was unable to muster, and the media was too politically timid and structurally compromised to cover it properly.

Babar focus is not just on rescue, but on preparedness too. He trains thousands annually, saying, 'the risk of floods will likely increase in the future. Everyone must be prepared.' Yet the media, obsessed with the political 'breaking news' – which are seldom as groundbreaking as it is claimed – has made no preparation for the potential climate disaster they ought to cover. The essential work of training journalists for such task, and providing with technical equipment needed is not being done. This preference for the sensational and the political over the existential ensures that the nation remains perpetually unaware and unprepared for climate emergency.

So the rescue work fall on the shoulders of non-governmental organisations. Taha Muneeb is the deputy secretary of the Markazi Muslim League (MML), a newly formed religious and political organisation with an extensive network of NGOs operating throughout the country - from Karachi to Khyber Pakhtunkhwa. The MML has a total of 13,872 volunteers carrying out rescue and relief operations throughout the affected areas of Khyber Pakhtunkhwa and Punjab. They were able to rescue more than 171,382 people, and to distribute food to those stranded in their homes. The rescue and relief mission lasted for more than a month, during which almost 3.8 million cooked meals were distributed, along with 128,463 ration packs and 1.9 million bottles of fresh drinking water. Muneeb also arranged two separate trips for digital media journalists to the southern part of the Punjab so that they could cover and understand the human tragedy that was unfolding there.

Muneeb says that the main hurdle in carrying out such an extensive, complex, and prolonged rescue and relief mission, was the lack of coordination between the government and the non-governmental relief organisations working on the ground. It seems to him that the state machinery was not well equipped to manage this disaster, and that it became dependent on the NGO volunteers. As an example, Muneeb narrates an incident where the boats deployed by the government of Punjab to carry out rescue operations were left stranded on the riverbank without trained operators. The local administration was left with no option but to hand over these boats to the NGO workers who knew how to use them. Muneeb points out another way in which state failure puts hurdles in the way of rescue operations. This is the reluctance of people to leave their homes and jump on a boat without any guarantee that their belongings will be protected by the state police. He tells a story of a man named Haji Rasool who was adamant that he would not leave his home, even after all his family members had been evacuated and the water had almost reached the roof. Haji Rasool insisted on staying to guard his house and belongings from looters. This is a common concern amongst people in areas adjacent to rivers.

Gondal reported another resource-related incident on his X account. A private company was charging hundreds of thousands of rupees to rescue the residents of Jalalpur Pirwala who were stranded in their homes. When this was brought to the attention of Maryam Nawaz Sharif, the sitting chief minister of Punjab, she asked the administration to ensure that boats operated by private companies were not taking advantage of the calamity to make a quick buck. The problem was solved the very next day. This incident shows how alternative media platforms (in this case, Gondal's X account, which has over 63,000 followers) can amplify people's concerns and highlight governance gaps in a way that the established media cannot. Gondal stressed twice that the mainstream media was busy running marathon transmissions about a highly anticipated India-Pakistan cricket match while South Punjab was facing one of the worst catastrophes in its modern history.

Haji Rasool sitting on a tree platform Photo: Taha Muneeb

According to Amar Guriro, a renowned independent environmental journalist based in Karachi, none of the mainstream Pakistani media organisations, as well as international organisations operating in Pakistan like the BBC and CNN, have the necessary tools to properly cover large-scale floods. To begin with, they are understaffed. They employ one reporter to cover every event in a city, from crime to politics, and if his city is hit by a natural disaster, they task him to report that too. The reporter is not provided with the technical equipment necessary to cover the subject. Ideally, drones, state of the art camera equipment and a medical team should accompany reporters covering climate disasters in the field. These expenses are burdensome for media organisations. As a result, they prefer to hire freelance local reporters rather than sending their own professional team.

The lack of expert journalists covering the floods can result in another kind of flood – an inundation of misinformation and disinformation. Even the country's most renowned outlets, like *Dawn*, AFY News, and *Daily Jang*, published sensationalist stories about anticipated 'super flooding' supposedly threatening areas of Sindh. Clearly their reporters did not understand the technicalities of the subject, or did not care. Guriro responded by writing a very comprehensive essay in Urdu (published in *The Independent Urdu*) debunking the 'super flooding' rumours. He spoke to several irrigation experts who explained that while the floodwaters from Punjab would eventually merge into the Indus River and reach the sea, the chances of a 'super flood', more of a sensationalised term than anything scientifically viable, in Sindh remained minimal. The Sindh government appointed former Sukkur Barrage control room manager Abdul Aziz Soomro as the focal person for flood monitoring. Over his forty-year career, Soomro had monitored water levels at nearly all of Pakistan's major barrages, dams, and rivers, including Guddu and Sukkur. Guriro quotes Soomro as saying, 'even when the eastern rivers are in extreme flood, large flood waves do not reach Sindh'. Soomro continues, 'Guddu Barrage can handle up to 1.2 million cusecs, and Sukkur Barrage up to 900,000 cusecs, which means that even with heavy flooding in the eastern rivers, Sindh is unlikely to experience a super flood'.

Soomro brings expert knowledge to bear on the issue. It is a great shame that no such experts appeared on mainstream Pakistani media to accurately cover the technical aspects of climate disasters and help the country navigate through them without needing to resort to fantastical scare tactics. Once the flood receded, and water levels returned to normal, another story surface. The displacement of large communities, the loss of millions of rupees worth of crop damage, the agricultural and economic consequences – none of this was covered by the mainstream media. We continue with the usual daily diet with members of the rival political parties shouting at each other on primetime news shows, engaging in petty point scoring, or a number of pandits and commentators shouting across each other on talk shows, while people continue to suffer the long-term effects of the floods on a scale which is beyond the scope of any NGO to tackle.

The latest data released by the Alkhidmat Foundation Pakistan, the country's largest NGO working in the rescue, relief, and rehabilitation of flood victims, shows the number of people affected by the 2025 flood to have reached almost seven million. Punjab suffered the most with 4.7 million victims, followed by Khyber Pakhtunkhwa with 1.6 million, and Gilgit-Baltistan with almost 356,000. Almost three million people have been displaced, 1,370 killed, and over 217,000 houses were damaged or destroyed. The figures concerning dead livestock and damaged crops are still to be ascertained, but the areas that were hit are considered the most fertile lands in Punjab. Alkhidmat and other NGOs aim to focus now on the rehabilitation of the displaced, giving them solar panels and tents so they can set up temporary homes until the government releases funds, and a proper policy can be devised.

Pakistan is blessed to have such NGOs, but surely less blessed with its media and governance institutions, whose failures are interrelated, a synergy of incompetence. Gondal explains that 'the reason mainstream media was awfully silent while half of the Punjab was under water is because [speaking out] would have highlighted the failure of the administration on the government's part'. The mainstream media does not have to courage to challenge or stand up to the government. Thus, they reply totally on the various PR departments of the state machinery. But there is another point worth mentioning: the lack of appropriate and adequate workforce, staff and personal in government departments and agencies. 'I used to criticise vehemently the bureaucracy of our country,' Gondal says. 'But when I saw one district deputy commissioner managing everything from revenue collection to disaster management, and even managing the protocols of the provincial ministers, it made me realise how overburdened all these people are, with very little capacity to do anything apart from day-to-day tasks'.

Pakistan has faced two massive floods in the past three years: in 2022 and 2025. Urban flooding has become a regular occurrence in Karachi as well as in parts of Khyber Pakhtunkhwa, where people are becoming accustomed to living under the constant threat of cloud bursts. Lahore does not have such risks of flooding, but smog and other forms of pollution have become a persistent problem for the city. Given this national reality, one would expect that a climate emergency policy would be in place, and that the crises would be discussed constantly in mainstream media.

The circus of the mainstream media fails to reflect the reality that people face on the ground. In the case of Lahore's smog, for instance, the mainstream Pakistani media peddle the state narrative about how successfully the government of Punjab is combating the crisis with 'smog guns' imported from China. Just how effective these smog guns actually are is an issue they have not bothered to explore. (Not much, I would say!) Independent journalists like Umar Daraz Gondal and Adeeb Yousafzai represent only a tiny minority of people who take their profession seriously, who are prepared to give up the comforts of their homes, and to listen to people's concerns and echo their complaints. This is undoubtedly why young Pakistanis, especially those of Gen Z and the rising Gen Alpha, have such an appetite and preference for alternative media platforms. given their refusal to evolve, he mainstream media is set to become totally irrelevant in Pakistan. The only hope is that they turn their eyes away from the interests of the ruling elite, spectacle and scandal, and towards the real concerns, issues and threats facing the people of Pakistan.

ASAD'S *THE UNROMANTIC ORIENT*

Josef Linnhoff

One summer's day in 1922, a young European Jew set sail for Palestine. He was one of an increasing number of Jews headed to the holy land in the years following the Balfour Declaration. He hailed from the region of Galicia in the Austro-Hungarian Empire, at the time a hotbed of antisemitism, and came of age in Vienna after his family joined the exodus of *Ostjuden* ('Eastern Jews') fleeing Eastern Europe for Austria in the early twentieth century. Despite both parents belonging to distinguished rabbinical families, this traveller was disappointed with his Jewish religious education. He was also disillusioned with Europe, sensing a moral drift, rootlessness, and restlessness at the heart of European society after the Great War. He was an aspiring German-speaking journalist not unlike Theodore Herzl himself. Though he was not a Zionist, all the ingredients were in place. Surely, after arriving in Palestine, it was only a matter of time? Not quite. Our visitor will be scandalised by much of what he sees on the ground in Palestine. The book he will publish upon his return will be deeply critical of the Zionists and express support for the Palestinians. His time in Palestine will spark an interest in the Near East that will eventually culminate in his conversion to Islam. And the young traveller in question, Leopold Weiss, will become far more famous under a different name: Muhammad Asad.

Born in 1900, Leopold Weiss converted to Islam in 1926, changed his name, and became one of the most famous Western Muslims of the twentieth century. Perhaps no single figure better captures the twists and turns of the twentieth century. Asad's remarkable life took him from Weimar Berlin to pre-Nakba Palestine, from the deserts of Arabia to the United Nations in New York. He witnessed the last gasps of the Ottoman Empire and the dawn of the Saudi and Pakistani states. Asad lost relatives in the Nazi Holocaust and experienced the horrors of Partition in India/

Pakistan. His career included stints as a journalist, diplomat, and statesman. But above all, Asad is known as a Muslim thinker and reformer. His writings traverse many fields of modern Islamic thought—from Qur'anic studies to political theory to Islamic law—to each of which he made a major contribution.

While Asad is best known for his iconic autobiography, *The Road to Mecca*, few are aware of its sequel, *Homecoming of the Heart*. And very few know about his earliest work, *Unromantisches Morgenland (The Unromantic Orient)* – published in German in 1924, two years before his conversion to Islam. This work is a journalistic account of Leopold Weiss's travels in Palestine and the Near East between 1922-1923. A close reading of *The Unromantic Orient* adds an important dimension to our understanding of the Israel-Palestine conflict. It sheds valuable light on the history of early Jewish anti-Zionism. It also shines a light on Asad's formative years before his conversion. The question of Palestine is, in turn, a useful lens through which to explore Asad's later life and career in the Muslim world.

The story goes that in the spring of 1922 a young Leopold Weiss, at the time a twenty-one-year-old aspiring journalist in Berlin, was invited to visit Jerusalem by an uncle who had settled there. Weiss accepted the offer and spent much of that year and 1923 travelling across Palestine and the region. This was his first experience of the Muslim world. Weiss kept a travel journal during this time and sent dispatches to European newspapers, eventually becoming a special correspondent for the *Frankfurter Zeitung*. He returned to Germany and published excerpts from his journal under the title *Unromantisches Morgenland (The Unromantic Orient)*, in 1924. This work is 159 pages, covers the period from 14 March to 10 October 1923, and includes fifty-nine black and white photographs that Weiss took himself.

It is a short but extremely valuable historical text. It gives us a firsthand account of life in Palestine in the years after the Balfour Declaration, at a time of heightened tension, twenty-five years before the creation of the State of Israel. Weiss's time in Palestine coincided with an important period known in Zionist historiography as the 'Third Aliyah.' Between 1919-1923, up to forty thousand Jews, mostly from Eastern Europe, migrated in the hope of establishing a Jewish homeland. This, in turn, led to increased frictions on the ground. The 1920 Nebi Musa riots and 1921

Jaffa riots preceded Weiss's arrival, with the 1929 Hebron Massacre around the corner. Not for the last time, Weiss was in the right place at the right time to witness the tectonic shifts of the twentieth century. *The Unromantic Orient* may also be one of the earliest works by a European writer to express clear support for the Palestinians. Weiss presents the Palestinians as the authentic, rightful inhabitants of the land, and in the opening pages he slams Zionism as a 'wound in the body of the Near East'. And yet, despite all this, this work has been largely overlooked by scholars. We do not hear Weiss's name nor see this work cited in the extensive literature on Israel-Palestine. The result is that important questions have not yet been asked. To what extent does Weiss give us a prescient early warning of what was to come? Does he anticipate themes that would later shape our understanding of the conflict? What can we learn, a full century on, from this early testimony?

The Unromantic Orient was remarkably ahead of its time, albeit in ways that a reader today might easily miss. Two examples will suffice. First, consider the fact that Lepold Weiss centres the Palestinians themselves. Almost every page mentions the local inhabitants. Weiss interviews them, acknowledges their fears and concerns, and paints a picture of a people with deep ties to the land and a clear sense of their rights and dignities. This sounds obvious today, but we should remember that the early Zionists tended to render the Palestinians invisible, portraying Palestine as an empty, abandoned wilderness in need of Jewish migrants to make the land 'bloom.' European travellers and British colonial officials fared little better. The text of the Balfour Declaration itself never uses the word 'Arab' or 'Palestinian' and alludes only in passing to 'existing non-Jewish communities' – which, at the time, were 95 percent of the population. Against this, *The Unromantic Orient* gives us another piece of evidence, as if needed, that Palestine was far from a 'land without a people'.

Second, consider how Weiss presents Zionism as an extension of British colonialism. Britain supports Zionism to keep a stronghold in the Near East on the eastern bank of the Suez Canal, Weiss writes, while the Zionists have 'willingly renounced' their own sovereignty by becoming tools of a colonial power. This, he writes, is the great 'fiasco' and 'self-condemnation' of Zionism.

Will Zionism die soon? The Arabs fervently wish it so...On the other hand, the leaders of the Zionist movement know well enough how they are basically serving a foreign power in order to subjugate a third nation; and in the light of this they willingly renounce their own nation's sovereignty for the foreseeable future; herein lies the fiasco, the self-condemnation of the movement (31 May 1923).

Again, this will sound obvious today, but Weiss is writing this decades before the theme of 'Zionist colonialism' started to gain traction in progressive circles in the West – which was only in the 1960s and 1970s, after the 1967 war and the emergence of figures like Edward Said. The young Leopold Weiss, still in his early twenties, seems to have had not only moral clarity but an unusually keen sense of perception.

In places, the work feels eerily relevant to our time. On the question of defining antisemitism from anti-Zionism, for example, Weiss cites a local Palestinian dignitary as saying:

Our struggle is not against Judaism, but against political Zionism, and it is the fault of Zionists if, today, the ordinary man sees Jews and Zionists as one and the same, and hatred is hurled against everything Jewish (12 May 1923).

These words are hardly out of place in 2025. In other aspects the book is clearly a product of its time. Weiss makes some basic errors about Islam, misnaming the al-Aqsa Mosque as the 'Mosque of Omar' and confusing Arab culture for Islamic teachings ('Muhammad Asad' will have much to learn). There is a romanticised Orientalism in some places. Weiss taps into mythical tropes of a 'timeless' Arabia, and his vivid descriptions of the beautiful, exotic women he encounters reveal a Western male gaze. The book sketches the diverse Arab and Jewish communities on the ground in Palestine, the latter including not only Eastern European but Sephardim, Bukharan and Persian Jews. While there is no sense in the text that its author is on the verge of becoming a Muslim, it *is* possible to detect a growing admiration for the Arabs. What starts as a political sympathy gradually gives way, as the journal proceeds, to a budding fascination for Arab culture and its people. At one point Weiss lauds the Arabs as 'blessed' and even speaks of 'my Arab people!' With hindsight, then, we catch glimmers in the text of the conversion and journey in the Islamic world to come, a journey that Weiss could hardly have imagined at the time.

Yet a close reading of *The Unromantic Orient* also raises questions. Did Weiss meet and interact with Zionists in Palestine? As a special correspondent with *Frankfurter Zeitung*, one would certainly expect so. There were many Zionists to meet and much happening in Zionist circles at the time. Apart from a brief reference to a conversation with the Zionist leader Menachem Ussishkin, however, the text is silent. The result is that the book gives a somewhat simplistic and one-dimensional account of a Zionist movement that was, in fact, broad and diverse. What might Weiss have made of notable Zionist thinkers like philosopher Martin Buber and economist Arthur Rippin, both of whom supported the Brit Shalom ('covenant of peace') initiative, set up in 1925 with the goal of peaceful coexistence between Jews and Arabs? What might Weiss have made of the cultural Zionism of Ahad Ha'am, which sought not a Jewish State but rather a spiritual centre and a thriving Jewish culture in Palestine? Or how might Weiss have reacted to a figure like Ze'ev Jabotisnky and his (in) famous essay, *The Iron Wall*, published in 1923? The founder of so-called Revisionist Zionism, Jabotinsky argues in this essay that no people in history have ever welcomed their colonization by outsiders, and thus the Zionists will have to use maximum force against the Palestinians:

> There can be no voluntary agreement between ourselves and the Palestine Arabs. Not now, nor in the prospective future...(I)t is utterly impossible to obtain the voluntary consent of the Palestine Arabs for converting 'Palestine' from an Arab country into a country with a Jewish majority...My readers have a general idea of the history of colonization in other countries. I suggest that they consider all the precedents with which they are acquainted, and see whether there is one solitary instance of any colonization being carried out with the consent of the native population. There is no such precedent...Native populations, civilized or uncivilized, have always stubbornly resisted the colonizers.

The irony is that Weiss would have agreed with much of Jabotinsky's analysis. He will have welcomed the recognition that there is already a community living in Palestine. He may have even respected the honesty and candour with which Jabotinsky states the problem and describes the colonial nature of Zionism. The difference, of course, would be the moral stance and conclusion that each would draw as a result.

To what extent can we trust the veracity of *The Unromantic Orient*? Is the text a historically accurate and faithful retelling of its author's experiences? If not, where does documentary fact meet narrative fiction? It is a question for future scholarship. But it is not, perhaps, the right question to ask. We should not let a focus on historical 'fact' blind us from the deeper truths and analysis that Weiss sought to convey. What is most striking about the text is how Weiss seems to have grasped, even at this time, the ominous direction of travel. The main theme in the text is that of two mutually exclusive claims – an indigenous population versus Zionist migrants backed by a colonial power – with the clear sense that something has to give. The centre cannot hold. In an entry from 20 April 1923, Weiss warns the Zionists that they will never be able to mobilise enough long-term force to silence the desires and demands of the Palestinians. In another entry Weiss talks of a Jerusalem 'brimming over' with hatred:

> Jew or Arab. Here they are brimming over with an intolerant hatred that leads them nowhere; for they will have nothing to do with each other. It is not a rebellion of weak against strong…but the hatred of rivals…(T)here is little air to breathe in Jerusalem. The voices cross continually, seeming to tell one another: You shouldn't be here (8 April 1923)

Fast forward two and a half decades, and Muhammad Asad would no doubt have been pained by the violence and dispossession of the Nakba, in 1948. But I do not think he would have been surprised. I think Leopold Weiss had already seen the warning signs – earlier and more clearly than most. I think we can read *The Unromantic Orient* as a prescient early warning of what was to come.

It is possible to still dig a little deeper to bring out the full significance of this text. The wider context here is key. One hundred years ago, as Leopold Weiss was writing and publishing his first work, Jewish anti-Zionism was the norm. Zionism started on the margins and only entered the Jewish mainstream in the 1940s, amid the horrors of the Holocaust. Until then, many Jews in Europe were assimilationists, seeing their future as full members of European society. Many feared Zionism would reinforce antisemitic tropes about the 'foreignness' of Jews in Europe. (It was on this basis that the only Jewish member in the British cabinet, Edwin Montagu, voted against the Balfour Declaration). There were Orthodox

Jewish critics of Zionism, then as now. Jewish socialist and Marxist anti-Zionism was a major force and is a story in itself, as seen in the example of the Jewish Labour Bund (1897–1920). Early Jewish anti-Zionism is a rich tradition that should be better known. The obvious question for our purposes is: where does Leopold Weiss fit?

None of these trends would have appealed to Weiss. Recall that Weiss was critical of both his European and Jewish upbringing. His anti-Zionism was neither assimilationist nor Marxist nor Orthodox. Weiss, in fact, had much in common with the Zionists themselves—both Weiss and the Zionists shared a disenchantment with Europe, a yearning for rootedness and community, and a romanticization of the East as a site of purity and authenticity. But what we find in the pages of *The Unromantic Orient* is a Jewish anti-Zionism that is based, above all, on the question of Palestinian rights. It is what we today would call 'pro-Palestinian' anti-Zionism, and we see this expressed by a young European Jew in the early 1920s – decades before the Nakba. Just how common was this at the time? How many voices were there, in European Jewry of the early 1920s, anchoring their anti-Zionism on a moral defence of the Palestinians? We do know of a few others – one such figure is Jacob de Haan, the Dutch journalist and literary writer. But we also know that this particular 'brand' of anti-Zionism was not yet common by the 1920s. It would seem, then, that Leopold Weiss was well ahead of the curve, an early voice in what would become a great tradition of Jewish defenders of the Palestinians, a forerunner of the Noam Chomskys, Illan Pappés, and Norman Finkelsteins to come.

Writing three decades later, Asad would briefly revisit his time in Palestine in this autobiography, *The Road to Mecca*, published in 1954. Excerpts from *The Road to Mecca* are lifted directly from *The Unromantic Orient*. But there are also differences. In his autobiography, Asad fills in many of the gaps and fleshes out the story behind *The Unromantic Orient*. He shares the details of how he came to live with his uncle in the Old City of Jerusalem and write for the *Frankfurter Zeitung*. He also discusses his friendship with Jacob de Haan, a Dutch Orthodox Jew, journalist, and prominent anti-Zionist who would later be assassinated by Zionist paramilitaries in 1924, shortly after Weiss's departure, in what was the Zionist movement's first political murder. But there is one aspect to the story in *The Road to Mecca* that stands out above all. Asad claims to have met in Palestine no less a figure than Chaim Weizmann, a leader of the Zionist movement, the driving force behind the Balfour Declaration, and the man who later became the first president of Israel. Asad's account is worth citing in detail:

> I still remember a brief discussion I had...with Dr. Chaim Weizmann, the undisputed leader of the Zionist movement. He had come on one of his periodic visits to Palestine...and I met him in the house of a Jewish friend...I had the disturbing impression that even he, like most of the other Zionists, was inclined to transfer the moral responsibility for all that was happening in Palestine to the 'outside world'. This impelled me...to ask:
>
> 'And what about the Arabs?'
>
> I must have committed a *faux pas* by thus bringing a jarring note into the conversation, for Dr Weizmann turned his face slowly toward me, put down the cup he had been holding in his hand, and repeated my question:
>
> 'What about the Arabs...?'
>
> 'Well – how can you ever hope to make Palestine your homeland in the face of the vehement opposition of the Arabs who, after all, are the majority in this country?'
>
> The Zionist leader shrugged his shoulders and answered drily: 'We expect they won't be in a majority after a few years.'

Ominous words by Weizmann, especially in light of the Nakba to come. But we should tread with caution and not rush to take Asad at face value. There are grounds to question whether the encounter with Weizmann happened exactly as Asad recalled. There may even be grounds to question whether it happened at all.

Part travelogue and part memoir, we already know that *The Road to Mecca* is not a reliable and historically accurate account of the life of its author. A major study of the text by Gunter Windhager, in German, has done much to separate fact from fiction. Asad's travelling companion Zayd, to give one example, is shown by Windhager to be a purely literary figure. And even on a surface reading, many of the dialogues in *The Road* to Mecca feel staged and stylised to fit into the text's dramatic narrative. Where might this encounter with Weizmann fall on the scale from fact to fiction? Asad is also recalling an exchange that allegedly took place three decades earlier, nor can we ignore the importance of the intervening years. By the time Asad wrote *The Road to Mecca,* he would have known of the forced expulsion of 750,000 Palestinians in the Nakba and the role Weizmann played in the State of Israel. How might this have shaped his memory and impacted his telling of the exchange? To what extent is an encounter from decades ago being retold and recast in light of later events?

Yet there is a bigger question still. Why, if Weiss met Weizmann in Palestine, is there no mention of this in *The Unromantic Orient*? This is the much earlier text, written at a time when memory of the meeting would have been fresh. For an aspiring journalist like Leopold Weiss, such an encounter with a Zionist leader would have been too big a scoop to miss. This is the stuff from which journalistic careers are made. We might add that Weizmann's alleged reply to Weiss, his curt dismissal of the Arab question, contradicts the public language of '*convivencia*' that he and other Zionist leaders were still adopting up until the 1930s. This is not just a scoop, then, but a potential scandal. So why is it missing from *The Unromantic Orient*?

There could be several reasons. Perhaps the importance of the exchange only dawned upon Asad in later years, after the Nakba and the founding of Israel in 1948 and the election of Weizmann as Israel's first president. Or perhaps this is a sign of censorship in *The Unromantic Orient*. It may be that the publisher did not want to attribute an inflammatory – and unsubstantiated – statement to a global statesman like Weizmann. Or perhaps Weiss, still a young journalist with a long career ahead of him, was choosing his words carefully. It is one thing to criticise the Zionists in broad strokes, another to expose its leader directly. But another possibility, alluded to above, is that the meeting with Weizmann did not happen at all – hence its absence from *The Unromantic Orient* – and is a narrative fiction worked into *The Road to Mecca*.

We simply do not know. All we know is that a significant encounter with a Zionist leader is included in *The Road to Mecca* and yet curiously absent from *The Unromantic Orient*. Perhaps one explanation lies in the story behind the writing of *The Road to Mecca*. It is little known that Asad started work on an autobiography after falling from favour and resigning as a diplomat for Pakistan at the UN. While working on the manuscript, he was a victim of a sustained smear campaign in the Pakistani press, forced to deny claims that he had left Islam, reverted to Judaism, and was working for Israel. The following extract is from a letter Asad sent to then-Pakistani Foreign Minister Zafarullah Khan, dated 6 July 1953:

> Dear Chaudhri Sahib,
>
> I am sorry that every time I write to you it is about something unpleasant, but I really see no way out of a difficult situation without placing before you the facts of the libel and slander to which I am now exposed. Since my resignation from the Foreign Service, a spate of malicious rumours, both oral and in the press, has been put into circulation to the effect that:
>
> 1) I have forsaken my allegiance to Islam and have reverted to Judaism;
>
> 2) I have exerted my influence in the Pakistan Foreign Ministry in favour of the Jews and have been advocating Arab rapprochement to Israel;
>
> 3) In the course of my recent tours of the Middle East I have surreptitiously visited Israel;
>
> 4) I have married in the United States a Jewess…

In another letter, from 16th June 1953, Asad is at pains to point out that his anti-Zionism predates, and was even central to, his eventual conversion to Islam:

> As a matter of fact, my opposition to Zionism and the idea of a Jewish state in Palestine was made clear even before I became a Muslim: for in my first German book, *Unromantisches Morgenland*…I strongly advocated the Arab cause and combated Zionist aims on moral grounds. Indeed, it was this realization of the injustice that was being done to the Arabs which drew me to them in those early years and thus became, indirectly, the initial cause of my interest in Islam and my final conversion in 1926.

The ostensible trigger for the smear campaign was Asad's decision to divorce his second wife for a Catholic convert to Islam. The real reasons are unclear. It is sad to think that Asad's early critique of Zionism and

ASAD'S THE UNROMANTIC ORIENT

defence of the Palestinians did not protect him from antisemitic smears in the Muslim world. But, for our immediate purposes, this could shed some light on our puzzle. If the encounter with Weizmann did take place, this smear campaign would surely have been a reason to include it in *The Road to Mecca*. Asad is setting the record straight and silencing his critics. If the encounter with Weizmann did not take place, this smear campaign would surely have been a reason to invent it. Asad is adding a fictional flourish to the truth of his longstanding anti-Zionism. What better way to prove his commitment to Islam and credentials as an anti-Zionist, at a time when both were under scrutiny, than telling the tale of his confrontation with Chaim Weizmann, factually or otherwise?

We therefore see how Asad revisited his time in Palestine in his later years, tweaking the story in subtle but significant ways, adding important details not previously disclosed. But we should not stop at *The Road to Mecca*. The story in *The Road to Mecca* ends in 1932, when Asad was just thirty-two years old. Asad lived until 1992, and in the years after publishing his autobiography Asad continued to write on a range of topics. He wrote a second book in German titled *Islam und Abendland* (*Islam and the West*) in 1960. He made a major contribution to Islamic political theory in *The Principles of State and Government in Islam*, in 1961. He completed his magnum opus, *The Message of the Qur'an*, in 1980. And he continued to talk about Palestine. In the 1970s and 1980s, Asad wrote a series of little-known articles and speeches that directly address the Israel-Palestine conflict. The titles alone are instructive: *Jerusalem: The Open City* (late 1970s); *A Vision of Jerusalem* (1982); *Jerusalem: A City for All People* (1982). Taken altogether, these works pivot on two core points: the question of the 'rightful' inhabitants of Palestine, and the spiritual significance of Jerusalem.

On the question of 'rightful possession,' Asad dismisses the Zionist idea that the Jews have a rightful claim to Palestine because they were settled in the land for several centuries in the pre-Christian era before being evicted by the Romans nearly two millennia ago. This 'fallacy' ignores the fact that history is full of stories of displacement. 'If moral validity could be attributed to such a claim,' Asad writes, 'then the Arabs could claim, with equal validity, the return to them of Spain.' But one wonders whether this is the strongest argument Asad could make. Does time alone trump morality? Does this really engage and rebut the nature of Zionist claims and the Biblical connection to Palestine? There is even a latent danger in the argument. Zionists need only occupy the West Bank and Gaza for a few generations more, one could argue, before 'time' grants them title to the land. It is perhaps for this reason that Asad tries another tack, this one far more effective. He identifies the present-day Palestinians as the descendants of the tribes that were originally settled in the land – the Amorites, Edomites, Philistines, Moabites, and Hittites – long before the arrival of the Hebrews. The Hebrews did not come to an empty country all those years ago, Asad tells us, and the original tribes continued to live there during the kingdoms of Israel and Judah and also after the Romans. Asad then writes:

> They are (still) living there – or in refugee camps nearby – to this day: and they are called 'Palestinian Arabs.'... The overwhelming majority of what we describe today as Palestinian 'Arabs' are in reality only the *Arabianised* original inhabitants of the country...In short, the Palestinians...are 'Arabs' in the cultural sense only; ethnically, they are direct-line descendants of the original, multi-racial inhabitants of Palestine; original in the sense of having lived there for untold centuries before the appearance of the Hebrews.

We seldom hear this argument in pro-Palestine circles today. But its value is obvious. Palestinians would seem to have a stronger claim to the land according to Zionism's own logic. Asad is tackling Zionism on its own terrain, utilising Zionist lines for anti-Zionist ends. If Asad is an original and incisive thinker in other areas, from Qur'anic studies to Islamic legal reform, why should his writings on Israel-Palestine be different?

On the question of Jerusalem, Asad draws on the Qur'an and core tenets of Islamic theology to argue for Muslim custodianship over the holy city. But he is keen to show this would not deprive Jews and Christians of their rights. His argument proceeds as follows. While a moral Jew may not abuse Jesus or Muhammad, nor can he or she revere them. A Christian may revere the Old Testament prophets but cannot be expected to hold the same for the Qur'an or Muhammad. It is only the Qur'an, Asad explains, that reveres all the prophets and stresses the essential unity of their religious experience. A Muslim cannot deny the earlier prophets for they are also his or her own (2:136). The Qur'an warns against reviling the sanctities of others (6:108) and explicitly orders Muslims to protect churches and synagogues (22:40). After a quick nod to history – the protection of Jewish and Christian holy places in Jerusalem under centuries of Islamic rule – Asad delivers his point. Jerusalem may be holy to all three communities, but only in Islamic hands can it remain an 'open city.' Only the Muslim community is morally and spiritually qualified to safeguard the sanctity of Jerusalem for all:

> Only the people who recognize all of the three monotheistic religions – Judaism, Christianity, and Islam – as being based on a truly divine revelation; the people who revere all the prophets of those three religions...It follows that in a conceivably free Palestine – a state in which Jews, Christians and Muslims could live side-by-side in full political and cultural equality – the Muslim community should be specifically entrusted with the custody of Jerusalem as a city, open to all three communities.

Yet there remains a polemical edge to these works. Zionism's attachment to Jerusalem as the 'birthright' of the Children of Israel, Asad tells us, is symptomatic of 'a people's narcissistic self-adoration'. While Zionists treat Jerusalem as a 'patrimony' or a 'piece of real estate to be "possessed"', Islam preserves the openness of Jerusalem for others. Asad's argument may appeal to liberal notions of religious freedom and pluralism. But it is anchored in Islamic theology, not in secular calls to international law or to any UN resolution:

> The all-embracing quality of the Islamic faith predisposes its followers for this sacred task: and predisposes them in a deeper, more truly historic sense that could be attained by any resolution of the United Nations.

Again, we seldom hear this kind of theological reasoning in pro-Palestine activist circles today. We see here what a learned and authoritative Muslim voice can bring to the discussion on Israel-Palestine. But we also see how the question of Palestine never left Asad. The fire still burned, long after his experiences in 1922-1923. Anti-Zionism is the common thread running throughout a rich and varied career from Judaism to Islam, from Europe to the Muslim world, from *The Unromantic Orient* (1924) to *A Vision of Jerusalem* (1982). Simply put, the question of Palestine bookends Asad's story.

Why, then, does the relationship between Asad and Palestine matter? In the years after publishing *The Unromantic Orient*, Leopold Weiss would convert to Islam, commit his life to the cause of Muslim revival, and it may be that his remarkable career in the Muslim world has distracted us from the Jewish part of his story. But we see here how the lessons from Asad's life do not begin with his conversion to Islam. The study of *The Unromantic Orient* sheds valuable light on the history of early Jewish responses to Zionism and the question of Palestinian rights. It also casts a fresh perspective on the life and legacy of Asad himself. If Asad is famous today as the author of *The Road to Mecca* and *The Message of the Qur'an*, we should also recognise the relevance of his earliest work. If Asad is known as a Muslim thinker who roamed freely throughout the Islamic tradition, contributing to many fields of Islamic thought, we should recognise that Asad's anti-Zionism is one of his greatest, and largely unrecognised, contributions. If many countries today can claim Asad as their own, from Austria to Saudi Arabia to Pakistan, perhaps the most formative link is with Palestine.

What started it all for Muhammad Asad, the beginning of the beginning of his story, was his first-hand witnessing Zionist colonisation of Palestine. It was his solidarity with the Palestinians that sparked his love for Arabs, and it was his love for Arabs that, ultimately, led to his conversion to Islam.

For Asad, the road may have been to Mecca, but that road started in Palestine.

THE SUWAYDA MASSACRES

Robin Yassin-Kassab

What a difference a dose of disinformation makes.

My first visit to Syria in 2025, the first for many years, was in March and April, late Ramadan and Eid. Though the first disaster of the post-Assad transition had just happened – I mean the chaotic response to an Assadist insurgency on the coast, which degenerated into massacres of Alawites – most people continued to give the new authorities the benefit of the doubt. I was able to sample the euphoria still lingering amongst most of the public since the long-awaited liberation the previous December.

My second visit – in July and August – began like this. As I had in March, I flew to Beirut and took a taxi to Damascus. But this time, shortly before the Lebanese border post, a soldier ran up to the car waving his arms. 'You've got Syrian plates!' he shouted. 'Turn around! They'll smash you up!' A couple of hundred metres behind him, an angry mob of Lebanese was roaring towards us, waving the multicoloured Druze flag. The driver was already doing a rapid three-point turn. 'The Arab people is a donkey!' he said, eyes on the road.

Fifteen minutes later he was engaged in a roadside conference with several other Syrian drivers. They decided on the safest route home, and reported that some cars had indeed been smashed. Some Syrian refugees in Beirut had also been beaten up. That was nothing new, but the pretext was. Lebanese Druze were up in arms – Israeli Druze were too – because the Druze in southern Syria were being attacked by militias loyal to the transitional government.

What had that to do with Syrian taxi drivers? Or with me? Presumably the disinformation swallowed by the protestors, or the disinformation already at home in their guts, was that all Syrians were guilty. In Syria, some Sunnis had decided that all Druze were guilty of treachery, and some Druze had decided that all Sunnis were irredeemable extremists. The events and their echoes in the media and social media were whipping up identity politics like never before.

Better focus on the detail. Most Syrian Druze live in Suwayda province in the south of the country. They border Jordan and are separated from Israeli-occupied territories by Daraa province. And they share Suwayda with Bedouin tribes. Perhaps 'dispute' is a better word than 'share', because the two groups have often squabbled. The conflict usually follows a traditional Cain and Abel pattern; depending on perspective, the thieving pastoralist tribes let their animals eat the crops of the agriculturalist Druze, or the Druze enclose open land that belongs to God alone. Today it feels that the conflict is intractable, but the shared history of Suwayda's residents has produced plenty of cooperation too. According to journalist Omar al-Asaad, 'the Bedouin had a cultural effect on the Druze, in terms of accent, poetry, and dress. And they allied sometimes, to resist Ottoman conscription, for example, or French taxes.'

Omar is one of my colleagues at the Prisons Museum. Nour Abo Farraj is too. Both are from Suwayda but now live elsewhere. I asked Nour to sum up why, even before the latest violence, the Druze community was generally suspicious of the new Syrian government and its Islamist tone. 'The community has a problem with any kind of conservatism,' she said. 'It's a closed group, but only a few people are religious.' The Druze faith, like those of the Alawites and Ismailis, is an esoteric offshoot of Shia Islam mixed up with neo-Platonic philosophy. As is the case with the Alawites, only initiated elders learn the secrets of the faith. 'The rest of us don't know anything about it. I, for example, am 36 years old, but I don't know anything about the religion except that there's a book called the *Hikma*.'

Beyond that, 'the Assads exploited the Druze. The educated people understood that, but still some felt protected under the regime. That assurance went when the regime fell.'

The Druze have good reason to be worried. In November 2013, the small Druze community of Idlib's Jabal al-Summaq were 'converted' to Sunni Islam at gunpoint. Even that didn't protect them. On 10 June 2015, Jabhat al-Nusra massacred twenty-three members of the community. The Nusra commander responsible was a Tunisian known as Abu Abdulrahman al-Tunisi, who was confiscating Druze-owned houses in which to settle his immigrant fighters. Nusra's leadership condemned the killings and briefly imprisoned al-Tunisi. Then in June 2022, Ahmad al-Sharaa visited Jabal al-Summaq and told the inhabitants there should be no compulsion in religion (echoing the Qur'an). He seemed to be telling them that they could return to public profession of the Druze faith. But they didn't dare de-convert.

Bassem Abu Fakhr is a spokesman for the Rijal al-Karameh, one of the most important Druze militias. He explains the distance that opened between some Druze and the revolution as the revolution militarised. 'It was a popular revolution against dictatorship,' he says, 'but it gradually took on a sectarian aspect. Shia powers supported the regime and Sunni powers supported the rebels. So, people in Suwayda said "this war isn't our war. It's a war of Syrians against Syrians which we want no part of."'

Therefore, as well as welcoming the displaced from other parts of the country, the Druze increasingly refused to send their sons to fight outside the province. This meant they had to avoid the regime checkpoints which ringed Suwayda.

'I have a cousin, for example,' says Nour Abo Farraj, 'who didn't leave Suwayda for fifteen years because he didn't want to serve in Assad's army. There's a whole generation of young men who limited their future careers because they didn't want to be part of the killing machine.'

But still the killing came to them. According to Bassem Abu Fakhr, 'there were sectarian attacks on the edges of the territory, and the regime wasn't capable of defending the area. So, there was a desire to defend the area from such attacks, and to defend the young men of the province from being sent to kill or be killed by other Syrians.'

In 2013, in response to these two desires, Sheikh Wahid al-Balaous established the Rijal al-Karameh, or the Men of Dignity. Men joined the militia rather than serving in the regime army, and they defended their own area, fighting battles on the frontiers with whoever attempted to infiltrate. These included a battle with Jabhat al-Nusra in 2014, battles with ISIS in 2018, and a battle with Ahmad al-Owdeh's Daraa-based militia in 2020. Continuous battles were also fought against regime-linked drug gangs. 'One of our slogans,' says Bassem, 'is "We Forbid Attacks By Us, We Forbid Attacks Against Us".'

Balaous was assassinated by car bomb in September 2015. A second car bomb exploded outside the hospital in Suwayda where the wounded were taken. A total of twenty-six people were killed, many of them founding members of Rijal al-Karameh. The Assad regime is presumed to be responsible.

Worse was to come. In March 2018, ISIS took over swathes of southern Damascus, including the Yarmouk camp for Palestinian refugees. This followed a regime-imposed starvation siege on the area which weakened the coalition of Nusra and Free Army militias that had held it until then. In May, the regime negotiated a deal whereby ISIS would surrender southern Damascus in return for its fighters being transported on buses to the Syrian desert near Suwayda. On 25 August, these fighters launched an assault on Suwayda and the villages to the east. 258 people were killed and dozens more were abducted. Most victims were civilians.

As well as unprovoked sectarian attacks, there was fairly constant violence connected to drug smuggling. In its final years, the Assad regime turned Syria into a narco-state, and Suwayda bore the brunt of it. The amphetamine Captagon was smuggled across the Jordanian border towards the large markets of the Gulf and Egypt by mafias linked to the regime, to Hezbullah, and to local gangsters.

'In its last stages, the Assad regime didn't protect the community,' says Nour Abo Farraj. 'There was a lot of violence, kidnappings, mass shootings, and the regime didn't do anything.' I know of a teenager from Damascus who was kidnapped in Suwayda. When his mother contacted the police, they gave her a phone number and said, 'this is the number of the people who kidnapped your son. We can't do anything. Go to the *mashayikh* and they will solve the problem.' The *mashayikh* means the sheikhs, the community's religious leaders. 'So, the regime didn't attack Suwayda, but neither did it defend it. And this is why the *mashayikh* became more powerful. Suddenly they began dealing with things that weren't their responsibility. It was the regime that established this status for them.'

There are currently three top *mashayikh* – holding the title of *sheikh al-aql* – or sheikh of reason – recognised by the Syrian Druze: Yousuf Jarboa, Hamoud al-Henawi, and Hikmat al-Hajari. These positions are hereditary, demonstrating the power of leading families rather than a particular level of religious knowledge. Sheikh al-Hajari, for example, ascended to his leadership position in 2012 when his brother died. He enjoyed good relations with the Assad regime, as did almost every religious leader in regime-controlled territory. 'He worked with the regime that was killing us and trading in our blood,' says Bassem Abu Fakhr. 'Once he asked us to give up our arms and to work with the regime, in other words to dissolve our movement.'

Khuloud al-Hunaidi – an activist and psychotherapist from Suwayda – goes further. 'Hikmat al-Hajari didn't just stand with the regime, he worked as a spy for it. And he refused to help those who were detained by the regime.'

By the time the regime collapsed, Suwayda enjoyed de facto autonomy from Damascus. This was a military as much as a political reality, though power in the province was always contested and plural. Up to 100,000 men were under arms, some in large, respected formations designed to serve the community, like Rijal al-Karameh, some in smaller, clan-based militias, and some in Captagon-smuggling gangs.

This autonomy – particularly its military aspect – was not only a threat to the central state, it directly contradicted it. A state, if it is to be a state, must have a monopoly of violence, and this determines how the transitional government sees both Suwayda and the northeastern territories under SDF control. It would view them through this security prism even if it didn't have a Sunni Islamist background. It wants to rule a state, and therefore it wants to disarm all competing militias. The large majority of the Syrian population also wants the militias to be disarmed. How can the war be ended otherwise?

The question is, how to achieve the disarmament? How to bring the province under central control while assuring its inhabitants that they will be protected?

How much support did al-Hajari enjoy before July, when the situation degenerated? The answers given by my interlocutors ranged from 'almost none' to '70 percent'. My impression is that less than half stood with him. His support certainly wasn't total, or solid. It could have been whittled away.

It soon became clear that al-Hajari was the Druze leader most clearly opposed to the transitional government, which he repeatedly described as *takfeeri*, that is, composed of Sunni extremists who declare non-Sunnis to be infidels. In Bassem Abu Fakhr's words, 'Hajari rejected the new government's entrance into Suwayda because there was no trust in its members. He declared it a terrorist, *takfeeri* government. We in Rijal al-Karameh, as well as the two *sheikh al-aql* other than al-Hajari, had a different, compromise position. Nobody trusted the government's cadres, so we suggested that the sons of Suwayda serve in the Defense Ministry and the Interior Ministry, and that they manage the security affairs of the province, and in that way Suwayda would merge into state institutions. But the government didn't want this solution. It wanted to manage Suwayda by itself. So, it started to make trouble on the Damascus-Suwayda road.'

This was the road that connected Suwayda to the rest of the world. The community relied on it for basic supplies, as well as access to the universities and hospitals of the capital. The road had suffered raids by Bedouin for years. Now checkpoints manned by pro-government militia added to the trouble. They were accused of insults, theft, even kidnappings.

In late April, the tensions escalated into outright violence when a forged audio recording of a Druze sheikh insulting the Prophet Muhammad spread across the internet. Which bad actor forged and spread the recording? Perhaps the Iranians, or the Israelis, or the transitional government – everybody has an answer to fit their political opinion. Whoever was responsible, they succeeded in catalysing trouble. On 27 April, Sunni students attacked Druze students at Homs University. Then on 28 April, armed Sunni militants attacked Jaramana, a suburb of Damascus which houses a Druze community alongside Palestinians and people from Deir ez-Zor. They killed at least six people. According to Omar al-Asaad, the attack was partly motivated by resentment that Jaramana was still intact. 'Some of those who attacked were from Jaish al-Islam. They came from Douma, which was destroyed by the former regime. So, some of it was the resentment of those who don't have homes directed against those who do.'

On 29 April, the Interior Ministry issued a statement debunking the blasphemous recording and establishing the innocence of the Druze sheikh accused of it. By then, however, the violence had outstripped its catalyst and spread to Ashrafiyah and Sahnaya, two neighbouring communities south of Damascus. Most residents of these towns are Druze and Christians, but people displaced from Deir ez-Zor, and from other parts of rural Damascus, had arrived there during the war. There had been tensions between the various communities, and this may have influenced the violence.

Once again armed Islamists attacked local self-defense militias. It seems the attackers had been permitted to pass through General Security checkpoints. A twenty-hour battle ensued, during which the General Security sometimes split into Druze and Sunni factions. At least sixteen members of the General Security were killed, but it's not clear if they were Druze killed by Sunnis or Sunnis killed by Druze. Less and less was clear, because a narrative of war had broken out in concert with the battles on the ground. On 1 May, Hussam Warwar, the mayor of Sahnaya, a Druze, would be assassinated along with his son shortly after welcoming government reinforcements to the town. But by whom? Nobody knew, so everybody interpreted. And two distinct stories began to emerge: one told by Sunnis, another by 'the minorities'.

Meanwhile, Druze fighters rushing north to assist their kinsmen in Sahnaya were ambushed on the road by Bedouin fighters. Dozens were killed. In response, Druze militias laid siege to Bedouin quarters of Suwayda. Perhaps in response to that – because now an escalatory spiral had set in – Bedouin militias attacked and looted Suwara al-Kubra on 30 April.

This was the hometown of Issam Zahreddine, a prominent Assadist general, and a war criminal who enjoyed having his photo taken alongside mutilated corpses. Killed in battle in 2017, he was buried in a large and garish mausoleum in Suwara al-Kubra, which the Bedouin now burnt. Most Syrians learned of the existence of the mausoleum at this moment, and were disgusted. Why had the Druze not destroyed it when the regime fell? Why were they celebrating this murderer of Sunnis? At the same time, the usually reliable @QalaatAlMudiq Twitter account posted a doctored image of a statue in Sahnaya. The supposed statue depicted Hafez al-Assad holding a helicopter dropping a barrel bomb. It was debunked shortly afterwards by researcher Aymenn J. al-Tamimi, but by then it had been widely shared, and had contributed to the emerging image of a treacherous, Assadist, sectarian Druze community.

Groups of Bedouin from Deir ez-Zor announced they were heading to aid the Bedouin in Suwayda. There was a sense that events were spiralling out of control.

Then on 30 April, Sheikh Osama al-Rifai, now the state's highest religious official, gave a televised address in which he urged the public to stand united against attempts to incite hatred. 'Do not listen to the voices of revenge and retribution,' he said. 'Every Syrian's blood is sacred.' He called on people to return to their homes and to re-establish calm, and said there would be no winners from civil strife, 'whose beginning is known but whose end and extent are unknown'.

And the violence began to calm. Druze militias in the settlements close to Damascus where fighting had erupted agreed to hand over their heavy weapons. Security was to be managed by Druze men commanded by the central authorities. On 1 May, a meeting of Suwayda notables including Yousuf Jarboa and Hamoud al-Henawi declared their belonging to Syria, supported a security force of local men under Interior Ministry control, and called on the government to guard the Damascus-Suwayda road. Hikmat al-Hajari attended the meeting but left before the final statement was made.

Al-Hajari later described the violence as a 'genocidal campaign' and called for 'international forces to intervene to maintain peace and prevent the continuation of these crimes'. By 'international forces' he surely meant Israel, which he described as 'not the enemy' to *The Washington Post* a few days later. Israel had been openly building relations with Syrian Druze since 8 December, for instance by allowing them to go on pilgrimages in Israeli-occupied territory. In March and April, hundreds of Syrian Druze visited the tomb of Nabi Shuayb in the Lower Galilee. In March, Israel offered permits for Syrian Druze to work in the occupied Golan Heights, but it withdrew the offer the following month.

Though a segment of the Druze under Israeli jurisdiction – including most of those on the occupied Syrian Golan – resist Zionist rule, another segment is allied to it. Druze soldiers serve in the IDF, for instance. And Israeli Druze were blocking roads in protest at assaults on their Syrian kin. So that was part of the motivation for Israeli involvement in Suwayda's affairs. A greater part was Israel's desire to keep Syria destabilised and divided, and to demilitarise the south of the country.

Israel flew drones and fighter jets over Damascus several times in late April. In the early hours of 2 May, it struck a hill near the People's Palace, the president's residence, presumably to show that it could. On the same day, Israel bombed sites in Damascus, Daraa, Quneitra, Hama, and Latakia provinces, and 'protected the Druze' by firing a guided missile which killed four Druze farmers.

Most Syrians, of course, considered Israel to be very much an enemy, including most Druze. Khuloud al-Hunaidi, for instance, told me, 'Israel is our first enemy. Not just of the Druze but of all Syrians. That is the general opinion in Suwayda.' At least it was when I spoke to her in May.

A couple of months passed. Then on 11 July, Bedouin tribesmen set up an improvised checkpoint on the troublesome Damascus-Suwayda road and abducted, robbed, and beat up a Druze vegetable merchant. The next day Druze fighters abducted Bedouin civilians in retaliation, and then Bedouin fighters abducted more Druze in retaliation to that. By 13 July, tit-for-tat abductions and rounds of fighting were spreading across the province. Bedouin fighters from Daraa were joining in too.

Bassem Abu Fakhr reports that, 'there were attempts to calm the conflict, but they were stopped. It seemed that the government was enflaming the problem in order to justify its presence. We were all surprised on the 14th when government forces entered without any coordination with the community. They attacked with tanks, drones and artillery. This was a response to the community's rejection of their presence, and it was the result of seven months of mobilization against the Druze. The Syrian, or Sunni, atmosphere was tense, and its anger was directed at the Druze.'

The fighting between the Druze and the Bedouin was perhaps the result, after fourteen years of war, of everyone owning a gun, and of the logic of collective responsibility, and of revenge. But the government's response went far beyond peacekeeping. It sought to use the opportunity to weaken the independent Druze militias and to strengthen those allied to Damascus.

According to the journalist Mazen Ezzi, the government operation was coordinated in advance with three loyal Druze militias – Laith al-Balaous's group, which advanced from al-Mazraa in the west, Adnan Abu al-Ezz's group, which came from Hazm in the north, and Suleiman Abdul Baqi's group, which moved in Suwayda itself. Ezzi claims that these men were promised administrative and military positions in return. Based on the testimony of a local reporter, Ezzi also claims that it was Abdul Baqi's militia which first attacked the Maqwas neighbourhood of Suwayda on 14

July. This is a Bedouin area, and tribesmen responded with indiscriminate machine-gun fire on various other neighbourhoods.

In response to that, and the unannounced arrival of government forces, most of the Druze militias put aside their differences in order to resist. A joint operations room was established including al-Hajari's National Guard, the Rijal al-Karameh, and others.

Right at the start of the deployment of government forces, a group was ambushed by Druze fighters. Eighteen were killed or injured. Others were taken prisoner, then stripped and humiliated. Some were forced to make animal noises, just as Alawites on the coast had been forced to, just as Sunnis had been forced to by Assadists before. These incidents were filmed and released on the internet. They enraged both the fighters arriving in Suwayda and much of the Syrian population, and in some minds, they helped justify the atrocities to follow.

On 15 July, Ahmad Dalati, the government's top security official in Suwayda, met with representatives of local factions and won their agreement to the presence of government forces in the province. Given that government forces could be heard shooting in the streets outside, the factions were formally accepting a fait accompli. On the same morning al-Hajari also issued a statement accepting the presence of government forces. Shortly afterwards, however, he rejected that statement, calling it 'submission and humiliation', and urged resistance.

Why was his position shifting so fast? It looked as if the Americans – who supported central government authority in Suwayda – had called him first, and the Israelis – who didn't – had called next. But it's just as likely that he was swayed by accumulating reports of massacres against the Druze. For example, thirteen people were killed on 15 July when pro-government fighters opened fire on a family gathering. Dozens of other residents were summarily executed. On 16 July, government forces shelled the city's National Hospital. Then they parked a tank at the entrance, killed several patients, detained the medical staff, and killed one of them too.

The situation was complicated further by Israeli strikes on government forces every day from the 14 July to the 17 July. On 16 July, with several tanks hit and dozens of its fighters killed, the government withdrew.

THE SUWAYDA MASSACRES

In those days I was receiving distressing voice notes from my friends Khuzama and Cedric. They were locked down in Khuzama's family home in Qaraya, a village to the south of Suwayda. They'd been using Qaraya as a base while making a film about post-liberation Syria. I'd planned to visit them there, to stay a few days to talk about politics in the province, but everything had blown up as I was arriving.

They'd gone seventy-two hours without electricity. The water supply was intermittently cut too, and the phone lines were down. They were hearing mortar fire from Daraa, and when they charged their phones from a neighbour's solar battery, and managed to get on the internet, they were hearing terrible news too. Khuzama's relatives and friends were reporting mass killings. Some Druze fighters were killing Bedouin civilians. The numbers of Bedouin victims were far less than those of Druze, but that didn't make these crimes easier for the Bedouin to swallow. Druze fighters were also forcibly displacing Bedouin from their homes. A mass exodus of tens of thousands headed towards Daraa.

At this stage at least 50,000 Bedouin fighters mobilised, representing forty-one tribes. Videos of their gatherings flooded social media. They came from Daraa in the south, Deir ez-Zor in the east, and Homs and Hama in the centre. Bedouin in Iraq, Jordan, and Saudi Arabia also declared their desire to come to the rescue of their kinsmen (there is no evidence that any actually crossed borders). Several Bedouin filmed themselves wielding scissors in their jeeps and trucks as they headed for Suwayda. This was a statement of intent to cut off the moustaches famously worn by religious Druze men.

Such a mobilisation had not happened before. The tribes were more accustomed to fighting each other than acting in unison, and throughout the war they had been divided, some fighting for Assad or the Iranian militias, some for ISIS, some for the Free Army brigades, and some for the SDF. Mazen Ezzi claims a source close to the government told him that it had planned a Bedouin mobilisation in the event of Israeli intervention forcing a retreat. What is certain is that the Hayat Tahrir al-Sham (HTS) had enjoyed strong connections with key Bedouin tribes since the days of Jabhat al-Nusra.

On 17 July, the Bedouin attacked Suwayda hard, murdering civilians, burning homes and shops.

Most Syrian media, meanwhile, was overblowing atrocities against the Bedouin. Reports of over 100 Bedouin killed in one go were not backed up by evidence. These and similar stories spread fast on social media. On Syrian and several pan-Arab TV channels, Bedouin survivors and displaced were given space to describe their suffering. Bedouin women recounted burnings, killings, and expulsions. Druze survivors were not given the same space. Victims of the Israeli airstrikes were also publicly mourned. The Israeli action may have forced a government retreat, but it did nothing to stop the tribes, and it further enflamed public opinion.

On 16 July, as well as striking Suwayda, Israel struck the General Staff complex at Umayyad Square in the heart of Damascus. I heard that one from the family home in Mezzeh. Most Damascenes heard it, and everybody saw it on TV. Umayyad Square is the symbolic centre of the capital, so this was like hitting Piccadilly Circus or Times Square. Dozens were injured in the strike, and at least three were killed, including the young mother Arij al-Rai, whose car had been passing by.

On 15 July, there'd been a demonstration in Hasakeh in support of Suwayda. On 16 July, after the bombing of Umayyad Square, there were demonstrations against Israel and in support of the government in Hasakeh, Idlib, Latakia, Aleppo, Homs, and Damascus. It seemed that a looming debate in society about sectarianism and governmental abuses was curtailed by the Zionist aggression.

That evening a large crowd gathered in Hama and chanted, 'The People Want the Declaration of Jihad'. The anger was directed equally at Israel and at the Druze community, which more people were now writing off as a treacherous collective collaborating with Israel, even as Israel was starving children in Gaza and gobbling up more Syrian land. One young man in the crowd waved a cardboard model of a giant pair of scissors. This was a reference to the Bedouin militias cutting off the moustaches of Druze elders, an act not only of personal humiliation but also of collective insult, because the moustache, along with baggy *sirwal* trousers, is symbolic of the Druze. And the Druze were becoming symbolic of everything that was unjust and dangerous. They were sheltering Assadist criminals and tormenting innocents in their secret dungeons. They were murdering Bedouin, no doubt out of hatred for Islam. They were trying

THE SUWAYDA MASSACRES

their best to make the new Syria fail, so the government had to hit them hard. So went the narrative.

Residents of Daraa cut the roads to Suwayda and called for a trade boycott. Sunni students attacked Druze students on the university campus in Damascus, and in Aleppo too. Two Druze brothers who had recently returned from Germany and opened shops side by side in the Barzeh neighbourhood of the capital were killed, probably for sectarian reasons. Once again, furious, wounded sections of the Sunni community were lashing out. The enmity towards the Druze came from society as much as the government, or perhaps the government was pushing and surfing this angry Sunni wave.

On the evening of 18 July, as violence continued to rage to the south, I attended a sit-in (or a *waqfeh*, which literally means a 'stand') outside the Parliament building, alongside perhaps about fifty people who were generally *musaqafeen*, that is educated middle-class people with progressive politics. I recognised the artist Yousef Abdelke and the activist Wafa Mustafa. I met Rindala there, a friend who works with an internationalist collective called The Peoples Want. She handed out some copies of The Peoples Want manifesto 'Revolutions of our Times'. Copies of *Alaan* (Now) were also being handed out. That's the new newspaper of the Communist Action Party, a faction which broke away from the mainstream Communist Party in protest at the latter's absorption into the Assad regime's tame Progressive Front, its adherence to the Soviet line, and its rejection of democracy. The paper's front-page banner reads 'Democracy for the Syrian People'.

Not everybody there could necessarily be described by the 'educated middle-class' label. I got talking with a young man called Mahmoud, for instance, who had been a refugee in a Jordanian camp, had returned home after the liberation and joined the new army, which he had recently left for reasons he didn't wish to explain. But perhaps his presence at the sit-in explained some of them. The protestors were holding signs which read 'The blood of a Syrian is forbidden to a Syrian'. The purpose of the sit-in as described on social media was to call for a ceasefire everywhere in Syria, and for the problems between Syrians to be solved by dialogue.

'The blood of a Syrian is forbidden to a Syrian' didn't seem to me a controversial slogan. It only echoed the words of the government-appointed mufti Osama al Rifai during the clashes in late April and May. Yet controversial it apparently was. After an hour or so, when the sit-in was thinning out, I went to meet somebody in the nearby Rowda café. I'd just ordered coffee when I heard shouts and screams. I and most of the Rowda clientele poured out onto the pavement to see what was going on. What we saw was reminiscent of the repression in the first days of the Syrian Revolution.

A group of about twenty men had arrived to beat and scream insults at the sit-in attendees. They were in plain clothes, but they were clearly organised. Every man carried the same type of baton. A couple carried axes. One of them grabbed a phone from someone who was filming, and hurled it to the road, smashing the screen. Once they'd dispersed the sit-in, the men chanted '*Qaidna lil-abad/ sayidna Muhammad*' (Our leader forever/ our lord Muhammad). In the context, this was almost blasphemous. During the revolution, this slogan – though its Islamic reference may have alienated non-Muslims – was a response to the regime's 'eternal leader' rhetoric deifying the Assads. Now, deployed by a new type of pro-power thug, it sounded uncomfortably like a reversion to repressive type. These men were claiming the Prophet rather than the President as their cosmic reference, but the message was the same as that of the *shabeeha* thugs who had arrived in vans with clubs and axes whenever Damascenes had gathered in 2011: You the people are not permitted to do politics. If you try, your heads will be broken. Politics belongs to the men of violence.

To be fair, this violence wasn't nearly as bad as the regime violence in 2011. Back then, the *shabeeha* had grabbed men and women and bundled them into buses, where they were beaten more severely, and then driven to security centres where some were beaten to death. But the intimidation was the same. The same thuggery. The same *tashbeeh*. And the same official approval. A uniformed, armed member of the General Security was standing outside the Rowda café with the rest of us. Most were gazing in horror at the scene, but he was nodding his pleasure. Several people on the pavement asked him to intervene. He angrily refused. 'Those people are Zionists!' he said. 'Today we found a child cut into pieces! A child in pieces in a box cut up by the al-Hajari militias!'

'Those people are civilians!' argued one man. 'Do you understand? Civilians! It's your responsibility to protect them.'

The security man disagreed. He repeated that they were Zionists, and then he repeated his story about seeing a dismembered child in a box.

It was unlikely that he personally had seen the bits of child. He was on duty in central Damascus, not on the frontline. What I presume he meant was that he had heard the story and had absorbed it as fact. Disinformation was flooding the street. It's true that other forms of disinformation were reaching audiences abroad, and perhaps 'minority' audiences inside the country. Israeli accounts were pumping anti-government nonsense. One viral story, for instance, claimed that President Ahmad al-Sharaa had fled the country. But the stories reaching most household living rooms in Damascus, as far as I could see, were pro-government and anti-Druze.

I had never known Syria free of disinformation. During the Assad era, many people had quietly swallowed the official lies, never examining them properly, so as to make life liveable. Many others had automatically discounted everything they heard from official channels. Now many of the latter category trusted the news they heard. This was their government now, the one they'd fought for, or at least suffered for. They wanted to believe it, so they did.

'There were some days when I was following what was happening on the ground,' says Nour Abo Farraj, 'but when I watched Al-Jazeera it was as if they were talking about a different planet. So, I don't blame individuals when there is such a disinformation campaign. The people's hope for the new system prevents them from seeing what is happening, and also from thinking logically. I feel sorry for these people. They have lived in war and fear for years. When you understand what motivates them to believe that the government is good and the future is assured, you can feel nothing but sadness.'

Fadel Abdul Ghany of the Syrian Network for Human Rights gave a rough estimate of 1,300 killed on all sides. At least 65 percent of the victims – up to 1,000 people – were Druze, and at least 30 percent of these were civilians. About 250 members of the government's forces had been killed, and about 100 Bedouin.

Special rapporteurs appointed by the UN Human Rights Council later reported the burning of thirty-three villages, widespread looting, destruction of crops, and killing of livestock. According to the experts – who did not document violations on the ground, but gathered reports – attacks on three villages alone, Ta'ara, al-Doura and al-Douweira, killed 1,000 people, 'including at least 539 identified Druze civilians – among them thirty-nine women and twenty-one children. At least 196 people, including eight children and thirty women, were reportedly extrajudicially executed.' The experts also 'reported abduction of at least 105 Druze women and girls by armed groups affiliated with the Syrian interim authorities, with eighty still missing. ... In at least three cases, Druze women were allegedly raped before being executed. Seven hundred and sixty-three persons, including women, remain missing.'

The result was predictable. The Druze closed ranks. At least half the community had been amenable to reintegrating into Syria before the massacres. Now none wanted to. The Rijal al-Karameh and almost all Suwayda's militias joined al-Hajari's National Guard, and al-Hajari himself spoke openly about separatism. Demonstrators in Suwayda's Karameh Square waved Israeli flags.

The story told by government supporters is that pro-government forces were sent to Suwayda as peacekeepers, but when they were attacked order broke down, and then rogue individuals committed crimes. Close analysis and expert witness testimony tells a different story. The assault on Suwayda was pre-planned. The government consists of former militiamen who had hubristically imagined that they could intimidate a whole community in the same way that they had once intimidated and dissolved rival militias in Idlib. State media had taken sides and so had failed to produce either objective journalism or a national discourse. Social media warriors had made matters even worse. All of this had weakened Syria and played into Israel's hands. Rather than showing the Syrian Democratic Forces (SDF), the US-backed Kurdish-led coalition of militias, how powerful the central government was by crushing the Suwayda militias, the disaster demonstrated government incompetence, and emboldened the SDF.

For a few days, as I moped in Damascus, the situation seemed hopeless. What to do when different communities cling not only to different interpretations but to different sets of facts? But then I began to hear conversations in which a more nuanced truth was dripping through. One woman, from a Damascene family that was pleased to see Assad gone, had called her old friend in Suwayda, a retired judge, and asked how he was. 'What can I tell you?' he replied. 'I see massacres all around. I see homes burning.' 'And do you trust what he says?' someone asked. 'Of course I do,' she replied. 'He's a judge, and he's my friend. I've known him for years.'

Slowly some of the social media warriors moderated their tone. More and more people realised that something had gone terribly wrong in Suwayda. And fewer people were willing to give the government the benefit of the doubt than they had in March, when Alawites were massacred on the coast. How had no lessons been learnt in the months between March and July?

In October, a video was released of Inas Matar describing the atrocities she had witnessed in Suwayda. Inas was a witness who couldn't easily be dismissed as a sectarian liar, because she was a Sunni, originally from the Damascus suburb of Daraya, who had moved to Suwayda when her home was destroyed by bombing. Her credibility was further strengthened by the fact that she was the sister of Ghiath Matar, one of the very well-known early martyrs of the revolution. It was Ghiath Matar who had developed the practice of offering water and roses to the Assadist soldiers sent to Daraya to shoot protesters, and who was later tortured to death by the regime.

However bad things are currently, there are grounds for hope that Suwayda and the rest of Syria, and the Druze and the Sunnis, can eventually be reconciled. Separatism for Suwayda is not a realistic proposal. The province has almost no water and no other resources to speak of. Jordan wants to deal with a unified Syrian state. Israel could airdrop arms and could continue bombing central government forces, but it can't incorporate Suwayda into its occupied territories without also incorporating Daraa, a province of millions of anti-Zionist Sunnis. To add to all this, Hikmat al-Hajari is establishing a mini-dictatorship in Suwayda which threatens anyone who speaks against it. The province is rife with assassinations and gun battles.

On the other side, there are clear signs that the government recognises it went wrong. Abu Ahmad al-Zakour, a former HTS official who is now Ahmad al-Sharaa's representative to the tribes, said while talking to a tribal audience in October, 'the tribes and the clans should be a key to goodness ... and they could have played a more positive role than they did in Suwayda'.

More importantly, several expert witnesses have told me that over 300 members of the pro-government forces have now been arrested for crimes committed in Suwayda. These arrests have not been publicised as they need to be in order to show Druze and other minorities that a state of law and order is being built, and the reason for the secrecy is the government's fear of having a public argument with its angry, traumatised, Sunni militia base.

But that's another story. As for the failure of most Syrian media and social media to accurately tell the story of the Suwayda massacres, the antidote seems to be traditional human communication.

Nour Abo Farraj argues for the importance of direct interactions. 'I write regularly for *al-Jumhuriya*,' she says, 'but the people who read *al-Jumhuriya* are not the problem. The educated people are like froth. We have no effect on society. We're just talking to each other. Civil society and the educated political class haven't developed their tools. There's a great distance between what's happening on the ground and the means we use to address it. When you write a paper or organise a conference, you're addressing the wrong audience. Face-to-face interaction is more important.'

WORKING FOR ALTERNATIVES

Saoussen Ben Cheikh

In this uncertain time, being human and caring for other fellow humans may sound naïve. Yet if we want to imagine and create a different future, we must begin with ideals.

In an ideal world, freedom of expression would be the bedrock of every society. Citizens would speak without fear and journalists would investigate without intimidation. Media would serve as a genuine watchdog openly pursuing truth, and power, no matter how entrenched, would always remain accountable to the people. In this democratic paradigm, media is not simply a business or a profession; it is a public good, a forum that empowers citizens to debate, decide, and ultimately elevate their society.

Yet today that ideal is everywhere in the world under severe strain. From disinformation floods and declining revenues in the West to authoritarian crackdowns and violent conflict in the Global South, independent media faces existential threats. The crisis is global. Media organisations are closing at alarming rates. Journalists are targeted by online harassment and surveillance. Public trust in news is eroding in polarised societies where propaganda and rumour spread faster than verified facts.

If journalism struggles to survive even in stable democracies, how much harder is the challenge in regions like Middle East and North Africa (MENA), where war, poverty, and repression intersect daily? While it is precisely in this volatile environment that critical information – the kind that empowers citizens to build their resilience, and that holds power to account – is most urgently needed. In the MENA region, free media has not only to contend with the universal pressures of the digital age, but also with deeply rooted authoritarian practices, fragile economies, and the daily risks of censorship, exile, or even death.

It is within this tension between ideals and realities that my own journey with alternative media has unfolded. Over the past decade, I have worked in media development, side by side with dozens of grassroots media initiatives across the MENA region. I have witnessed young journalists risk their lives to publish stories that might otherwise remain buried. I have seen entire communities come alive when their voices were finally heard, reclaiming their own narrative. My journey took me from the rubble of Aleppo to the crowded impoverished neighbourhoods of Sana'a. I witnessed collective blogs springing up in Tunisia after the fall of Ben Ali, and met journalists scattered in forced exile across Europe, piecing together new media platforms and using storytelling to cling to the memory of their homelands.

These encounters taught me a fundamental lesson: while equipment, funding, or protection may be scarce, courage and imagination are often abundant.

My path into this media space was not accidental. Coming from Tunisia, the country that sparked the Arab Spring, I was acutely aware of how narratives shape realities. Growing up under authoritarianism taught me what it meant to live with censored media, where the evening news was nothing more than a theatre of praise for the regime, and the real stories circulated through whispers in kitchens, or via underground networks.

I use the term 'alternative media' not because these newsrooms were marginal or peripheral, but because they represented a true alternative to the forces that have long suffocated public discourse in our region: state propaganda, rigid censorship, and commercial capture.

These initiatives were in fact experiments in freedom, driven not by profit but by the ideal of democracy so desperately demanded in the region.

When the uprisings broke out back in 2011, I felt naturally drawn to those who dared to challenge the silence. The Arab uprisings were a rupture in the region's media as much as in its politics. For decades, state-run television, tightly controlled newspapers, and a handful of loyalist radio stations had monopolised the public sphere. Now, empowered by the wind of change, young people armed with mobile phones and frequenting internet cafés began livestreaming protests, documenting police brutality, and uploading testimonies directly on social media, particularly Facebook and YouTube.

I vividly remember meeting a group of Tunisian youth who had created the online platform Nawaat in their determination to amplify citizen voices during the revolution. They had no professional studios, only laptops and enthusiasm. What they published was raw and sometimes chaotic, but it was alive. It carried the pulse of the street, and it reminded everyone that truth does not need polish. It needs courage. In Syria, I sat with young men and women who had transformed cramped apartments into makeshift newsrooms. Their tools were a cracked camera lens, a car battery powering a router, and an unyielding conviction that the world must know what was happening. They worked while bombs fell, verifying footage between air raids and publishing eyewitness accounts at dawn. Some were later killed or imprisoned, yet the archives they risked their lives to build still testify to their bravery. In Yemen, the spirit of defiance was equally strong. I met women who had crossed checkpoints to reach rural villages, determined to record stories of drought, child marriage, and displacement. For them, journalism was not a mere profession; it was an act of defiance against invisibility. They refused to allow their communities to be reduced to numbers in humanitarian reports. They brought to light stories to confer dignity on their people.

But even amid the inspiration, I could see their fragility. These initiatives were powered by passion, volunteerism, and occasional injections of donor funding, but they had no safety nets. I remember a Syrian collective that had built an impressive online following. Their reports on corruption were cited by international organisations. But when their grant ended, they had no reserves to call on and no Plan B. Within months, the initiative closed, their website went offline, and their archives disappeared. It felt as if a whole library had burned down. This fragility was not a matter of individual failure or incompetence. It was fundamentally structural. How do you build sustainability when freedom itself is criminalised, when audiences cannot afford to pay, and when advertising markets collapse under war?

Over time, I witnessed the slow, painful shift from the euphoric energy of the early 2010s to the democratic contraction we face today. Across the region, authoritarian regimes have regained significant ground.

In Egypt, hundreds of journalists have been jailed. In Syria, nearly all independent media was pushed into exile, and is only slowly and tentatively rebuilding now. In Tunisia, even the fragile gains of the revolution are under threat, with laws now once again restricting press freedom. Simultaneously, digital platforms, once seen as liberating, now feel like traps. Algorithms reward sensationalism and hate speech while burying careful reporting. Worse, some of these platforms cooperate with governments to censor dissent, removing the pages or accounts of independent collectives overnight, silencing them with a flick of a digital switch.

When the conflict in Gaza escalated in October 2023, the major Meta platforms suppressed, hid, or removed content produced by Palestinians and their supporters. As reported by Human Rights Watch, between October and November 2023 over 1,050 takedowns or suppressions of peaceful content in support of Palestine were documented. In another investigation by the BBC Arabic team, twenty media outlets in Gaza and the West Bank reported a 77 percent drop in audience engagement on Facebook pages after 7 October 2023, while comparable Israeli media saw a 37 percent increase. These data show that rather than being neutral arbiters of free expression, social media platforms in this case helped amplify – or at least did not meaningfully resist – mechanisms of erasure. They limited the visibility of independent media in Gaza, making it harder for voices from the ground to reach global audiences, and thereby assisting in silencing them.

And yet, despite the closures, the jails, and the digital traps, journalism stubbornly persists. I think of a Yemeni team that pivoted to producing educational videos for NGOs in order to keep their newsroom alive. Or Syrian exiles in Europe who launched investigative podcasts, bringing stories of war crimes to international audiences. Or Tunisian youth experimenting with newsletters and satire to bypass censorship. Their very survival, in the face of such overwhelming pressure, is in itself resistance.

I share these reflections because the story of alternative media in MENA is still unfinished. It deserves to be told, not only as a chronicle of what happened after the Arab Spring, but as a mirror for the questions we continue to wrestle with today: Can we keep our ideals intact in the face of overwhelming pressures? Can free media survive in contexts where freedom itself is retreating? Can journalism truly belong to the people it serves, rather than to donors or investors?

And beyond these questions lies a deeper one: how can journalism in our region be both a public good and a viable profession? How can newsrooms not only defend democracy, but also live decently from their work, producing high-quality content? These are not easy questions anywhere in the world, but in our region – marked by conflict, poverty, and instability – they are even more urgent.

Passion alone cannot sustain a newsroom. This became painfully clear as the years went by. Most of the initiatives I worked with faced the same dilemmas, slowly draining their energy and, in many cases, forcing them to close their doors. The first and perhaps most visible trap was donor dependency. International organisations often arrived with funding, but the money came tied to rigid thematic priorities. One year the buzzword was 'women's rights', the next 'countering violent extremism', and later 'digital literacy' or 'migration'. Small newsrooms twisted themselves into knots to fit into these ever-shifting boxes, adjusting their editorial lines not according to the needs of their communities but to the conditions of their funders.

I recall a Yemeni outlet that began as a bold voice against corruption but found itself producing glossy 'success stories' for a donor campaign. The reporters were frustrated. They wanted to investigate land grabs and militia abuses, yet they spent months writing profiles of entrepreneurs chosen by external agendas. The more they complied, the more they lost the authenticity that had given them credibility in the first place.

Even when editorial independence remained intact, economic realities hit hard. Advertising markets in conflict zones or fragile economies are virtually non-existent. Who can buy ad space when businesses themselves are collapsing under bombs or sanctions? Meanwhile, local audiences, struggling daily with poverty, cannot pay for subscriptions or memberships. I remember a group in Syria who tried to launch a small online subscription model, charging the equivalent of just one dollar per month. Even that symbolic fee proved impossible for most of their audience, who barely had enough to cover their daily subsistence.

To make matters worse, some governments actively blocked alternative funding streams. In countries like Egypt or Algeria, foreign funding for media is treated as a crime, and local businesses rightly fear placing ads in outlets that might anger the authorities. Independent media is thus squeezed from every side: the economy offers no lifeline, and the state tightens the noose on any external help.

The digital transition should have been our great equalizer. In theory, it's the cheapest upgrade in history. Done right, technology can make publishing smarter, lighter, and cheaper. In much of the West, the transition has been relatively smooth. A journalist can record, edit, and publish an entire multimedia story on a single device. AI now speeds up transcription, translation, fact-checking, and even first-draft writing. Cloud services back up archives instantly. Algorithms, for all their flaws, also make it possible to reach thousands of readers in minutes. Running a newsroom costs far less than it did two decades ago, and the barriers to entry have never been lower.

But in our region, the digital transformation has been more difficult. Here, the digital promise often collides with harsh financial and physical limits. Many newsrooms do not even have reliable laptops, let alone the luxury of experimenting with AI tools. I have worked with teams where the 'newsroom' was a single Android phone on a power bank rationed like water. Electricity cuts out for hours every day. Internet connections are unstable, expensive, or throttled. Journalists carry power banks like lifelines, sprinting to upload files in the short window when electricity returns. A Syrian colleague once described how his team used a car battery to keep their router alive long enough to send a story. A Yemeni editor told me she timed her publishing schedule around the hours when her neighbourhood's generator would hum back to life. And the gap between us and the West is widening. While Western reporters worry about being 'too dependent on AI,' many of their counterparts in the MENA region are still struggling with the basics: having a device that works, a reliable internet connection, or a safe place to store archives.

The paradox of digital transition in our region is that it promises lighter costs and wider reach, but this gap in access keeps growing. For those with the right equipment and stable infrastructure, digital tools are multiplying possibilities. For those without, the digital future is still an uneven struggle, widening inequalities between North and South, urban and rural, privileged and precarious.

Beyond money, perhaps the most silent but destructive vulnerability is institutional fragility. Many collectives began as groups of friends or activists who suddenly found themselves running newsrooms without the essential training or tools to manage them. They knew how to capture footage and verify testimonies, but they lacked basic systems for human resources, financial management, or long-term strategy. When crises hit, and they always did, these weaknesses proved fatal. I recall one Syrian collective thriving with powerful investigative reports, yet when their lead editor was arrested and another staff member fled, they had no structure to sustain operations. Within weeks, the team unravelled.

Similarly, a Yemeni radio station I worked with faced a similar fate when their small office was raided. They lost their equipment, but what destroyed them was not the raid itself, it was the absence of backup plans, reserves, or institutional resilience. Too many projects have collapsed not because they lacked vision, but because they were never given the chance to grow roots strong enough to withstand the storms.

The tragedy of these closures is that the vulnerabilities were never failures of individual journalists. They were structural, built into the hostile environments where these media operated. Passion may ignite a newsroom, but without sustainable business models, legal protections, and organisational support, even the brightest sparks risk being extinguished.

The central question remains: can alternative media stay true to its civic ideals while overcoming the structural pressures that seek to extinguish it? I believe the answer lies not in a single, fixed model, but in courageous experimentation across multiple, adaptive fronts.

Community-supported journalism offers one path that has shown promise, particularly when it is framed not as a transaction but as a civic act. When readers are invited to become members rather than customers, the relationship changes; people begin to feel they are co-owners of a shared public good. In Tunisia, I watched a small investigative team host monthly open newsrooms, offering coffee, a gathering space, and a chance for neighbours to participate and ask questions.

Where membership alone can't carry the economic weight, hybrid models step in. I have seen outlets keep their editorial independence by building a small studio that serves two masters: during the day, they produce public-interest journalism; in the evening, they rent the space to NGOs, universities, and social enterprises for trainings, filming, and live panels. One Yemeni digital magazine survived a funding winter by launching a lean production arm: they created short educational explainers for local organisations – how to access water trucking, how to navigate school enrolment – while ring-fencing their investigative desk from donor influence. Similarly in Palestine, a women-led radio station balanced grant cycles by hosting ticketed cultural nights and audio storytelling workshops; these events successfully doubled as both an audience revenue stream and a community engagement opportunity.

Regional solidarity can also change the arithmetic. When newsrooms stop behaving like isolated islands and start functioning like an archipelago, costs go down, and reach goes up. During a cross-border collaboration between Amman and Gaziantep, two small teams co-reported a series on food prices and smuggling routes. They shared translators, pooled datasets, and co-published on the same day, each outlet introducing the story with local framing and voices. None of them could have carried that investigation alone. Together, they built a sustainable ecosystem rather than simply chasing a single headline.

Diaspora engagement remains a reservoir we have not fully tapped. Millions from the region live abroad, carrying valuable skills, professional networks, and a deep hunger for credible information from home. When invited deliberately, this community becomes far more than just a source of donations. I've witnessed a Syrian French developer volunteer to harden the security of a site repeatedly targeted by Distributed Denial of Service (DDoS) attacks; a Yemeni American lawyer spend weekends training a newsroom in basic media contracts; and a Tunisian filmmaker in Montreal mentor young producers on sound design and help them pitch to podcast festivals. The money mattered, but the mentorship mattered more. It multiplied capacity and reduced dependence on the next grant cycle.

Crucially, none of these models is a silver bullet, and each carries tension. A membership drive can slide into pleasing the base; a service studio can drift into mission creep; a regional network can fracture under politics; a diaspora campaign can be accused of exporting an agenda. The point is not to pretend purity is possible, but to design robust guardrails and keep the editorial heart visible. I have seen teams write their red lines on the wall – literally – so every intern, donor, and guest could read them: no pay-to-play content, no prior approval of editorial, no advertising from entities under sanctions, no data sharing without consent. These humble, public rules build trust far faster than any slogan could.

When all these approaches begin to breathe together, they produce something sturdier than a mere business model. They produce a civic habit. To truly grasp this synergy, imagine a week in the life of a small, independent newsroom in Sanaa or Sousse. Monday, the editor hosts a one-hour open meeting on Zoom for members and curious neighbours, taking three questions on upcoming investigations. Tuesday, the studio rents out for a social-enterprise pitch night, covering two reporters' travel for the month. Wednesday, a cross-border Slack channel hums as colleagues in Beirut and Marseille exchange leads and double-check a dataset. Thursday, a diaspora mentor drops in to help a producer clean up audio levels and set up a backup server. Friday, the team publishes a story and sends both a newsletter and a WhatsApp summary, followed by an Instagram Live where a reporter explains the methodology in simple language. The result is messy, human, and underfunded but it is also alive and recognisably accountable to the people it serves.

In a region where authoritarianism thrives on silence and secrecy, community ownership is revolutionary precisely because it makes the newsroom a public square again. It says the microphone belongs to those who live with the consequences of what is reported and what is ignored. It anchors journalism in habits of listening, answering, and co-deciding. And it turns media from a product into a common, something we tend together, defend together, and pass on intact to those who will tell the next chapter of our story.

After a decade of media development, I carry both scars and hopes. I have seen too many closures, too many broken dreams. But I have also seen the unbreakable will of people to tell their stories, no matter the risks, no matter the cost.

So, can alternative media in MENA survive? Yes, but not by replicating Western models, nor by relying solely on donors. They will survive if they root themselves in their communities, if they embrace experimentation and innovation, and if they see themselves not as businesses alone, but as collective global movements.

Today's struggle for truth is no longer an East vs. West dynamic; it is an intertwined, transnational movement. The challenges we face, from the pervasive disinformation that warps elections to the realities of climate change and cross-border conflicts, are simply too big for any single newsroom or nation to handle alone. The lessons forged in the rubble of Aleppo or the digital traps of Cairo are equally vital to media resilience in Paris or New York. The task of building a just society demands a rising together of communities, both South-to-South and South-to-West, where expertise, capacity, and accountability flow in all directions. Because alternative media is not just about journalism; nor is it a luxury. It is the foundation of democracy, the backbone of development, the lifeline of freedom. If we allow it to disappear, we risk losing not only stories, but our very capacity to imagine and build a just society.

HRANT DINK— THE JOURNALIST AS MARTYR

Boyd Tonkin

'I am sick and tired of both the suffocating embraces and the exclusion that forces me to lose sight of the fact that I am no more than a common, ordinary citizen' – Hrant Dink, *Agos*

I

Journalists in Britain, as in many other places, do not expect to be remembered with much respect – let alone reverence. The best that most of us can hope for is a fast-fading reputation for honesty, tenacity, and (for the lucky few) a decent style. Most, and probably justly, will not even achieve that. When the former assistant editor of *The Pioneer* in Allahabad (Rudyard Kipling) published his 'Epitaphs for the War' after the carnage of 1914-1918, all that he wrote on behalf of his original profession was 'We have served our day'. 'Tomorrow's fish-wrap,' my colleagues used to sigh as night fell and the fruit of our diurnal toil rolled out into the world – a vanished world, now, of print-only papers delivered in the dark on thundering trucks and chip-shops with relaxed hygiene rules.

So, to visit a secular shrine to a newspaper editor and columnist feels strange. Even stranger, as the subject of this memorialisation – even veneration – is framed here not just as a dauntless truth-teller and campaigner, but a martyr. You prepare to visit the office of an inky hack, albeit one renowned for his courage and integrity. You enter what feels like the chapel (or maybe *türbe*) of a saint – but one often treated as a demon by his peers.

North of Taksim Square in Istanbul, broad boulevards run through the thriving district of Şişli. Originally dominated by the cosmopolitan merchant class of late-Ottoman Turkey, many of them Greeks, Jews, and Armenians, the neighbourhood was later peopled (like much of the modern city) by Muslim incomers from rural Anatolia. No signs will direct you from the Osmanbey metro station to the 1920s Sebat Building on Halaskargazi Avenue. Once there, however, a plaque on the pavement outside explains why you have come.

Here, on 19 January 2007, the newspaper editor Hrant Dink opened the front door. He had taken a mobile phone call, rushed downstairs without his coat from the office of the bilingual Turkish-Armenian weekly *Agos*, and gone out into the street. Three 7.65mm bullets, fired at point-blank range, pierced his skull from behind. He died on the spot. The agent of the assassination – although not its instigator – was a seventeen-year-old in a knitted cap named Ogün Samast. Eyewitnesses claimed that, after he pulled the trigger, he had shouted 'I shot the infidel!' And that, just before, Dink had said: 'Don't do it, son'. Samast eventually received a twenty-two-year jail term but was released in November 2023.

Easy enough to visit the site of a notorious killing; much harder to grasp its human reality before, and beneath, the layers of interpretation poured over the event. The Turkish journalist and writer Ece Temelkuran, who hurried to the scene, had blood on her shoes that day. When, in the stairwell of the Sebat Building, she handed Dink's wife (now widow) Rakel a glass of water, Rakel knocked it away. The glass shattered. With her daughter Sera and son Arat, Rakel sat on the stairs, and howled. 'Lifting her face from her daughter's face, Rakel screams, her eyes on each one of us, one by one: 'The state's pure! Our state's even purer now!'... Rakel's hands, clawing the air, clutching at the screams, falling to her side: 'Is your blood purer now?' Rakel turns to Temelkuran and says, 'we trusted you, we stayed in this country! We trusted you! And now this?'

'This' was the murder with the connivance of state actors – at which level remains, as with so many Istanbul mysteries, a matter of endless dispute – of the foremost Turkish Armenian, or Armenian Turk, of his time. Dink had co-founded *Agos* in 1996. Over the next decade, he turned the paper – printed in both Turkish and Armenian – not only into a unique platform for debate and dialogue between two mutually suspicious peoples. It, and he, became an advocate for a broader, more open Turkish identity; for an idea of nationhood that embraced every strand of the region's many-sided heritage.

'I am a citizen of Turkey,' he insisted. 'I am an Armenian... And I am an Anatolian right down to my bones.' He sought not just redress for historic wrongs but release from the immobilising dualism that made Turk and Armenian each other's perpetual spectre or shadow. He called not merely for Muslim Turks to embrace the present and past of their Armenian kin but for Armenians to release themselves from the mythical, devilish 'Turk' that envenomed their dreams and their politics – especially in the diaspora abroad. And he did so as a proud Turkish citizen who believed in a pluralistic national community.

So, I went to the former *Agos* offices to find a journalist who, in life and death, had brought as much honour to our sometimes grubby trade as any columnist and editor could. On a sunny Saturday morning in September, the suite of rooms that commemorates Dink felt like a placid refuge from the crowds outside. The *Agos* HQ now functions as the '23.5 Hrant Dink Site of Memory'. Why 23.5? On 23 April 1920, the new Turkish National Assembly proclaimed popular sovereignty and so began the dissolution of the Ottoman Empire. That date, also 'Children's Day', became a public holiday for the newborn Turkish Republic. But on 24 April 1915, a round-up of leading Armenians in Istanbul had launched the successive waves of state-backed massacres, starvation, and forced marches that most historians, some Turks among them, now designate as the Armenian 'genocide'. Behind the still-contested terminology, more than a million people indisputably died. Over 2 million strong before 1915, Turkey's Armenian Christian population now numbers around 70,000 – although many more 'crypto-Armenians' who chose to practise as Muslims after the persecution retain elements of traditional culture and belief. Dink had no qualms about invoking 'genocide', a word still taboo to official Turkey, but often employed other terms as well. 'My ancestors, using the Anatolian phrase for it, called it "slaughter",' he wrote in *Agos*. 'I choose to call it "devastation".'

Dink positioned himself, and his work, midway between Turkish festivity and Armenian mourning: precisely on 23.5 April. He could enjoy 'the holiday of 23 April with all its fervour' but also 'partake in all the grief of the following day'. 'How many people experience such a dilemma on the surface of the planet?' he asked. 'This is neither easy to understand, nor to explain.' But explain it he eloquently did, to Turkey, Armenia, and later – posthumously above all – to a worldwide audience.

The 'Memory Site' on Halaskargazi Avenue serves as museum, archive, gallery (with installations by invited artists) and – most of all – as shrine. Sections of the *Agos* floor remain as they looked on the day of the editor's death: notably, Dink's editorial office (enviably large) with its bookshelves, award certificates, souvenirs, family photos, and its wide desk scattered with knick-knacks. It feels, spookily, as if the editor has just left his chair to pop out on an errand. Other rooms store the *Agos* archive and illustrate the paper's bridge-building work, or dive into Dink's life and career: his youth in an Armenian orphanage and formative summers at the Tuzla Armenian children's camp outside Istanbul; his painful spell of military service; the torture he underwent when arrested as a leftist after the 1980 military coup; the multiple lawsuits and court battles that continued until his death. In the corridor, cuttings and photos trace the Turkish history of his time. Video clips show Dink speaking and debating, at conferences or on television. Articles from *Agos* and elsewhere feature on leaflets printed in Turkish, Armenian, and English. The well-curated, amply illustrated displays, and sophisticated audio-visual aids, are overseen by the Hrant Dink Foundation. All testify to a project that does not lack for funds.

As Şişli bustles and barters down in the street, here a hushed stillness reigns. I have toured plenty of memorial houses dedicated to canonical authors and artists, but never a place of pilgrimage of this kind for a journalist. Yet humour, and defiance, undercut the solemnity. Dink evidently had the madcap geniality that shines through in video extracts and quotations from his work. Aghast at the proposed French law designed to outlaw 'denial' of the Armenian genocide, he offered to go to France – explicitly to deny the idea of genocide that his Turkish foes constantly accused him of promoting. He claimed for *Agos* the role of 'village idiot' among Armenian Turks, the naive witness who blurts out what others won't admit and becomes 'the spirit of a spiritless community'.

II

Though Ogün Samast pulled the trigger, Hrant Dink died, beyond doubt, at the hands of an arm of the state. However, as soon as you begin to investigate political violence in Turkey, you grasp that the state has as many arms as the goddess Mahakali. Moreover, some may move without, or against, the others' will. After Samast's conviction, getting on for two decades of further trials have widened the circle of culpability without defining the ultimate source of the hit. In 2021, twenty-seven people received prison sentences (including four life terms), among them local police and intelligence chiefs. In February 2025, after an appeal against undue leniency in that process, nine life sentences were handed down. On the face of it, official Turkey seems to have redoubled its zeal to see justice done. Yet it appears that, as often, one faction within the state seeks to exploit the case in order to undermine another. Many of those accused of conspiracy to murder Dink, Samast included, allegedly had links with the Gülen movement: the far-reaching religious network which began almost as a technocratic upgrade of the Sufi orders of Ottoman times. Originally a Gülen ally, President Recep Tayyip Erdoğan has fought its followers for a decade as a (real or imaginary) menace to his total supremacy. So, the Gülenists have become a handy one-stop shop in the search for the culprits of every murky deed.

Dink died at a peculiar, and short-lived, moment. First elected in 2002, the so-called Islamist government of Erdoğan and his AK (Justice and Development) party still then enjoyed at least tactical support from many of Turkey's non-religious democrats. They approved the AKP resistance to the shadowy power of the military. Authors of three brutal coups (in 1960, 1971, and 1980), the Turkish armed forces and their allies in the state had severely curtailed political and civic life since the creation of the post-Ottoman nation by Mustafa Kemal (Atatürk). It has always been unwise, if not impossible, to reduce the swirling kaleidoscope of politics, ideology, and faith in Turkey to a binary conflict of 'religious' against 'secular' interests or values. For a while, Erdoğan seemed to offer release from the iron hand of military tutelage to Turks of many persuasions.

Shortly before Dink's death, I recall sitting on a rooftop terrace in Sultanahmet – with the domes of the Blue Mosque and Aya Sofya glinting in the evening sun behind us – to hear an impeccably cosmopolitan group of Turkish authors explain why they preferred an AKP government to the fatherly grip of the Kemalist generals. Erdoğan, they hoped, promised an adult politics, difficult but free, in place of the childish manoeuvres of an elite forever in thrall to their uniformed guardians. Meanwhile, the multi-coloured patchwork of the past on this disputed ground became a source of growing pride. At a literary dinner I told fellow-guests how much I appreciated the gourmet Ottoman cuisine served to us. 'Ah,' a Turkish author next to me replied, 'but long before that, it was *Byzantine* food'.

For advocates of a fully democratic Turkey, the years before Dink's assassination felt, despite setbacks, like a spring of hope. Foreign attention often seized on the prosecution of writers, journalists, and academics for 'insulting Turkishness' under the notorious Article 301 of the penal code. This was a replacement for the previous Article 159, modelled on a similar provision in Mussolini's Fascist code. Orhan Pamuk, Turkey's first winner of the Nobel Prize in Literature, felt the heat of Article 301 after he talked about the Armenian slaughter to a Swiss newspaper. Novelist Elif Shafak incurred a lawsuit when characters in her book *The Bastard of Istanbul* discussed genocide. Dink himself suffered a triple dose of drawn-out 301 cases. One, in 2005, led to a six-month suspended sentence, even though the court's own learned opinion had rebutted the prosecution case. He had referred to 'the poisonous blood to be shed after freeing oneself of the "Turk"': in other words, to self-liberation from harmful obsession and paranoia. The expert report agreed.

Article 301 made a loud global noise. Yet the free-speech campaigners missed a large part of the picture. Prosecutions under this rubric often originated from local lawyers and judges: a hard-right nationalist attorney named Kemal Kerinçsiz instigated many. Plenty of them stalled, failed outright, or were annulled in higher tribunals. The cases served as ideological 'lawfare' for mostly secular nationalists, who wanted to push back against the newly raised profile of pluralism in Turkey. It was not, at that stage, any sort of concerted crackdown by the Erdoğan government to silence dissent. Sadly, that arrived later.

If the early AKP administrations did not exactly welcome Dink's pleas for rapprochement between Armenian and Muslim Turks, they lifted some of the barriers that had hindered genuine exchange. Turkish historians such as Taner Akçam and Müge Göçek explored the massacres of 1915, threw fresh light on the orders that prompted them, and chronicled their aftermath. When Akçam called his book *A Shameful Act*, the title came from a remark about the Armenian slaughter by Atatürk himself. A historians' group united Turkish researchers with scholars from Armenia. It led to a landmark conference staged at Bilgi University in September 2005, on 'Ottoman Armenians during the decline of the empire', after nationalist lawyers had the gathering banned from other campuses.

Dink himself spoke at the symposium. As always, he presented Armenian-Turkish dialogue and reconciliation not just as a route to recovery for Armenians but an essential step along the route to a better Turkey. 'Armenians will not heal as long as Turkey does not democratise,' he said. 'They are like twin spirits. As one undergoes surgery on the operating table, the other suffers for its twin.' His peroration tackled the abiding Turkish fear that Armenians, or rather their grasping heirs, will return to claim lost lands if granted firmer rights. 'Don't worry, our aim is not to take these lands away,' he said, 'but to come and one day be buried deep in them'.

More than 100,000 people joined Dink's funeral procession. They carried banners asserting 'We are all Hrant', or 'We are all Armenian'. The vast bulk of them had no prior connection with the Armenian cause. For Ece Temelkuran, the popular protests expressed anger at 'that crushing sense of being unable to change things', and a need to grieve 'this unstoppable wheel of death' – of Kurds, Armenians, Assyrians, leftists – in 'this country founded on death'. In a sense, the public reaction to Dink's murder marked a high tide for the liberalising Turkey that had become an EU candidate nation in 1999.

That mood of inclusive hope did not last. Soon enough, as Temelkuran records, the backlash began. A 'flashfire of ultra-nationalist sentiment' swept the country. Recently dead Turkish soldiers, killed by the Kurdish separatists of the PKK, ousted the fragile memory of long-dead Armenians who died as a result of ambiguous orders that scholars still struggle to attribute. Erdoğan's autocratic turn, and a renewed ideological fusion of faith and nation, would make the mass grief and rage that greeted the Dink murder look not like a beginning, but an end. By 2016, when the state moved ruthlessly to quell the coup attempt, calls to resist the army mutineers were not only sent to mobile phones by telecoms networks but broadcast from the minarets of the country's 86,000 mosques.

To survive, and to flatten their opponents, Erdoğan and the AKP had made their peace with some elements of the old 'deep state' while seeking to sideline and eliminate others. By around 2013, the reborn sultan had started to gallop down his authoritarian track. The botched coup attempt of July 2016, conveniently blamed on the Gülenists, furnished the perfect pretext for an escalation of repression. A comprehensive purge cleansed Turkish education and media of supposedly disloyal voices. In 2025, Turkey has sunk to 159th place (out of 180) on the World Press Freedom index. More than 500,000 people across all professions and institutions have been detained during the state's long-drawn-out revenge for the 2016 fiasco. The anti-AKP mayors of Turkey's major cities languish in jail on ever-changing, politically motivated charges: Istanbul's Ekrem İmamoğlu, likely presidential candidate of the opposition CHP party, prominent among them. Also imprisoned, as it happens, was the borough mayor of Şişli itself: Resul Emrah Şahan.

III

A visit to the 'Memory Site' should remind any journalist why it matters to do our job with as much candour and bravery as we can muster. Journalists love the image of the fearless heretic who courts vilification and rattles the fixed prejudices of the majority. Along with the figure of the dogged investigative reporter, whose incendiary exposés topple governments and corporations, the intrepid maverick who stands up to received opinion offers a favourite model of the media hero. In many Western countries, however, writers who set up shop as gadflies, contrarians, and provocateurs are not much more than harmless licensed jesters. They fire only paper – or, these days, pixelated – darts. Manufactured 'controversy' is the junk snack of the grazing media consumer. The present online surfeit of ephemeral outrage has reduced its nutritional value to zero.

Dink's career, in contrast, incurred the cost of principled dissent in a strongly normative culture. He became scapegoat, whipping-boy, and punchbag for fulminating chauvinists. Many columnists court cheap applause; Dink voluntarily put his head in the stocks. As Oscar Wilde (himself a brilliant journalist) wrote after his downfall and disgrace, 'it is a very unimaginative nature that only cares for people on their pedestals. A pedestal may be a very unreal thing. A pillory is a terrific reality.' Dink did not seek, but neither did he flee, his pillory.

Reading his words, and listening to his voice, I understood that his work sometimes led to acute stress and anxiety not simply because he risked the wrath of the many media attack-dogs for Turkish majoritarianism. Hundred of death threats resulted. He also fought, at a deep level of feeling and identification, against himself – or, the part of himself that yearned above all to belong as a good Turk at ease and in tune with friends and neighbours. One video extract shows his anguished response to the seemingly abstract charge of 'insulting Turkishness'. It meant, to him, that the butcher, the baker, the greengrocer on his street, would brand him a pariah. 'At the end of the day, you have to live with these people.' Yet such a stigma would mark him as an alien, an outsider, a traitor. He never wanted that. Unlike Dr Stockmann, the archetypal whistle-blower and free-press militant of Henrik Ibsen's play *An Enemy of the People*, Dink never comforted himself with the delusion that 'the strongest man in the world is he who stands alone'.

Dink recalled that, when he performed military service in the Turkish army, all the friends in his intake duly gained the rank of sergeant. He alone was denied promotion and assigned a menial job in the barracks garden – excluded as an Armenian, as a known student leftist, or as both. His commanding officer, otherwise kindly, explained that Dink had a 'despicable character'. For much of that day, he admits, he wept. He desperately sought to belong in the cosy family of Turkishness but grew up at a time when that family had ousted its marginal members and raised the fences around those who remained.

Journalists who campaign against injustice often want to 'shame' the perpetrators. Dink's predicament was different. He felt compelled to challenge the monolithic and amnesiac culture of the modern state. 'My only wish is to talk freely about our shared past with my beloved friends here in Turkey,' he wrote. Yet in doing so he sensed that he had, in some way, shamed himself. He faced ostracism, ridicule, the loss of liberty and livelihood. And still he knew, from inside out, how and why his accusers and tormentors felt and acted as they did. WB Yeats once wrote that 'we make out of the quarrel with others, rhetoric, but of the quarrel with ourselves, poetry'. Journalism offers plenty of platforms for the rhetoric of soapbox self-righteousness. Some of its strongest voices, however, know how to find, and share, a private poetry of quest and doubt. As Dink did.

The press that – in Turkey as in many other countries – did so much to nurture and enforce a univocal nationalism also created small spaces for that other kind of voice to speak. Turkey itself came late to this process of majority shouts and minority whispers in print. Famously tardy in its adoption of mass printing (the first Istanbul press for Turkish-language publications started in 1727), the Ottoman Empire continued to rely on local oral culture for the transmission of its edicts long after rotary presses had begun to strengthen central power elsewhere. A Turkish-language paper had launched under Sultan Mahmoud II in 1831 at the dawn of the 'Tanzimat' era of state modernisation. But low levels of literacy (under 10 percent for Muslims during the imperial twilight) and the technical problems presented by the Arabic script of Ottoman Turkish meant that newspapers channelled more the gossip of the elite than the alleged voice of 'the people'.

Atatürk's revolution aimed to 'catch up' with Western media, as with so much else – to use the master-metaphor of the Kemalist age, superbly satirised by the great Istanbul writer Ahmet Hamdi Tanpinar in his novel *The Time Regulation Institute*. Close associates of Atatürk founded the *Cumhuriyet* newspaper in 1924: then a state cheerleader, more recently a pillar of opposition politics. Frequently renewed, Atatürk's Press Law of 1931 granted sweeping powers of media censorship to the state. Language reform boosted literacy rates and so broadened readership: first the quick-fire replacement of Arabic with Latin script in 1928 (the 'Alphabet Reform'), then the thorough purge of a vast, rich Arabic and Persian vocabulary from the old Ottoman Turkish language. What remained was, supposedly, a pure tongue for the pure people of a pure modern nation.

Yet everywhere the grit of impurity endured, in the guise of Armenian (despite the massacres), Greek, Kurdish, Assyrian, Jewish, Roma, and other minority cultures. Even – or especially – the house of Islam itself hosted innumerable local and sectional mansions. Many resisted the Kemalist bulldozer, from the suppressed but still-enduring Sufi orders to the huge Alevi community. Turkey stubbornly refused to set in a single Kemalist mould. It took further waves of repression and expulsion to approach an ideal homogeneity: in 1923, after the population exchanges mandated by the Treaty of Lausanne; in 1955, after a secret false-flag operation had blamed a bomb in Atatürk's Thessaloniki birthplace on Greek militants; and again in 1964. After that round of 'cleansing' violence, the writer and translator Maureen Freely – who was brought up in Istanbul – remembers that 'almost overnight, the city I had come to know, where Turks of all ethnic backgrounds lived intertwined lives, where everyone seemed to speak about five languages, became a city in which non-Muslims listened carefully to the state-sponsored injunction: "Citizen, speak Turkish!"' Further east, that command equally targeted Muslim Kurds.

IV

With his bilingual newspaper and unabashed pluralism, Dink represented not only a possible Turkish future but – in his way – a Turkish past as well. Or rather, one side of that past: the jigsaw coexistence that he praised rather than the communal hatred he sought to 'abandon in its dark cave in history'. He did not seek, as many diaspora Armenians did, to worship and weaponise the pain of memory. In *Deep Mountain*, her fine book of reportage about Turkish-Armenian relations, Temelkuran reckons that 28,000 studies have presented the genocide/slaughter/devastation of 1915 from the Armenian perspective; around 700 have put the official Turkish line that accepts mass deaths but denies genocidal intent. In the global memory match, the Armenians have played the Turks off the pitch. But Dink the stalwart son of Turkey had no desire to profit from foreign plaudits. 'I feel offended when people in Europe and America use my problems, past or present, for political capital,' he wrote in 2004. 'I sense abuse and rape lurking behind their kisses.' His journalism seeks not to amplify grievance and entrench division. Rather, it gropes towards a complex citizenship that would leave history's toxic waste forever in its cave. Freely notes that 'for him dual identity was at the core of a new patriotism'.

The heyday of *Agos*, in the decade after 1996, also coincided with the last gasp of print-first journalism. A title with a limited circulation could still find a voice strong enough to speak with bigger names on almost equal terms. Soon after, the online deluge and social-media tide would – in

Turkey as elsewhere – help to deepen rifts, magnify suspicions, and make that 'dual' or hybrid identity harder than ever to defend amid the sloganeering din of cyberspace. Accusations of a non-Turkish heritage still cling to political figures who dare oppose the AKP. Ekrem İmamoğlu himself, who hails from the Black Sea coast, has for years had to counter noisy media claims that he is 'really' a Pontic Greek. The sensible response – 'So what?' – still seems difficult to handle. Predictably, Greek nationalist outlets have conversely hailed the ascent of 'one of theirs' in the place that still counts for many as the one and only *polis*: Constantinople.

Constantinople always haunts Istanbul – indeed, Dink reported that diaspora Armenians bridled whenever he chose to use the Turkish name. In Orhan Pamuk's memoir of his youth, *Istanbul: Memories and the City*, the novelist suggests that the distinctive Istanbul melancholy – *hüzün* – he finds everywhere stems from the sadness of 'lives amongst the ruins' of a vanished multi-national empire. For Pamuk, however, this mist-shrouded existence amid the remnants of a 'glorious past' had failed to awaken a Turkish hunger for lost diversity. On the contrary: *hüzün* brought about 'an erosion of the will to stand against the values and mores of the community'. Defeated passivity encouraged docile citizens 'to be content with little, honouring the virtues of harmony, uniformity, humility'.

In novels such as *The Museum of Innocence*, Pamuk gives incomparable expression to the stoic, obedient, mustn't-grumble *hüzün* of the everyday Istanbul he knew, that 'black mood shared by millions'. Pamuk's work both cherishes and resists the charms of the 'monotonous, monolingual town in black-and-white' in which he passed his youth. That climate, however, has itself passed into history. Come the new millennium, and it turned out that, in the AKP era, official reverence for custom and piety could partner a cult of brash, aggressive capitalist modernity. If the journalism of Dink and his associates strove to restore multi-cultural colour and contrast to the monochrome scene, then Erdoğan had his own cure for Istanbul melancholy. His populist blend of futuristic economics and faith-based nostalgia would drive the fogs of *hüzün* into the Bosphorus and out to sea.

Go to the Hrant Dink 'Memory Site' if you wish to witness the resilience of multi-faceted, mosaic Turkey as championed by its most outspoken journalistic voices. Down by the waterfront, however, another kind of cosmopolitanism seems, on the surface, to flourish. Opened in 2022 after years of delays and controversies, the Galataport development – a pet project of Erdoğan's – stretches for 1.2km along the Kadiköy shore. Sealed from the city by securitised access points, its 250 brand-name stores and chain restaurants face a promenade flanked by gigantic cruise ships. All bright lights and slick surfaces, this ancient public space of docks, warehouses and cafés has become an electronically guarded theme-park and shopping mall. When I visited, the line of moored multi-storey giants that blocked the historic view to the Asian side of the Bosphorus included the Carnival line's towering vessel, 'Miracle'. It is a sort of miracle, I suppose, that a government ostensibly devoted to religion and tradition should so eagerly open Turkey to the crushing spectacle of globalisation imposed by debt-laden financial syndicates. In any case, Galataport has 'caught up' with any other citadel of high-security consumerism.

To their credit, many Turkish journalists have objected robustly to Galataport. Yet its buzzing crowds on a weekend night reveal the appeal of a model of social life that has little to do with Dink's ideal of warm and frank dialogue among equals. Rather, all differences dissolve in the collective pursuit of international designer labels and fast-food menus. In the city of the seething Grand Bazaar, only an idiotic snob would complain that Istanbullus enjoy their markets. But no one haggles over prices here, or tarries for tea with a stallholder. These rites of consumption – uniform, sterile, monitored, delocalised – feel like a pilgrimage of a newer kind as shoppers queue up to pass the security gates. Around the world, authoritarian populists pose their various risks to the civic plurality and multiplicity that Hrant Dink and his paper championed. But so, as well, does the homogenised monoculture of the mega-mall and the cruise liner. For journalists, and citizens, Galataport should feel like a frontline of threatened freedoms too.

SYSTEM FAILURE

James Brooks

Much can be learnt about journalism in the era of advancing climate breakdown from the story of Roger Hallam, the otherworldly co-founder of environmental protest groups from Extinction Rebellion to Just Stop Oil via Insulate Britain and others best forgotten – Burning Pink, anyone?

On his website, Hallam claims to be 'the UK's number one climate campaigner' and even accounting for the occasional misfire, that's not an idle boast. Together with Swedish teenager Greta Thunberg and her school strikes movement, Hallam was at the vanguard of the wave of mass participation civil disobedience reinvigorating environmental protest at the end of the last decade.

Hallam's media star rose highest in the summer of 2019, which was also the heyday of the first widely known group he co-founded, Extinction Rebellion. In April, after less than a year of existence, XR had gone from a handful of unknown activists meeting at a café in the Gloucestershire market town of Stroud, to many thousands blocking bridges and intersections in central London – and over a thousand arrests. That summer, XR activists were gearing up for a second, bigger, more disruptive London shutdown in October.

In a pattern repeated in all the groups Hallam co-founded, XR claimed to be non-hierarchical, yet Hallam was ever-present as something between its figurehead, eminence grise, and leader. In August, he was summoned for an interview on the BBC's *HardTalk* programme. In a baggy brown t-shirt, with his scraggly beard and oddly unplaceable accent tallying with his former job as a vegetable farmer, Hallam cut an unlikely figure. *HardTalk* usually called in global statesmen, or those who had their ear, to face the steely, forensic questioning of its host, Stephen Sackur, over half-hour face-to-face interviews.

Yet Hallam's dressed-down appearance and rural accent did not offset his preeminent characteristic – simmering, barely contained intensity. Hallam acts like a man who is always *living* the climate crisis. Looking hard at his inquisitor during the interview, it was as if Hallam was also gazing at a raging forest fire consuming a mountain range just beyond. Such eschatological intensity was implanted deep within XR, which distinguished itself from earlier environmental activist groups by foregrounding doomy forecasts of civilisational collapse over more hopeful messaging, sometimes venturing beyond even the grimmest scientific predictions.

In the *HardTalk* interview, Sackur ceded the scientific ground early. Hallam cited a couple of stats on the relentless rise of global carbon emissions and Sackur responded: 'On the science, there's no disagreement.' We all knew, apparently, that the biosphere was in a perilous state. Hallam was then free to deliver his stock-in-trade warning of collapse. Starting with a phrase he would repeat several times in the following twenty-five minutes, he said: 'The fact of the matter is, we're facing mass starvation in the next ten years, social collapse, and the possible extinction of the human race'. There's enough scope for ambiguity in that sentence for Hallam to have eked some scientific plausibility out of it if challenged – *regional* mass starvation would happen in the next ten years, not total social collapse and human extinction – but he wasn't.

Instead, the Hallam statement picked up in both social and traditional media came later, when Sackur challenged him on 'encouraging [children, young people, the elderly] to put themselves in harm's way' on XR actions. Not so, Hallam replied, people were already terrified by imminent climate collapse and were angry at their governments for failing to protect them. XR had just given them a conduit to vent their frustrations and push for action. Then there was this exchange:

> Hallam: Teenagers are shitting themselves about what's happening for the future. They've got another fifty, sixty, seventy years to live on this planet. By that time there could be only a billion people left. I mean, that's six billion people that have died from starvation or been slaughtered in war. I mean, the scale of it is beyond the imagination, isn't it? And this is the biggest problem – the elites and the BBC and conventional media have simply not grasped the enormity of what's happening.

Sackur: Never mind the elites. It seems that many people even who were involved in the early days of Extinction Rebellion like yourself think you are going far too far.

Hallam: You haven't heard what I've said and this is the fundamental problem.

Sackur: I'm listening very carefully to you.

Hallam: No, I don't think you are. You're listening but you're not emotionally connecting, and this is the problem. You know, I've just spent a year doing interviews like this with journalists, and journalists are not emotionally connecting with what's happening. I'm talking about the slaughter, death and starvation of six billion people this century. That's what the science predicts; that's the trajectory we're on and that requires absolutely desperate measures to stop it.

If Hallam was incensed by Sackur's lack of connection, emotional, or otherwise, with the allegedly scientific prediction of six billion deaths from climate change by the century's end, he should have been satisfied by the wider response. The statistic quickly became a talking point on social media and filtered into traditional media commentary, most often as an example of the hysterical alarmism and scientific illiteracy allegedly driving XR. The remark was still doing the op-ed rounds over four years later when *The Telegraph* offered financial services bigwig and climate denialist Neil Record a column to ridicule the Hallam-led spin-out group, Just Stop Oil. The headline – 'What could happen if we just stopped oil? Six billion might die'.

All this was perhaps to be expected of the right-wing press, which, thanks to its owners' fossil-fuel heavy financial portfolios, had always been antagonistic to XR. But there was also pushback from supposedly less politically partisan commentators and institutions, or liberal ones. Until then, these had shared with right-wingers a tendency to focus on the group's civil disobedience tactics rather than XR's core message of imminent climate collapse and the 'absolutely desperate measures' needed to avert it. But the self-evidently dubious six billion deaths comment, everyone went for.

Fact-checking website Climate Feedback (now Science Feedback) examined Hallam's comments and the resulting article went as viral as possible for such dry, scientist-approved content. Its withering assessment that 'counter to Hallam's statement, published studies have not predicted six billion human deaths this century and there is no credible mechanism referred to justify how this could happen' chimed with similar cool-headed remarks in broadsheet columnists' copy as they returned from their summer holidays. And then, three weeks after it was broadcast, the BBC revisited the interview on its popular, stats-checking radio programme *More or Less*. Perennially perky host Tim Harford pulled out some World Health Organisation figures and waxed sceptical on Hallam's powers of prophecy. The segment ended with comments from Andy Haines, professor of environmental change and public health at the London School of Hygiene and Tropical Medicine. In authoritative upper-middle-class tones, Haines stated the need to reduce carbon emissions, describing the need for mitigation as 'a good news story, because many of the strategies which we need to put in place to cut greenhouse gas emissions are also beneficial for human health'. It was never explained why that coincidence was such good news, presumably because in the minds of all concerned it was self-evident. Of course, governments, or at least good, democratic western ones, would want the best for their populations. Sensible emissions-reducing climate policies and robust public health went hand in hand, and so of course would become the preferred approach. There was no need to glue yourself to the road in protest. The world wasn't about to end. The route over some potentially treacherous ground could be plotted with confidence.

Fast forward to mid-January 2025 and Hallam is in prison, put there by the actions of a journalist. In July the previous year, he had been sentenced to five years in jail – widely reported as one of the longest sentences in modern British history for nonviolent protest – which was reduced to four on appeal. Hallam had been found guilty of 'conspiracy to cause a public nuisance', a charge brought onto the books as part of legislation introduced by the government expressly to crack down on environmental and antiracist protest. Despite its sweeping curbs on civil liberties, the Police, Crime, Sentencing and Courts Bill barely registered in the mainstream press until a Bristol protest against it flared into a riot, and a Police van was set alight. Even then, discussion of the bill's contents barely went beyond a couple of op-eds in *The Guardian*.

The conspiracy precipitating Hallam's imprisonment was a November 2022 Zoom call planning motorway shutdowns for Just Stop Oil. The plan was for JSO activists to climb and affix themselves to gantries along the M25, London's orbital motorway, and block traffic for hours as emergency services scrambled to remove them. Disruption and illegality are hallmarks of Hallam's brand of activism, his goal being to throw a spanner in what he sees as ecocidal business-as-usual and force a mediatised confrontation with power. This time, though, the media was ahead of the game. Three or four days of motorway shutdown were scuppered by a journalist hidden among the Zoom meeting's attendees. She shelved an immediate scoop and instead passed her recording to the police.

Scarlet Howes, the journalist, still got a decent amount of copy out of it, though. First, upon Hallam and his JSO associates' arrest, four days after the Zoom call, and then a year and a half later following their trials and convictions. The first article adhered rigorously to the editorial standards of the organ that published it – Rupert Murdoch's *The Sun* – complete with punning headline, 'JUST STOP FOILED', and compressed standfirst description of Hallam as 'mastermind of eco-mob'.

'We need to step up,' Hallam is quoted as saying on the call, but the reader is left unclear as to why. The words 'climate' or 'environment' figure nowhere in the report and 'eco' only in hyphenated conjunction with 'mob', 'idiots', or 'zealots'. We're left to assume that Hallam's 'yobs' are motivated purely by a nihilistic, attention-seeking drive to sow anarchy and 'cost billions to Britain's already battered economy'.

The online version of Howes's confessional report published after Hallam's sentencing opens up another possibility, hidden in the video at the top of the page. There we can view a segment of the Zoom call where Hallam – more frazzled and excitable than under *HardTalk*'s studio lights – lays out why, in his opinion, activists 'need to step up'. He mentions that James Hansen, one of the world's foremost climatologists, whose powerful 1988 testimony before US congress raised the topic to unprecedented levels of both popular and political awareness, had recently issued a memo. In it, Hallam relays, Hansen and his colleagues 'say that they now expect the world to go over 1.5 degrees [Celsius] in 2024 – in two years' time'. Global temperature rise to this extent over pre-industrial levels was widely agreed upon as a guardrail limiting entry to a future of irreversible ecosystem damage and possibly disastrous and unstoppable 'runaway' climate change. It was a barrier, therefore, not to be breached. But it was – in 2024, just as Hansen had said. This startling reality was apparently far from Howes's mind at the trial, however. Instead, she connected emotionally with the matter at hand: 'When I heard the verdict I was elated – despite the concerns that I and most other people share about the future of the planet'.

Back to 16 January 2025, with Hallam safe in his cell in Wayland Prison in rural Norfolk. *The Guardian* website publishes an exclusive write-up of a report from the Institute and Faculty of Actuaries, the UK's chartered body for risk analysts, giving its assessment of the long-term economic impacts of climate change. As the headline states, the IFoA concluded that these are potentially catastrophic, with up to '50 percent loss in GDP between 2070 and 2090 from climate shocks'. A halving of gross domestic product fifty years' hence is abstract and distant enough not to cause alarm for most people. The same cannot be said for the information in the story's fifth paragraph, that at three degrees Celsius of global temperature rise by 2050 – a 'plausible worst-case' scenario – 'there could be more than four billion deaths, significant sociopolitical fragmentation worldwide, failure of states (with resulting rapid, enduring, and significant loss of capital), and extinction events'. Leaving aside the bizarre parenthetical recontextualisation of mass slaughter in financial terms – 'I didn't realise how bad climate change was until I understood the significant loss of capital it may entail!'– and the dry, actuarial language, this is global calamity on an even shorter timescale than in Hallam's predictions. Yes, we're talking about a 'plausible worst-case scenario', and yes, it's still not 'what the science predicts', but that's mostly because science, or at least the peer-reviewed literature, just doesn't deal in numerical forecasts of medium-term climate-change-related death. Nonetheless, as Hallam himself later noted on social media site X, where he uses a screengrab from his *HardTalk* appearance as an avatar: 'The Institute and Faculty of Actuaries are in the business of making accurate insurance judgements'.

Quite. So, who held whom to account in the aftermath of that interview? The self-assured, rational-minded journalists pooh-poohing visions of societal collapse, or the strange man straining to convey them to and through an emotionally detached elite media class? Who was right? Shall we wait and see? If it was Hallam, shall our children and grandchildren applaud him from their early graves?

I did not want to write this essay, even though, for once, I'm qualified to do so. I don't work specifically on climate, but I'm a science journalist and have covered the topic several times. Also: I was one of the eco-mob for several years, active in XR from its first major central London action – blocking bridges in November 2018 – until probably its final one – a week of expressly law-abiding protests outside government ministries in April 2023. I was arrested at an XR roadblock in October 2019.

Blessed with neither the career ambitions of my professional peers, nor the time and aptitude for activist organising, I've never been a deep insider in either world. But I've had enough experience in both to be able to mine my memory for raw essay material fairly easily. Yet I didn't want to. Why? Because I would be forced to emotionally reconnect with the bleakest possible knowledge about the fate of life on Earth, humanity, and, finally, my own children.

'It is worse, much worse than you think,' as New York journalist David Wallace-Wells wrote as the first line of his 2019 book, *The Uninhabitable Earth: Life After Warming*. That sentence is the first of two observations essential to understanding journalistic treatment of the climate crisis, because it is essential to first understand the abject failure of journalism to communicate our current predicament.

The opprobrium heaped upon Hallam for his six billion deaths statement was not borne of any journalistic or scientific motivation for accuracy in public discourse. It came from an opposing impulse – an opportunistic desire to be proved superficially correct on a wayward detail and thereby keep a much bigger and wholly untenable argument afloat. We can note that, despite using similar 'alarmist' language, comparable scorn was not visited upon United Nations secretary general António Guterres after his presentation of the latest Intergovernmental Panel on Climate Change report in April 2022 (IPCC reports are well-known for being both comprehensive and conservative in their assessment of climate risk). Yet his language is hardly less lurid than Hallam's:

We are on a fast track to climate disaster. Major cities under water. Unprecedented heatwaves. Terrifying storms. Widespread water shortages. The extinction of a million species of plants and animals. This is not fiction or exaggeration. It is what science tells us will result from our current energy policies.

In the same speech, Guterres also said: 'climate activists are sometimes depicted as dangerous radicals. But the truly dangerous radicals are the countries that are increasing the production of fossil fuels.' He did not dwell on who was portraying activists that way, or why those who pride themselves on speaking truth to power would instead buttress power against the truth, but then his words were intended to inspire a sense of urgency among UN-member governments, rather than a professional awakening among journalists.

In that, he failed. Just as everyone who has tried to convince a wider group locked into dominant narratives of climate discourse – that we aren't facing cataclysm, or that the socio-economic system has it within itself to avoid it – has failed. I have failed; Roger Hallam has failed; David Wallace-Wells, with his compendium of high-level scientific studies all pointing inexorably to calamity, has failed.

And still, 'it is worse, much worse than you think' holds true for us all. For example, we now know that the Earth's oceans have likely crossed a chemical tipping point, with one study showing that 40 percent of surface waters, and 60 percent of the ocean subsurface (down to 200 metres depth) have become too acidic for shell-forming species to survive. The oceans absorb between 25 percent to 30 percent of human-produced carbon dioxide emissions, acting as a 'carbon sink' and reducing wider climate impacts, but carbon dioxide acidifies the water. We are only now understanding how sensitive sea-life is to this process.

As I learnt from a recent study, coral reefs, those resplendent polyp colonies that form over thousands or millions of years, have crossed their own tipping point and are now functionally extinct, as a result of ocean acidification and heating. The oceans absorb more than 90 percent of the excess heat energy from global warming, at the rate of five or six atomic bombs of the size that destroyed Hiroshima exploding every second. As I also learnt, just in recent weeks, the unprecedented ocean and marine heatwaves that decimated sea-life in many regions and horrified climate and ecological scientists (but barely troubled public consciousness) in 2024 have hardly abated in many areas, and gravely worsened in others. The North Pacific has experienced record-breaking heat, continuing an exponential trajectory that began around 2010. In October 2025, one of the most severe marine heatwaves ever recorded developed in the Yellow and East China seas, with temperatures reaching up to 5.5 degrees Celsius above normal.

On most climate models and in much climate discourse, oceans are treated as eternal carbon and heat sinks, unproblematically neutralising humanity's poison byproducts. At barely 1.5 Celsius of global warming we can already see what nonsense this is. To be anthropocentric about it, ocean acidification and coral extinction will further sink global fish stocks which are already plummeting because of overfishing, and fish are the primary source of animal protein for around one billion people globally. To take a broader view, climate change is rendering our oceans and seas uninhabitable to animal life, and less able to absorb the excess energy we uncaringly pump into them, with profound and terrifying consequences for all life on Earth.

I cannot stress this enough: according to the laws of physics, the situation for the oceans, which I've barely begun to describe, along with the situation for almost every ecosystem, can only get worse, much worse. Human civilisation was only possible – is only possible – because around 12,000 years ago we entered a period of environmental stability known as the Holocene. This stability is held delicately in place by myriad interlinked geophysical and biological processes. Push them too far and they will break, and tip the whole biosphere into unliveable chaos. Humans are pumping carbon gases into the air at a geologically unprecedented rate – the equivalent of 53 gigatonnes of carbon dioxide in 2024 – that is still rising. If you thought there was an 'ecological transition' happening, you were misinformed. I'm not even talking about oil and gas; we are burning more *coal* than ever before. Globally, renewables are supplementing rising fossil fuel use, not replacing it. Those geophysical and biological processes are buckling, and soon they will break.

I'm failing again. *You're not emotionally connecting, and this is the problem.* True, no? The functional extinction of coral, the desertification of the oceans, 53 gigatonnes a year, 1.5 degrees Celsius, 5.5 degrees… This litany of disaster-detail leaves most people stultified and numb. Certainly, that was my own reaction to Wallace-Wells' book. I viscerally understand Hallam's frustration during the HardTalk interview. I, too, want to tell you that six billion people will die, that's what the science says, and rouse you to panic. I want to lose it like Jennifer Lawrence's doomsday-comet-spotting astronomer invited on a chat show in Adam McKay's climate allegory *Don't Look Up,* yelling: 'we're all 100 percent for sure gonna fucking die!' But this isn't the place for that, and more to the point, it wouldn't be true. The likelier scenario is the one sketched by John Schellnhuber, director of the International Institute for Applied Systems Analysis in Austria, on the sidelines of a conference a few years ago. It's a video that often does the rounds on climate activist social media due to Schellnhuber's status as a big beast of climate science, and his candidness in the clip. In it, a calm, collected Schellnhuber matter-of-factly pronounces his view that, considering humanity's current trajectory, 'there is a very, very big risk that we will just end our civilisation. The human species will survive somehow, but we will destroy almost everything we have built up over the last two thousand years.' There are similar clips of other senior climate scientists speaking equally frankly, but they never get anywhere near mainstream media broadcast. You have to wonder why.

The second observation that helps us understand journalism in the climate crisis – and makes Hallam's treatment by journalists, rather than just his eschatological fervour, legible – is that journalists are emblematic members of the *professional-managerial class* (PMC). In their 1977 essay that introduced the term, Barbara and John Ehrenreich described PMC members as 'salaried mental workers' whose role in society is to ensure 'the reproduction of capitalist culture and capitalist class relations' – that and nothing else. Not to find out the truth, not to hold power to account, and not to protect a habitable environment for humanity.

The truth of this kind of functional class analysis can be hard to grasp, especially when it concerns the middle-class professions like journalism. For sure, almost no-one believes we live in the 'classless society' promised by neoliberals in the final decades of the twentieth century. We all instinctively tag people, including ourselves, as working or middle class, often applying subdivisions within those categories. We know that the working class exist for functional reasons within capitalism – to make or do things at a wage low enough for their employer to extract a profit. But when we look at the less productive, or even unproductive, middle classes – those who are paid more for less arduous work – our functional analysis hits a wall. In the case of journalists, we might attempt to apply the same schema used for the working class – that they make or do things at capitalist-friendly rates – but that falls down fast. Few media owners are turning much of a profit from journalism these days, many are making losses, and yet there's no shortage of billionaires keen to acquire and run journalistic outlets. Furthermore, in the UK, the corporation employing the most journalists – around 5,500 worldwide – is publicly funded and supposedly independent from government, yet has an editorial line markedly similar to the main commercial broadcasters and oligarch-owned broadsheets, whose journalists are invited on to discuss current affairs with surprising regularity. Clearly, something other than capitalist labour-value extraction is at work. Everything points to the preeminent importance of media control in protecting capitalist – or, in the case of the BBC, and assuming a separation that may not exist, establishment – interests. Journalists are the employees who perform that function.

We may also find this analysis difficult to accept because it would appears to rely on top-down control, as if journalists would need to be constantly reminded of their duty to capital as they carry out their daily tasks. Such thinking follows the cultural narrative of journalism existing as a 'fourth estate' – a truth-seeking counterweight to other houses of power – when it is in fact more legitimate to speak of a 'politico-media class' within the PMC, so intertwined have the two professional worlds become. To give just one quick but telling example, unrelated to climate, Declassified UK is an independent foreign policy-focused outfit employing only a handful of journalists but it has done more to expose the British state's military support for the genocide in Gaza than the rest of the media combined. You might think that revealing state involvement in the livestreamed war crimes that have transfixed and horrified millions of people in the UK would be universally hailed across the fourth estate, maybe with a hint of jealousy. But no, Declassified's work has been overwhelmingly shunned by mainstream sources, and its journalists refused parliamentary press passes on spurious grounds. So does the politico-media class act as one to protect capitalist and establishment interests.

The assumption that top-down media control would be needed to enforce media compliance also overlooks journalism's overwhelmingly middle-class make-up, which becomes predictably upper-middle class (private school, Oxbridge) as you reach the upper echelons. Young journalists already possess a PMC outlook as they start their careers, and it becomes fully entrenched as their professional and family lives advance within their tightly circumscribed PMC milieux.

The class system's production of self-regulating journalistic compliance was perhaps best expressed by polymath media theorist Noam Chomsky in a BBC interview from February 1996, spurred by a testy Andrew Marr, then political editor of *The Independent* newspaper:

Marr: How can you know I'm self-censoring?

Chomsky: I'm not saying you're self-censoring. I'm sure you believe everything you say. But what I'm saying is if you believed something different you wouldn't be sitting where you're sitting.

What is the PMC outlook? Obviously, the PMC is not a monolith, and its members may have differing political allegiances, but their thinking is united by a cast of mind where the dominant neoliberal frames of reference are utterly axiomatic. Within that system, journalists are capable of brilliant work in exacting conditions. I work for a subscription publication in higher education and science policy, and I'm always struck, when I compare the size of our staff and our available resources with those of other, much larger outlets, at the quality and quantity of original journalism we produce. We ask tough questions of government, probe alleged wrongdoing in universities irrespective of whether they are our subscribers (frequently, we don't even know) and challenge the top-down institutional policies that ruffle our rank-and-file readership. But all that happens within the marketized, neoliberal framework for higher education and academic research with its watchwords of 'excellence', 'innovation' and its 'global race' for technology, skills, and 'talent'. Those shibboleths, whose meaning or worth is never examined, all have their place in the wider PMC worldview in which every problem has an in-system solution.

As a result, mainstream 'environmental journalism' is not worthy of the name. Real environmental journalism would cover the multitude of crises unfolding in our ecological and climatic systems; it would make the complex underpinnings of those systems legible, and present honestly the radical changes necessary to limit their collapse. There are a handful of journalists that do this, who are mostly freelancers and/or lone wolves with crowdfunded blogs and YouTube channels. But overall, mainstream environmental journalism, which is mostly not written or delivered by specialists, is a thin slurry of tech boosterism and superficial political reporting, focusing endlessly on what is promised and never on what is delivered. We get stories on electric vehicles, on the 'net zero transition' and annual reports from the UN's COP meetings where news on the eventual deal is frequently delivered with an admission that the result 'is unlikely to satisfy climate activists' – as if the only consequence was a few disgruntled hippies rather than an ever-increasing risk of civilisational collapse. Such a presentation serves to perpetuate the suicidal myth that with just some minor tweaks, few of which will ever meaningfully impact our day-to-day lives, we can 'solve' climate change, as one frequently used and wrongheaded formulation has it.

Journalists aren't deliberately misleading their audience. Most are simply unaware that the idea of an in-system fix for climate change in 2025 – now we've broken 1.5 degrees of temperature rise, brought nearly every major ecosystem to the brink of collapse, and are still pumping geologically unparalleled quantities of carbon dioxide into the atmosphere – is so transparently absurd. For them, the technocratic consumer-capitalist system is real and unmovable and it is nature that is somehow negotiable.

Hallam was optimistic. It's not that journalists aren't emotionally connecting with the climate crisis – they aren't connecting at all. How could they? To acknowledge the true scale of the climate crisis would mean admitting that the socioeconomic system whose propaganda they have imbibed and now unthinkingly further, is the most catastrophic project humanity ever undertook. They might then also understand the paradox that the system has not failed, even as the biosphere comes crashing down around it. The purpose of a system is what it does, as the eccentric British management consultant Stafford Beer noted. And the purpose of this system is the growth of capital and accumulation of profit by capital's owners. It did those things brilliantly, on a scale and with a rapidity never seen before in human history. Stewardship of the planet's resources was never part of the plan, only ransacking them was. And, well – success!

I didn't want to disregard any sense of journalistic composure or rationality but *the scale of it is beyond the imagination, isn't it?* Of course Hallam's truth-telling and willingness to confront power could only ever meet the responses it did from a media committed to protecting the ecocidal status quo – arm's length engagement and rationalistic dismissal from the liberal media and broadsheet press, and collaboration with the state security apparatus from a well-known tabloid.

In truth, the wave of mass participation civil disobedience that Hallam spearheaded had started to break well before Scarlet Howes shopped him to the police. Some of the most committed activists were already in jail, many more were burnt out or bogged down in legal matters, and the occasional joiners were becoming increasingly occasional. By now, late 2025, the movement is all but dead. Which should make Howes, and many of her media peers, glad. In spite of myself, I dearly hope their confidence in the system to 'beat climate change' is justified. We shall see. As activists say: nature bats last.

JOURNALISM HAS FUTURES

C Scott Jordan

It is very difficult to discuss the futures of things that are dead. And few things have been heralded as often as the 'death of journalism'. Our mourning garbs never have time to collect dust in the closet they are withdrawn from on a nearly daily basis. The death of democracy – whatever that is – the death of history – whomsoever that may belong to – truth, tradition, morality, even common sense. Postmodernism, that wicked branch of philosophy that has tainted the soul of at least two generations, has not just normalised such farcical funerals, but made them routine.

It is summed up in how popular opinion tends to concentrate around films and television, occasionally leaking out into the real world. It is where a character dies, or rather is telegraphed as dead. Whether by prudence or clever writing, not all deaths need be explicit, in gory detail. Think of famous off-screen deaths. Without a corpse or some irrefutable evidence to the contrary, the public cannot help but speculate as to the fact at hand. A Schrödinger's Cat to infinity and beyond, or at least until the show runners run out of ideas, or the cascade of diminishing returns that is the contemporary notion of a cinematic universe demands the return of a beloved character that the over-paid actor has grown tired of portraying. And this is before we even get to the metaverse at the disposal of every uncreative creator. Until then conspiracy upon conspiracy. And this does not just happen on the endless streams of content. Think of the last time a world leader goes without being glimpsed on the nigh seamless surveillance cloak our devices muster. Putin, Xi, and Trump could fill scrap books with headlines asking if their deaths were being withheld from public knowledge. Imagine if Kier Starmer managed to miss a day of showing off an expression of seemingly incurable constipation to the media's all-seeing eye. Oh, the conspiracies we have for one another! And now we have no comfort or satisfaction. Because truth has eroded such that one need not dig to make a sufficient grave. And in the fog of it all, we did not even think to ask where is the corpse which we intended to lay to rest.

In the end, it is all simple fear of change. We draft eulogy after eulogy, yet the papers continue to be dropped upon door stoops, though to a lesser and lesser extent. The same old rags fill racks in corner shops, yet take up so little space, they are often hard to find at first glance. Headlines are still updated, even if people do not read beyond their spiny language. And the twenty-four-hour news cycle continues to twenty-four-hour, even when there is nothing to be said. Or nothing that is desired to be spoken of. Indeed, democracy trudges along. History has not ended. Truth, tradition, and even morality remain, even if they garner fewer champions and are increasingly hard to decipher from the rest. Concepts, we find, are hard to kill indeed. Just ask the US-led Coalition how the war on terrorism is going! This grand act of drama then is all at the service of our inability to cope with change. We simply double-down on the sum of our fears. Journalism did not die when the noble reporter sold his soul to the businessman, or media mogul. Journalism did not die at the hand of a grand conspiracy to snuff out press liberty. And technology is not the slow death of journalism. Ironically, the birth of journalism as we know it today was the result of technological innovation. Throughout its history, these moments that have been labelled apocalypse for the press were just snapshots of change in journalism. This series of change we might refer to as evolution. It has always been a give and take. Rules and regulations were needed to keep things honest, yet when the screw turned too tight, freedom and novelty was needed to remake the press in the times it found itself within. The struggle between the state and the people, the common and the special interest, have played their essential role. But when we play to the copout of the death of journalism, we numb ourselves to the real change that is taking place and abandon the agency we have over the direction that change may take. So, while the quantity and quality of what we might traditionally know as the beating heart of media, the press, or journalism appears in decline we must not give into the bias driven belief that death is upon us. Change is what is upon us. And change is something we can embrace and engage with and, in so doing, shape. But to appreciate the change on our doorstep, we need to ask ourselves what is the thing that is changing.

The answer behind what journalism is really, is not as intuitive as it may sound. Part of the reason we do not exactly know what journalism is derives from the amnesia that results in us not having much of a sense of where it came from. Often, we think it was always a part of our society. The great fourth estate! And this, in a sense, is not incorrect. Before journalism took on a form in and of itself, we simply had the conveyance of information. This took on two forms. The first was word of mouth gossip, which remains as powerful today as it has ever been, passed around fires, community centres, or up and down trade lines. The second was official ordinances or records, which we often forget were handwritten by humans and thus equally as subject to the imperfections and bias of humans – a fact often overlooked in our amazement that records from such and such an era have existed for all this time. The formalisation of this information transmittance, which would still be considered pre-journalism, was more formalised in medieval town criers or messengers, even in 'public' announcements posted throughout the Roman Empire. I think it is important to note this pre-journalism because we often lose sight of the essential nature of journalists as conveyors of information, missing out on this first principle often leaves for a weak approach to the higher defences journalists take on such as what it means to be informed or what it takes to be a good citizen.

Many like to pinpoint the birth, or perhaps baptism by fire, of journalism at the invention of the printing press around 1440 by Johannes Gutenberg. But innovations in and of themselves rarely spark revolutions. Quite often, they just maintain the status quo, but more efficiently. In such reductions we lose sight of the ecosystems, often quite complex environments, where real change comes about. Gutenberg's press produced more Bibles, but it took eighty or so odd years before Christians started really thinking about their religion. Many of the innovations in journalism place us on quantum leaps, but it is not just the ability to more rapidly get word out, but the advancements in systems of education, innovations in labour so as to produce that oh-so delightful leisurely time, and spaces for public intelligence and discourse that shape our societies. So, we can say the press, for which contemporary journalism takes its moniker, was a nice ignition spark, but it took a lot more to get the machine rolling. At the same time, we cannot leave out two important concepts that must be viewed as progenitors for journalism: democracy and capitalism. Both require the people in a given society to make informed decisions. However, as an important asterisk, both of these and early journalism were for the most privileged. Democracy, so high upon its pedestal, has been more often than not for the few and not the many. Doubly likewise for capitalism, or at least control of its levers. Through its early growing pains, what we might call journalism remains a means to inform and, thanks to its availability to the privileged class, gossip.

Journalism did not take on a new identity until the eighteenth century when it became a means to communicate directly with large masses of now, at least, somewhat educated and somewhat individually motivated public. Journalism became a tool for power. It rallied, subverted, and undermined the poles of power throughout the eighteenth and nineteenth centuries. Words can be as important as bullets in a revolution, and faster acting than innovated technologies – just wait until the two become common bedfellows! However, Newton's Third Law of Motion pertains to history as well. And just as journalism could be used by the people to take the power they were denied, the twentieth century saw to an equal and opposite reaction. States did not sit by idly and let the hysteria of the masses have all the fun. States also wielded the power of journalism to craft narratives and, in the most efficient cases, produce propaganda machines. And while states were most effective at this in the twentieth century, we must not overlook the individuals who also saw the power they could wield. And just as state-owned media grew, so too did the media controlled by press barons and media moguls. So much so that today one can hardly call themselves an elite if they have not at least dabbled in being a mogul.

It is important to also not downplay the innovation in technology running side by side with the ways in which the press were manipulated into a tool. As the press became bigger and faster, telegram cables, radio waves, television circuits, and internet networks, made the world a smaller place and brought more and more people together. In the beginning, this means that the power wielded in journalism becomes greater, but something else happens, particularly with the advent of television. With the US war in Vietnam, many could watch war for the first time from the comforts of their homes. To see and hear takes us to a strange new world. This, of course, elicits more emotions, but in television we have the first instance of the eye that can see itself. The camera's lens could see more and could see all. So, while an awareness existed of the propaganda machines all around, the camera lens allowed for a greater picture to be seen. The seems in propaganda were now noticeable. The journalism of the eighteenth and nineteenth centuries rallied the masses around the concepts of truth, justice, the privilege granted simply by being informed. These noble pursuits become mottos of major news sources. And as happens with buzzwords, the more they are used, reproduced, and pushed on without consideration or reflection, the less of their original meaning is retained copy upon copy upon copy, the resolution of that beautiful image made distorted and ugly.

Now today, we stand at the precipice for journalism. But we mustn't be so quick to lay out our black apparel or begin drafting eulogies and obituaries. In this very brief history, we have seen that journalism has taken on many identities. A stream of information, a splattering of gossip, an instrument of education, a mode of upward mobility – to be informed in an often underappreciated privilege, especially in democracies – a tool for harnessing power, both in terms of revolution and in maintaining a status quo, a machine for propaganda, and a reiterative and reflective looking glass – the eye that can see itself. While all of these identities have their own flaws, they should be equally seen as important to what potentials lie ahead in the future of journalism. So, as we return our black garbs to the closet and embrace the change that must take place, what do we have to look forward to?

When looking to futures scenarios, a logical place to begin is with the status quo. While the status quo does not readily get us to the 'future' in the sense that those in the futures studies community look to investigate, it serves as a control for the real possibilities out there. So, before we get to the future, per se, there is one impediment that trips up a lot of individuals attempting to cope with the so-called 'death of journalism'. This hurdle comes by way of Edward S. Herman and Noam Chomsky. In their work, *Manufacturing Consent*, they give fantastic analysis of a variety of case studies, critiquing the actions taken by mainstream US media. In summation, despite the high-minded rhetoric put forth by American journalists, they in fact play into the bubble prism of American exceptionalism and have done little, if anything, for the sake of truth. While the analysis is brilliant, the work overall does not offer any way forward. It does preach that greater democratisation of the media is perhaps a step in the right direction. Interestingly, my 2022 trade paperback copy from Pantheon has made a peculiar design choice. Over the title, the cover is punched through the 's' in 'Consent' with the punch shape of a 't' conveying a hidden title: Manufacturing Content. I had wondered if this might be a window into how the propaganda model put forward by Herman and Chomsky might extend to how social media has taken over as the 'mass media' and that the filter bubbles created by the algorithms of such platforms as Facebook actually manufacture their own realities through content. The problem is, this undermines the pro-democratisation thesis put forward in the original 1988 book, written long before the idea of social media, and none of the updates in this addition touch on that. So, perhaps clever by half, but not. While it is an essential read, the problem is that, thirty years on, the propaganda is not just commonly known, we are on the verge of a common appreciation for the fact that journalism cannot help but be biased at least in one way or another. Certain media sources are propaganda, so what? We cannot help but be biased when we speak, thank you, but what now? How do we progress?

Let us lean into this dethroning of the mainstream media. Stephen Cushion, professor at the Cardiff University School of Journalism, Media and Culture, takes on this thesis of the further democratisation of mainstream media, tracing the rise of alternative media. However, even in the label 'alternative' an enemy becomes apparent for the mainstream, regardless of which side or flavour of bias the major media sources prefer, they can find common enemy in these alternative means. And they use the typical ad hominem attacks of alternative media being unprofessional, unregulated, and lacking a certain sophistication – as if the mainstream media outlets have not also lost their lead in these arenas. And frankly, the public are largely exhausted with the bullshit of the mainstream. The slightest common understanding of propaganda and a pinch of awareness has generally equipped folks to not be surprised when the BBC or *The New York Times* give you exactly what they give you: the same old rubbish about the royal family, the same scripted debate on school shootings, and, even on slow news days, any old American or British whatever when catastrophic climate events, political revolutions, or transforming events take place in other parts of the world but are not given coverage or even a few words. Cushion notes how we often rely on alternative news sources, yet do not consider them 'news' in the traditional sense. However, numerous statistics show that we largely get our news from social media. Cushion argues for a more sophisticated appreciation of alternative media, but again as these alternatives pop up in new and exciting ways through social media and beyond, the pace will be too quick for these sources to gain the 'prestige and dignity' that the mainstream commands and works to keep exclusive. Cushion gives us a nice introduction, but we need a method by which to judge new forms of media and journalism so that we can transcend the problem of innovation without anything really changing. For let us not forget, that these alternatives can so easily take on the same flaws the mainstream pretends do not exist, and all the work would have been for nothing.

It might help to point out a few trends that are driving the status quo future for journalism both in mainstream and alternative forms. First, technological innovation and exponentially rising complexity have delivered the public to an endless sea of information, both authentic and manipulated. Not only are we overinformed, but we are also not sure if the information thrown at us is real, fake, or partially real. Watching the news is no longer a spectator sport. In fact, for those attempting to be good, informed citizens, it's exhausting work. Ironically the more informed we are the less we really know about what exactly is going on. Second, now that we know journalism cannot help but be biased, the apparent solution is to double down on one's bias and that awareness absolves one of any sins. What is the result of this, well you have a hyper polarising media ecosystem. The problem with this is, that generally the average person is not that radical, but their radical tendencies are easily cranked up with the right messaging, especially if likes, views, and other metrics are at stake, made bread and butter through monetisation. The media ecosystem becomes this disgusting polar binary of difference. Now, we know difference is not bad, in fact it is quite good, but this sort of difference is aggressive and, often, defensive. In the weaponisation of difference, discourse is shoot first and ask questions later, which is not really discourse and is certainly a hell of a long way from what we might call dialogues aimed at coexistence. Third, it is clear that non-western, Other voices and that news outside the US and Europe are clearly less than completely 'newsworthy'. This again is not new and those non-western and Other voices are growing louder and louder. One only wishes that they not make the same mistakes or try so hard to be accepted by western mainstream media that they in turn become the very monster they rose to surpass. Fourth, regardless the storied history of journalistic ethics and the good work being done there, no one seems to give a damn about ethics or integrity. Most journalists cannot even agree on the common right to a free press and what that entails, how can there be a common system of morality where a free press can mean everything from a protected, yet respectable voice to 'I can say whatever I want with impunity'. A toxic utilitarianism has made it so that the truth, or at least my version of the truth – because don't forget we haven't resolved postmodernism, so my truth is mine and yours is yours – regardless of how I got there, is paramount. Truth is what journalism is all about, right? So how can that end not justify any means. Well, but then there is Gaza. So, fifth, it turns out there are things we might commonly see as wrong, and maybe, just maybe, there is a pretty close thing to the universal principle of justice. It sounds utopian, but well, the genocide taking place in Palestine, seen through the eye that can look at itself and the millions of other eyes that manage to get uploaded to the cloud before being blown to oblivion, has everyone who has not wilfully plugged their ears with wax or buried their head in the sand, saying 'that ain't right'. Regardless of our differences.

It is all quite messy. But such are postnormal times. However, the same tug-of-war can be tracked, even as the participants change and the sides one pulls for makes increasingly confusing and even quite shocking bedfellows. Two status quo futures also stick out, futures which are already, to an extent, taking place in our present. The first image is that of ignorance being bliss. It's a mess right, and it's all too much and simply trying to live one's life and be informed is like having a nagging parttime job that never satisfies and is never satiated. But maybe it is not so bad. Who needs to know everything. And one is certainly a lot happier when not watching the news of child mutilation and assault or of the unravelling planetary disaster that is modernity. But we live in two systems that do not benefit the ill-informed. Democracy, which is still dependent at least on nominally fair voting, and capitalism, which is not just an economic system, but now an all pervasive political and cultural system. So, in a future where ignorance is bliss, voting empowers the minimally clever party without ethics and capitalism allows the further inequality of that society so that those minimally clever, completely unethical, powerful few can run amok. Not so nice is it, when put that way.

The second image is based on the adage if one cannot beat them, join them. The world is increasing in complexity, so too shall journalism and the media. Disregarding, if you will allow me, the first estate, clergy, if the second and third estates, the nobility and the working class, can be so complex in stratification, why not the fourth estate also. This is an image where there is not just media, but a second tier of media that holds the first-tier journalists to account. Democratic governments around the world are riddled with checks and balances, why should not the systems that inform. It seems the only reason journalists come together around the world is to defend one another against persecution. Would it not be nice if journalists came together to hold themselves to account? After all, who watches the watchmen? And who watches them? While this is happening in a highly democratised way from tit-for-tat editorial exchanges between mainstream outlets to influencers hurling '*j'accuse*' to their millions of followers, perhaps larger organisations could spring up that would be able to levy fines, if not influence over the journalistic world instead of just patting themselves on the back with extravagant and exclusive award ceremonies.

In looking at these status quo futures, which are really just the extension of the present – extended present in postnormal times theory – we should be weary of the potential for stagnation. Here we should note decreasing attention spans and the abundance of amnesia the public has demonstrated throughout history. It follows foreseeable logic that the media will continue to democratise into new fringe elements, apps, and platforms. This does not mean the big names are going anywhere, if there is any wisdom left in their editorial boards, they would do best to lie low, keep up with the technological jumps, and focus on the power their headlines command, corrupting what good writers they can get their clutches on and manage to pay. Meanwhile the democratisation could likely flow like streaming services have done, forcing several major studios to get in on making their own apps and services. However, very quickly it all becomes a bit much. And although cable television is effectively dead, these providers have stayed alive by packaging streaming apps in much the way cable networks would package certain channels. The game has completely changed and the game has stayed exactly the same, all at once. Blogs were once thought to obtain these same feats, but the difference now is that the emperor has been revealed to have no clothes. Faith and trust in the mainstream is in a pretty bad state. With such spaces as YouTube and its many lookalikes, or Substack, content creators, the new identity journalists must embody, at least for the short-term future, are at their most democratised. And all it takes is someone to package this pool of talent just right for commercial consumption. Perhaps new mainstream media outlets will rise from the ashes of Gaza, but more likely than not, new packaging methods will see the rise of the future of journalistic content. But, come what may the integrity of future journalism relies now on the writers themselves, not editorial boards in smoky boardrooms. Many of the great writers and thinkers throughout history started as journalists and throughout history had to conform to certain styles and editorial oversight. For the time being, that is almost out the window, so it is essential that young writers pave their own ethical way forward and stand strong in their convictions as the new ships in pursuit of truth and justice are being built. At the moment, the sea is full of lifeboats with writers typing at their computers or phones, and one way or another, bigger ships will come about to pick them up. But for the first time in history, writers have the means to stay in their lifeboats until something truly worthy comes along.

But there are future images a bit further out. So let us venture into what we may call the future proper. Now as we explore this new frontier, lets return to the idea of journalism as a source of, or even as a power, in its own right. Perhaps that power is too great to leave to any state, conglomerate, or rich individual. Why not give it to AI? We are already on track to let AI do most of our mundane thinking for us, why not let it keep us 'informed' on what really matters or what is important to keep 'in-mind'. Perhaps we will see the error in 'ignorance is bliss' and realise we can have both mental wellbeing and be informed on global events. Of course, AI at the moment is riddled with the bias of its creators, limited to what inputs are already out there and are being put out there, and there is the pesky issue of AI hallucinations and AI slop. But those are the issues of now, with a more mindful and sophisticated approach, AI can be set up to correct for such flaws. While it may not be perfect, it will certainly be better than any man at such a problem-laden task. And suppose that AI is also doing all the business of governance and economics, why not also journalism? At least the three will keep each other honest, even if it is all just for show. While it easily looks dystopic, the more we think and plan for dystopia, the more we can design AI to avert it. This is the hubris of certain AI thinkers. At the end of the day, AI needs to be seen as other innovations and not just leapt upon so that we may make further quantum leaps. Instead, it must be kept as a tool and constantly worked alongside the other myriad problems we need to work out in the future. After all, we like the futuristic idea of pushing a button to solve problems, but that is not science fiction, it is fantasy. We are tool users, fair enough, and let us use the tools we can create that lead us forward. But we cannot allow the tool to become the hammer that makes every problem a nail and we must not allow ourselves to become tools in the process. And let us not compromise on our most important tool, our brains. No one tool fixes all and I think we would be wise to keep a decent sized toolkit, regardless of how heavy it may become. It does not hurt to slow down and revisit old ideas.

There are many other images of futures open to us that we should look to and imagine, if we can. One idea might be as simple as an ecosystem where journalists are protected so that they may ethically do what they are asked to do and that the training and education is there so that they can see out these ends properly. Simple and doable and something that can be projected into a variety of complex arrangements in the future. But if we want to get into the unthought futures out there, we have to reconsider everything up to this point. Look at all the identities and images journalism has taken on, decouple it from what it has always been tethered to, and ask what we really want it to be. And at this moment, postnormal times grants us an agency to choose where certain concepts go. Journalism is a critical element that we need to generate a greater discourse on what its role will be in the future and how it may look. This requires us to look at journalism beyond democracy and capitalism. That means that the media industry needs to cease to be an industry. Maybe this is just what is needed to get at the truth that so many journalists have pursued and so many good journalists have failed in their devotion toward.

In this analysis, one future stands out to me. It is a future where journalism does not exist. At least not as a job in the traditional sense. Instead, it could be called a vocation, but it is so elementary and critical towards what it means to be a human that we do not spend much time thinking about it on its own. My hope is that a future will come to pass where we do not exactly know when journalism began or ended. Perhaps we call it something entirely different in this future. But a spirit endures. This spirit propels humanity to be informed as much as is humanly possible, be this through reading or through experiencing. It drives humans to engage in community and discourse to advance understanding and widen worldview. It grants the power of true communication between Others and is a tool for individual and communal empowerment and agency. This spirit is, in fact, beyond what we today call collective or individual. It appreciates perspective but knows truth lies in wait of discovery. Ethics and morality are so innate they are not discussed as such, but constantly refined as new situations arise. Many other tools and technological innovations will be discovered to help us take on this monumental task. We will be able to critically look back at past records and leave behind clear records of our own time that will keep pushing our capacities forward in a balanced and good trajectory.

I have a fascination with media mottos. Many of them were crafted over a century ago and are often riddled with an uncomfortable frankness and a level of arrogance that is usually befitting those above the law – many of them thinking they are more powerful than God. But there is one I really like. The Aspen Daily News has a circulation of about 16,500 and runs out of Colorado in the United States. Its motto is 'if you don't want it printed, don't let it happen'. It's very American, but it carries an air of parental wisdom. We will keep watching, but we have a choice over what happens. We have agency. That is at the root of futures thinking and journalism. Journalism is the eye that can see itself and there is no point hiding the flaws. We will determine what comes next, even if no one is explicitly watching. But make no mistake, all it takes is for someone to open their eyes to see what is going on. Because of this, journalism will never die, but it might just become something we cannot yet perceive in thought, right now. And at this moment we are making journalism what it will be in the future. I hope that we do take seriously ethics moving forward and set a standard fit for what is printed and broadcast in the future. We have to stop observing the give and take, tug-of-war, and participate in it if we want to ensure that democracy does not die in darkness and that facts remain sacred. Fair and balanced need not be a utopian dream. As more and more voices put out more and more words, we must make sure we craft the ecosystem around journalism to set it up as a compass through the unknown ahead.

Keep informed. Keep reading.

ARTS AND LETTERS

REDESIGNING MOSQUES *by Abdullah Geelah*

SHORT STORY: JAMEEL'S TREE *by Ibrahim N Abusharif*

SHORT STORY: 'I MARRY YOU MYSELF'
by Hamida Riahi

FOUR POEMS *by Wietske Merison*

THREE POEMS *by Saba Zahoor*

REDESIGNING MOSQUES

Abdullah Geelah

Prophet Muhammad established the first central mosque within his seat of power at the site of his residence. From then on it became a vital cornerstone of the city-state of Medina. The Prophet personally pioneered and participated in its construction. The mosque was a modest mudbrick structure: its walls crafted from beaten clay and its pillars and roof fashioned from the stumps and fronds of Medina's abundant date trees. It could not be more simple: a rectangular (53 by 56 metres) enclosure with rooms for the Prophet and his wives. Plus, a shaded area on the south side of the courtyard for prayer.

Although devoid of aesthetic ambition, the mosque was profoundly disruptive to the prevailing architectural paradigms of its time, whether Christian-Byzantine, Jewish, Sassanid-Zoroastrian, or pagan. Prophet Muhammad's Mosque was neither ornate nor derivative of existing temples; it abjured statues, instruments, objects, and imagery. Its unassuming functionality enabled remarkable versatility while avoiding distractions from its primary role as a place of worship. Absent of confession, sacraments, or song, its liturgy consisted solely of the Qur'an, recited – like the *athan* – in the simple and unadorned human voice. Here the faithful bowed and prostrated in regimented unity, barefooted, first oriented towards Jerusalem, and later to Mecca. It was symbolic of the new religion's simplicity and unique identity.

As the hub of the nascent Medinese community, Prophet Muhammad's Mosque soon became integral to the religious, social, economic, and political affairs of the city. Its multifaceted use as a building catered to the wide-ranging needs of the *ummah*. While early mosque design in newly conquered lands adhered to the Prophetic model (due to praxis rather than prescription), the subsequent conversion of non-Islamic religious structures into mosques shaped the trajectory of Islamic architectural styles. These distinctive regional approaches to mosque design – Mesopotamian, Persian, Byzantine, Visigothic, and Indian – often drew inspiration from both the external and internal stylistic elements found in temples specific to their respective geographical contexts. The sole Quranic injunction of mosque design, it seemed, concerned its purpose as a 'place of prostration'. Over the course of Islamic history, these borrowed aspects of mosque design transmuted into precepts; the minaret and dome became the norm. The mosque's functionality, beyond its central purpose as a place of worship, became lost or obsolete in the ever-changing Muslim societies.

Buildings which are associated with Islamic architecture include mosques, *madrasahs* (religious schools), palaces, and caravanserais. Among these, mosques are emblematic of Islamic architectural principles because they epitomise Muslim worship and community. Despite the existence of secular structures in regions of Europe formerly under Islamic rule, such as the Alhambra in Spain, mosques remain the most significant representations of Islamic architecture in the West.

Mosque architecture in the United Kingdom presents a complex challenge, encompassing both aesthetic and socio-cultural dimensions. Historically, many mosques have been established in repurposed residential or commercial structures, resulting in a lack of architectural coherence, design ingenuity, or optimal facilities. This issue is further compounded by the necessity of harmonising traditional Islamic architectural elements with the local British architectural vernacular. Moreover, there exists a tension between creating spaces that fulfil the religious requirements of the Muslim community and those that promote broader community engagement and integration.

Public debate and scholarship on British mosque architecture and functionality have been both intense and interesting. Young British Muslims have been active in efforts to interrogate the existing orthodoxy within the traditional mosque landscape. In my conversations with young British Muslims, I have found that they overwhelmingly consider 'mosque politics' as having led to complexity in their own construction of identity and community. Two prominent themes emerged around 'mosque politics': design and diversity. The last was particularly pertinent and timely. Plans for the opening of a women-led mosque in Bradford,

England in 2015, for example, reinforced the exclusionary nature of mainstream mosques; and underlined the argument that traditional mosque architecture in western contexts creates confused identities for Muslims. Coupled with the ethnocentricity of British mosques, this has often complicated the desire for young British Muslims to integrate their faith and national identities. The question is posed: could a cohesive British Muslim identity be formed if the mosque fulfils its original and historic role as an open communal space? To answer this, it is important to explore the socio-spatial role of mosques in shaping a cohesive British Muslim identity, with a particular focus on design and diversity.

'Socio-spatial' refers to how social relations shape and are shaped by spatial environments. In *The Production of Space* (1991), Henri Lefebvre argues that space is actively shaped by social relations rather than serving as a passive setting for human activity. From an architectural perspective, this approach underscores the role of design in influencing social interactions, fostering community cohesion and ensuring equitable accessibility. Building on Lefebvre's ideas, Akel Ismail Kahera in *Deconstructing the American Mosque: Space, Gender, and Aesthetics* (2002) examines the potential for an American Islamic architectural idiom, tailored to the complex transcultural and spatial realities of American Muslims. Drawing inspiration from Prophet Muhammad's Mosque in Medina and his *sunna*, Kahera identifies this sacred space as a foundational 'spatial paradigm' evolving over time to balance architectural convention with symbolic meaning. He introduces the term 'spatial *sunna*' to encapsulate the principles – belief, order, space, materials, and symbols – that shape mosque architecture. This term is helpful in illustrating the role of the mosque as both a religious and social space, using Prophet Muhammad's Mosque in Medina as an idiom.

The Cambridge Central Mosque, inaugurated in 2019, is the first purpose-built mosque in Cambridge, England. It was conceived to address the growing needs of the Muslim community which had outgrown the capacity of existing facilities. The project was spearheaded by the Cambridge Mosque Trust under the guidance of Tim Winter, a prominent Islamic scholar and Cambridge academic. The mosque's creation was a decade-long endeavour, marked by extensive fundraising efforts and a vision to establish a space that would serve not only as a place of worship but also as a cultural and educational hub for the wider community. Designed by Marks Barfield

Architects, the firm renowned for their work on the London Eye, the mosque is a triumph of Anglo-Islamic architecture. Visitors are welcomed by a meticulously manicured *chahar bagh* with English oak benches and crab apple trees adjoining an octagonal stone fountain. The soft murmur of flowing water provides a soundtrack of tranquillity, inviting contemplation and spiritual solace. The mosque's vaulted timber structure – an intricate lattice of interwoven wood – mimics the organic geometry of a forest canopy. The vast, light-infused prayer hall is punctuated by majestic columns that ascend skyward. Its exterior marries traditional Islamic motifs with contemporary design sensibilities. 'Say: God is One', the expression of Islamic monotheism, covers the walls of the mosque in geometric Kufic script and assembled skilfully in Cambridgeshire Gault brickwork. Most remarkable is the edifice's commitment to sustainability: its integration of solar panels, rainwater harvesting systems, and natural ventilation indicating a profound respect for creation itself, and making it Europe's first eco-friendly mosque. The use of sustainably sourced materials and the emphasis on reducing the carbon footprint reflect a deep commitment to environmental stewardship, aligning with Islamic principles of respecting and preserving the natural world. Unlike traditional mosques, the Cambridge Central Mosque embodies a modern interpretation of Islamic architecture and caters to a multi-ethnic and non-sectarian British Muslim polity. It is a pioneering model for sacred architecture in the twenty-first century and, more importantly, it is the first serious attempt to articulate an indigenous approach to mosque design in the United Kingdom.

The iconic double-minareted, onion-domed architectural forms often associated with mosques in British cities should not be misconstrued as triumphalist declarations of Islam's presence. Instead, these designs were an aesthetic homage intended to evoke a sense of familiarity and nostalgia for immigrant communities, offering a visual connection to their homelands while they adapted to life in a new, unfamiliar cultural environment. However, this architectural narrative increasingly feels discordant for younger, more diverse generations of British Muslims. These individuals, whose identities are deeply rooted in the fabric of contemporary British society, perceive such designs as less reflective of their lived experiences and their multifaceted cultural identity.

Front entrance of the Cambridge Central Mosque with the Quranic inscription: 'Verily, I am Allah: There is no god but I: So serve thou Me (only), and establish regular prayer for celebrating My praise', in Kufic script.

The Cambridge Central Mosque provides an antidote to this prevailing architectural paradigm. By seamlessly integrating English design with elements of Islamic tradition, it redefines what a mosque can and should be in the twenty-first century. Its innovative timber structure and open, inclusive ethos resonate closely with the aspirations of younger British Muslims. Rather than drawing heavily from nostalgic motifs of the past, it exemplifies an almost avant-garde vision that feels both authentic to Islamic heritage and profoundly attuned to the realities of modern British life. In doing so, it reclaims the mosque as a space where faith, culture, and contemporary identity can coalesce harmoniously.

Cambridge Central Mosque, interior, with interwoven, canopy-like colonnades.

Communities in the United Kingdom considering adaptive mosque architecture may find inspiration in the Noor Cultural Centre in Toronto, Canada — an example of innovative design that fuses tradition and modernity. Originally designed in 1963 by Raymond Moriyama as the Japanese Canadian Cultural Centre, the building was a sanctuary for a community scarred by historical injustices, blending Japanese architectural elements such as lattice windows and rain chains. In 2001, the Lakhani family acquired the building and, inspired by Quranic principles of diversity and mutual respect, envisioned it as a progressive Islamic cultural space. Renovated in 2003 under Moriyama's guidance, the transformation revolved around *noor* (light). Intricate Arabic calligraphy was added to the wooden lattice screens, seamlessly merging Islamic artistic traditions with the building's Japanese heritage. Eschewing the minaret-dome archetype, the Noor Cultural Centre embraced a timeless aesthetic that encouraged contemplation and cross-cultural harmony. Central to its mission was a commitment to gender equality, articulated by Azeezah Kanji, granddaughter of the founders, who shared that her late grandfather aspired to create 'a space where men and women have equal authority.' The lockdowns brought on by the Covid-19 pandemic tragically led to the closure of the centre's physical space. A poignant loss to its community. Nonetheless, the Noor Cultural Centre endures as a symbol of how adaptive design can harmonise cultural legacies with contemporary values, offering a model for sacred spaces that inspire both reflection and inclusivity.

Nasser Rabbat, the Aga Khan Professor of Islamic Architecture at the Massachusetts Institute of Technology, whom I interviewed, is critical of mosque design more generally. 'Mosque design is one of the least advanced areas of design in the Islamic world. Mosques are extremely traditionalist in the way they are designed. And every now and again, you'll have a revolutionary design which is shut down.' He continued, 'as an architectural historian who has looked at the history of the mosque across time, I don't think that the dome and the minaret are essential requirements of the mosque. Mosques can be built without them. Therefore, the cost [of building domes and minarets] could be diverted to something else, some other way of creating an impact in the community, for example, especially as a minority living in a larger community of non-Muslims.'

It may be contended that a puritanical fervour underpins the abstention from constructing opulent mosques—a sentiment deeply rooted in historical tradition. Prophet Muhammad himself established the first major mosque in Medina using only beaten clay and palm leaves. This austerity is echoed in the architectural ethos of revivalist Muslim movements such as the Deobandis (and to a certain degree, the Salafists) whose doctrinal rigor prioritises the mosque's spiritual function over its ornamental or aesthetic dimensions. When I presented this perspective to Rabbat, he responded with an interesting anecdote drawn from the medieval Arab geographer al-Maqdisi. In the tale, a young al-Maqdisi questions his uncle as to why the Umayyad caliph al-Walid I chose to deplete the state's treasury on the resplendent Great Mosque of Damascus rather than channelling resources into public infrastructure. His uncle rebukes him, explaining that its grandeur was conceived as a response to the opulence of Byzantine ecclesiastical architecture. It is an attitude of self-conscious superiority mingled with a formal repudiation of the very world one seeks to emulate. Indeed, the allure of revivalism in mosque architecture is ultimately misplaced. Such designs often align with revivalist movements in Islam that aspire to resurrect an abstract and idealised vision of the past.

Noor Cultural Centre, Toronto.

Practical concerns aside, the notion of erecting a 53-by-56-metre mudbrick structure in cold and overcast Britain is both impractical and incongruous. A more thoughtful approach would be to engage with the Prophetic model on a conceptual level. The spatial *sunna* shuns ideological and doctrinal preoccupations. It focuses instead on the spatial and geographical dynamics, employing Prophet Muhammad's Mosque as an analytical framework to reconceive mosques as social and spatial community hubs.

What is stopping British mosques from fulfilling this socio-spatial role? In numerous focus groups I conducted with young British Muslims, participants consistently cited a lack of diversity as a primary factor in their disengagement from traditional mosques. The gendered segregation in British mosques, as elsewhere globally, diverges significantly from the spatial *sunna*. Kahera explains that, while Prophet Muhammad's Mosque upheld gender segregation in the ritual space – with women praying behind men and the imam facing the *qibla* – the physical space itself remained integrated. This deviation from the *sunna*, Kahera suggests, stems from the influence of entrenched customs prioritising women's segregation. In the rare mosques across the United Kingdom that deign to offer female spaces, the facilities are often nothing short of woeful. Women are relegated to obscure back entrances, slipping in with the discretion of conspirators, perhaps clutching the faint hope that this indignity will at least grant them access to a transcendent Tardis-like haven. Alas, they find themselves unceremoniously deposited in some dreary alcove of the sacred establishment – a curtained-off recess in a forgotten backroom, a clammy basement that smells of mildew, or within uncomfortably close proximity to the kitchens and restrooms. There, as the scent of disinfectant mingles with the tang of leftover *dhal*, the atmosphere seems to whisper, and some men might muse, this is where they belong.

Such exclusionary dynamics have become intolerable for many young people. In recent years, the emergence of 'third spaces' has introduced a compelling socio-spiritual phenomenon, providing alternative environments that blend spiritual and social activities. These spaces are uniquely designed to address the needs of Muslims, particularly younger generations, who often feel alienated from traditional mosques.

Functioning as inclusive and culturally relevant platforms, they offer both spiritual engagement and communal interaction, acting as 'enabling environmental infrastructure' that bolsters the spiritual wellbeing and identity of their members. Unlike conventional mosques, these third spaces are not necessarily intended to replace existing religious institutions, except in cases where traditional mosques fail to meet the needs of specific Muslim communities. Instead, they often operate as complementary spaces, focusing primarily on socio-cultural enrichment rather than formal religious practices like regular congregational prayers. Their informal, welcoming atmosphere appeals especially to younger Muslims in western contexts, providing avenues for spiritual development and meaningful social connections.

A notable example of such a space is the Inclusive Mosque Initiative, established in London in 2012. Rooted in the principles of 'intersectional feminist Islam', the organisation creates inclusive, accessible spaces for worship and engagement. It adopts a broad definition of a mosque, maintaining that 'a mosque is made up of a community, not bound by a building'. Although the initiative aspires to construct permanent, inclusive, carbon-neutral mosques, it currently operates nomadically, hosting activities in rented venues. By rejecting the linguistic, ethnic, political, doctrinal, and sectarian divisions that often characterise traditional mosques, the initiative boldly advocates for marginalised communities through alternative religious practices. However, its unconventional approach has elicited mixed reactions. Some, like a female participant in my focus groups, found practices such as mixed-gender congregational prayers led by female imams unfamiliar and disconcerting. 'It felt weird and quite uncomfortable.' Others questioned the compromise of fundamental Islamic principles, highlighting instances where participants prayed without performing *wudu*. 'I respect the group's inclusive aims but not at the expense of basic religious principles.'

Interestingly, the emergence of third spaces like the Inclusive Mosque Initiative is not confined to progressive movements. Examples such as Rumi's Cave in Kilburn, London, demonstrate how third spaces can operate within the bounds of theological orthodoxy while addressing the diverse spiritual, social, and cultural needs of local Muslim communities. Functioning as an arts and community hub rather than a traditional mosque, Rumi's Cave fosters an informal and dynamic environment. During my visit in 2018, the community was embroiled in a campaign against local council plans to demolish the centre and nearby buildings to make way for luxury flats. The centrality of this space to its community was underscored by a focus group participant's fervent declaration: 'I would rather see all the mosques closed down than to see Rumi's Cave demolished'.

Roots Community Space, located in Irving, Texas, is another example of a popular and successful 'third space'. Housed in a modest former office building, the space exudes a welcoming yet simple atmosphere, its exposed brickwork and *Suhbah* ('companionship') coffee shop forming its key features. On my Monday evening visit, I found a lively mix of attendees (Muslim-born and converts, men and women, black and white) seated on the floor in true Prophetic tradition, their discussions enhanced by the aroma of freshly brewed coffee. At the helm was Imam Abdul Rahman Murphy, an Islamic scholar of Egyptian and Irish-American heritage, whose sessions span *tafsir* (Quranic exegesis) to modern societal challenges. His vision for Roots is clear: 'a community space… collaborative and supplementary to the already existing community initiatives'. Free from rigid rules, Roots fosters authentic connections with faith, rooted in Prophetic custom. 'What you find [with traditional mosques],' Imam Murphy notes, 'is everything is heavily focused on the educational experience and not at all focused on the social experience… We believe that the Prophet Muhammad socialised in a way that benefited people… People were learning from him by eating with him, standing with him, talking with him.' Imam Murphy, aware of the faith's growing disconnect with the youth in the West, highlighted Roots's unique response: 'In the US and Britain, we have seen people leaving the religion at an incredible rate…It's not the faith which is irrelevant but the way it's articulated.' Hence, Roots combines spiritual and social elements in its programmes, facilitated by its coffee shop, creating a sacred yet conversational atmosphere. Despite his reverence for the early mosque founders in the United States, Imam Murphy laments their slow adaptation to contemporary needs. 'The greatest adaptation which they have made [to these mosques] is building a multipurpose hall that could include some iteration of a basketball court. And this was not authentic enough to compete with established community centres that people go to and they would rather play at the gym. So, it was not fully bought in to the needs of the young people.' His attempts to reform mosque governance during his seven years as an imam proved unfruitful, leading to the establishment of Roots as an independent third space. Imam Murphy has maintained Roots's unique identity as a supplementary Islamic space despite interest from certain benefactors to turn it into a *musala*. 'We do not provide *Jumu'ah* here; we only pray *salah* if we are here. We do not want this place to be "*masjid*-centric". That is not our purpose. There is no need to have another *masjid* here when there are others nearby. It is inauthentic to what we are, we are not here to compete with anybody. That is where Roots came from: it is providing a solution to an age-old problem. Everyone knows the answer but no one knows how to get there. So, we thought of a social spiritual space.' While practical, cultural and institutional barriers hinder the incorporation of such 'third spaces' into traditional mosques, Imam Murphy remains optimistic yet cautious. 'At Roots, we have non-Muslims and unveiled Muslim women, would they feel comfortable entering a masjid? The masjid needs to be a neutral space; it cannot exclude people. It needs to be a culturally relevant experience for people but authentic to the Prophetic tradition.'

These 'third spaces', though not architecturally distinctive or conventionally defined as mosques, represent a fascinating evolution of the mosque's role adapted to fit the complex identities of new generations. Their focus on socio-cultural enrichment contrasts with the rigid, segregated dynamics of many traditional mosques. This divergence reflects broader tensions within the Muslim community between progressive and orthodox practices, as well as between the spatial *sunna* and cultural praxis. The potential of third spaces to influence future mosque design cannot be overlooked. Rabbat emphasised the importance of integrating cultural dimensions into mosque architecture: 'It would become absolutely crucial that British mosques should double as cultural centres. This has to be repeated for the benefit of the British Muslim community. I know that the clerics are probably resisting [the idea of mosques as cultural centres] based on the accusation that art is not Islamic. This is beyond short-sighted, in my opinion. It is a big, missed chance for them to integrate, to improve their image and to weed out some of the activities that are taking place in mosques.'

Care must be taken to avoid recommendations that may appear overly prescriptive, and this caution stems from three principal considerations. First, the absence of rigid religious directives in mosque architecture affords Muslim communities the flexibility to shape their places of worship in ways that align with their unique needs and aspirations. It would be unwise to impose rigid definitions of acceptability, as these are ultimately informed by subjective preferences and the specific requirements of local contexts. Indeed, this flexibility is a valuable asset that should be championed more assertively, fostering creative reimaginations of inclusive, harmonious worship spaces tailored to the British cultural landscape, thus overcoming entrenched stagnation in mosque design. Second, grassroots initiatives within the United Kingdom, led by Muslim organisations, are actively reshaping the paradigms of mosque architecture and governance. For example, the Muslim Council of Britain (MCB), the most diverse representative body of British Muslims, provides training on good governance in this field. Other local organisations, unaffiliated with the MCB, are undoubtedly also advancing similar efforts. Allowing these initiatives to take their course is prudent. Third, it is impractical to reconstruct the existing mosque landscape to align with a more culturally relevant architectural style. Despite their limitations, the mosques across the United Kingdom reflect a distinct historical context, bearing witness to a bygone era and motivating future architectural evolution. The Cambridge Central Mosque exemplifies such progress, with its innovative design serving as a compelling model.

The mosque embodies a remarkable polyvalence, extending far beyond its primary function as a place of worship. Historically rooted in Islamic societies, mosques have served as sanctuaries for prayer while simultaneously acting as vital social institutions – centres for interaction, events, discussions, and communal support. Prophet Muhammad's Mosque in Medina exemplifies this multifunctional role, acting as the nucleus of the early Muslim community and establishing the spatial *sunna* that informs mosque design. This legacy underscores the necessity for contemporary mosques to address the spiritual, cultural and social needs of their communities, particularly in the West. Efforts should focus on restoring and adapting existing British mosques to meet the evolving requirements of local Muslim communities, with emphasis on better accommodation for women and the inclusion of social and cultural activities. Where such adaptations are impractical or cost-prohibitive, supplementary 'third spaces' must be encouraged. These spaces are crucial for fostering community cohesion, particularly in diasporic contexts, by offering inclusive environments for young and marginalised groups to negotiate cultural and religious identities. By mitigating social isolation and serving as informal networks of support, third spaces play an instrumental role in promoting resilience and strengthening social cohesion within Muslim communities.

The future of Anglo-Islamic architecture therefore stands at the intersection of tradition and modernity, poised to craft spaces that reflect the evolving British Muslim experience. Achieving this vision requires a delicate balance – a fusion of Islamic design motifs with contemporary British aesthetics. Innovations such as sustainable practices, exemplified by the Cambridge Central Mosque, present opportunities to create environmentally friendly, functional, and spiritually resonant spaces. As seen with the Noor Cultural Centre in Toronto, adapting existing buildings demands creativity, drawing on the spatial *sunna* for inspiration while embracing new forms and materials. The adaptability and fresh perspectives of young British Muslims will be pivotal in driving this evolution. This architectural renaissance necessitates a parallel revival in thought, where creativity becomes the bedrock of mosque design. The social mobility and cosmopolitanism of young British Muslims will inspire the creation of inclusive, utilitarian, and vibrant spaces that embody the shared ethos of Islam and Britain. Anglo-Islamic architecture, as a result, can emerge as a celebrated symbol of cultural synthesis – an enduring reflection of British Muslims' distinctiveness and the society's progressive transformation, resonating with all Britons as part of the nation's evolving narrative.

SHORT STORY

JAMEEL'S TREE

Ibrahim N Abusharif

I was eleven years old when I first touched a dead person. I combed my fingers through his thick white hair minutes after the old man's chest stopped moving and the colour in his face had started to change. Quiet sobs moved around his small room in a Chicago hospital, but when the sobbers noticed sweat bead up on the man's forehead, they whispered that sweat on a newly deceased person means he has received mercy on the other side of *barzakh*, an Arabic word for a barrier that separates the living from the dead and the dead from the living.

The information felt more than new. It was a dart, a sacred puncture breaching an otherworldly barrier to let me know that a gracious escort received a man who planted a cherry sapling on the day I was born and named the thing after me. As long as I can remember, it was known as 'Jameel's Tree' and nothing else.

After my grandfather's funeral, guests came to our house to condole more. It went on late into the night, and they had similar religious things to say. My parents demanded that we kids shake hands, serve Arabic coffee, and absorb the dignified custom so that we may never become severed from Arab tradition. I had no problem with the custom but had to run out to the backyard because I needed to know if a tree could survive the loss of thick hands that kept it pruned and straight its whole life. I didn't really think the tree would die but had a storybook hope for something extraordinary, like the tree moaning or weeping, another missive from beyond *barzakh*.

I pressed my palm against the bark and closed my eyes, waiting for something to happen or howl. It meant very little, as it turned out, a frustrating blank contact, which repeated itself when I pressed harder. My palm and feelings hurt, I fell to the earth. When I was done bawling, I looked at our moonlit yard that was as empty as ever, though this time it made less sense. Something was taken from the yard, like a verb. Was that the howl?

We never had any suburban furnishings in our yard, not a blade of grass. Other than a small concrete patio and a couple of wooden benches, it was fence-to-fence garden – one large sown field and a fruit tree in the right-hand corner. Neighbours noticed that the yard was unusual. My friends too thought it was strange, using words they must have borrowed from their parents. But the friends got over it, especially in the winter when we'd play tackle football or with toy plastic army men on the great battlefield.

In the summers, rows of vegetables and spices were everywhere, plus lush grapevines along the red wooden fence that, on windy days, looked like the outfield walls of Wrigley Field. Before he got a motor tiller, my father used a pick and shovel to move the ground hardened by winter. With the soil picked to submission, my mother brought trays of sprouts and moistened seeds. My grandfather managed the work, in a general way, pointing and offering land stories and advice, a Palestinian thing. Every morning, they sipped sweetened tea looking over the crops. They said it was important to look because land can survive drought but never apathy.

But things change. It's terrible to report, but it began when my parents sodded half the farm. About the same time, there was a rise in vitriol. At a large square white table on the patio and cheap lawn chairs, relatives gathered on weekends to sip, eat, chain smoke, and gravitate like addicts toward debilitating arguments about Palestine and Arab ineptitude. The events that lit the fire of quarrel never did bode well for Palestine. There was always bad news, some kind of loss – noxious gas of analysis and paranoia that went uncontested on the table. Forced to be there – the same tradition pretext – I heard the political scientists of my family, spill their raw anger and psychological diasporas.

To be fair, they were good at some things, like mocking. They were great mockers, in fact. I fell victim to the mocking culture because I sounded like a foreigner when I spoke Arabic and fell down a lot. To recap: Arab adults finding nothing better to do during the intermission of their fracas than mocking kids for not knowing what their parents never taught them.

It all produced a great strain on young minds. The deliberations frightened me at a private level, made me think that the world was bad and the great life I knew with my neighbourhood friends was a fraud ready to show itself because my friends were 'Americans' whose parents and priests kept the wrongdoing in the Near East well funded and well prophesied. It had been difficult to pull off these kinds of discussions during my grandfather's reign. He was a prophetic-looking figure with a dense auric field: wide bright forehead, a scalp full of thick white hair, large eyes, full Arab lips, and crescent shaped eyebrows. All he needed was a staff and a faintly glowing toroidal halo.

He disliked fake experts and gassy people who thought that intelligence was best demonstrated when finding the ugly of life; they were folks suspicious of happiness, which apparently sedates people in preparation for the final take over.

Despite his death, the tree lived on and produced fruit with indifference to the kind of talk that you'd think would have killed everything moist within listening distance. Each year, late July, the earth around it turned deep red, coloured by fallen cherries that attracted bees and wasps, which we kids turned into fantastic games of dare.

I realise how widespread tree culture and human memories are intertwined; still I feel privileged that a player of a homemade flute thought to plant a metaphor the day I cried for the first time.

The vulgar pressures of adulthood press hard. We were struggling with jumpstarting careers and with bank stresses, including sisters divorced from unfavourably complex men who invested their measure of self-worth in the events of the east and who saw in their wives a solution for their sense of violence and in other women a solution for their wounded manhood.

The Mensons now lived in our house. A friendship of convenience developed between us shortly after my siblings and I closed the sale and divvied up the proceeds, months after our mother passed on, years from my father's passing. A few days after we closed, I visited the Mensons on good impulse. I did feel some duty for their smooth transition, but there was something else. The Mensons seemed happy with my visit and said it was thoughtful. I helped them move a table and showed them which living room outlet was controlled by a light switch near the front door that had mystified them since nothing happened when they clicked on and off. They were too cheerful about the disclosure, an exaggeration that irritated me. Right before sunset, as I was about to head back home, a two-bedroom apartment forty-five minutes southwest, near a Catholic university where I teach English, I walked the couple out to the yard and narrated the short history of the tree and its name.

'That's interesting,' Mrs Menson said nodding her head slowly. 'Ever get confused when your family talked about the tree? You know, thinking you were being called or something?' That's what the woman wanted to know, something about my fucking confusion.

'Actually, no,' I obliged, wondering why a light switch would evoke a more robust reaction than a resplendently gracious deed of a grandfather bred in sacred land. Revealing one of my superpowers, I told them, 'Whenever I heard 'Jameel' I just knew right away who they were talking about.' I tightened my lips and looked down to let them know I wouldn't add more to the suburban chatter.

The Mensons showed me that they were impressed with my genius and looked toward me with raised eyebrows, both Vivian and James, the postmodern bastards who now had control over the tree. They then traded glances and offered me what I think I had hoped for: they had no problem, they said, if I wanted to come once in a while to sit in the yard. James started the sentence slowly, looked toward Vivian, who completed the proposal at normal pace.

'You sure?' I spoke. They insisted that it would be nice if I dropped by, just in case they needed to learn more about the house, a standard suburban issue, a three-bedroom split level, one of a dozen on the quiet block, none with mysterious doors or cellars guarded by metal-armoured guards or sprites. I thanked them, almost drifting, as I looked toward the tree and felt that frustrating blankness again emanating from the thing. Nostalgia never gives what you think you want. Certain kinds of people, paralysed by early associations forced upon them, have the strongest attachment to nostalgia. There was more here. The Mensons said other things, but my mind was not with them. They saw the passport on my sad face, a look of powerlessness, and they stopped talking.

'I'm sorry,' I said uncomfortably. They gave sympathetic smiles. We walked leisurely back through the garage. I saw a shiny new shovel hanging on the pegboard. Mr Menson looked toward it, and I was sure he was thinking of using it as a weapon, and it's possible I was thinking the same thing.

The following spring and summer, I made regular trespasses unmolested. I checked in on the tree and the Mensons, who had their own idea about what my visits meant. I noticed that they enjoyed talking about it with neighbours, a splendidly peculiar thing to indirectly boast about: my relationship with them, the tree, the informality with a former owner, an Arab Muslim ethnic to boot who had 'fascinating' or 'very interesting' religious narratives. I'd never come without asking if they needed help with something, and they often did, like drilling a metal spice rack into the wall beneath the microwave.

Like legions of other Americans, my wife and I had convinced ourselves of our dissatisfaction with life which has only one cure: buy something as big as a house and as oppressive as a bank debt. Cured, I made a case to buy something near my old neighbourhood, an affordable seventy-five-year-old bungalow on Lavergne Avenue, not far my high school, the railroad tracks, and Stoney Creek. My wife surprised me and liked it. When we moved in this past winter, I drove to the Mensons and told them about our move, and they seemed content, but not more than that. Mrs Menson right away asked me if I could do something about a large hole in the drywall of the garage ceiling that their 'insane' grandnephew had pounded in with a hockey stick. 'You can tell who's going to grow up a criminal!' she complained bitterly. She put on a face I had never seen before.

'I'll fix it, but not until spring,' I said. The cold will keep the plaster from setting right, and it's better to paint when the temperature is above fifty. I didn't know if that was true.

'It won't get worse?' she asked with disappointment. I assured her of my performance. She acquiesced but did not comment on my new dwelling. She seemed different. Not sure why.

My penultimate backyard visit formally began on a beautiful May day, the first Saturday after I had submitted my final grades of the spring semester. In an act of heresy, I had no choice but to fail four students, something I had never done before. I did not enjoy it at all. They were not stupid. They simply did not care. Apathy is not easy to confront.

To take a leisurely walk for about fifteen minutes to my former home felt pleasant. I looked around, up, and down, ready to say 'hello' or 'good morning' to any soul that got near. No one did. These were the same sidewalks I once took to Roy Clark Elementary School, the same cracks we kids avoided to spare our mothers' backs. I walked down Lamon Street and ambled past the Mensons' large front bay window. I saw Mrs Menson pacing in the living room while talking on the phone. She saw me and waved me by, granting me permission with an animated face. Frustration or excitement? I walked to the far side of the garage and unlocked the chain-link gate, wondering if the new arrangement would change how I felt about my visitations. I had made an important adjustment in my living system and had some expectation that it would alter other things, pulling connected cords. I closed the gate behind me and walked past the side of the garage and looked toward the corner. It did feel different in a way. A few things came to mind, some of them weird, like how dropping something when confronted with strong feelings is not caused by a temporary loss of motor function, but an intellectual shifting of priority and ownership. The coffee in my hand did not fall and splash against the concrete and my shoes; I dropped it because I decided that coffee meant nothing to me, nor did the newspaper. For understandable reasons nonsupernal, I felt no blankness at all. I felt befuddled and, I think, damaged as I looked toward the stump.

I sensed colour changes in my cheeks. I felt blood move through my flesh. My eyebrows and forehead were also doing something. I had never felt so aware of myself; and for a very brief moment, I became intensely curious about how my face looked. 'I don't get it,' I whispered. 'My God, where is it?' With no suburban pace in my legs, I walked to a six-inch peg. I stared at it. Then I marched back and aggressively opened the gate and heard it smash against the brick wall of the garage. I knocked hard and fast on the side door of the house. I heard someone walking quickly. She opened it.

'Oh, Jameel, it's you. I don't remember you coming to this door before.'

'Mrs Menson, what happened?' I asked her hurriedly.

'Sure. But ... ah ... what do you mean?' she said investigating my meaning.

'The tree. What happened?'

'O that old tree,' she said, fanning down her right hand. She then looked nonchalantly away, waiting for my turn in light-hearted bantering.

'Why did you cut it down?'

She tapped her cheek and looked past my head. I watched her aging eyes scan May clouds. She pursed her lips and chuckled: 'It just had to go.' She then sped up: 'And guess what? Mr Menson and I are going on a vacation. A group of us from St. Linus are going to the Bahamas this time. We're leaving in a couple of hours. A limo to O'Hare. Can you believe that? A limo!'

'I loved that tree, Mrs Menson. You knew that.' I was now more visibly irritated, a slower pace of words, a sign of difficult self-control. 'You know its history. I sat in your yard reading my paper and looking out at the tree.'

'Yes, you certainly loved that tree. I remember,' she said with a casual smile, slowly nodding her head. She gazed again at the horizon then back toward my face. She understood my indignation. Finally. 'Well, you can still sit in the yard, Jameel. We won't mind.' She raised her eyebrows as if tempting a child with ice cream. 'In fact, when we go to the Bahamas, you can come every day. O Lord, I hope we don't get lost in that Bahama Triangle, you know.'

'Mrs Menson.' My eyes fixed. 'It was my tree.'

James joined Vivian and asked what was going on. He looked toward the garage from the kitchen window. He probably wanted to see if I had taken the shovel and hid it behind my back. She casually told him about my concern, and then Vivian turned toward James and asked about packing for the trip. I didn't hear what he said. She then looked at me and quickly toward the pegboard: 'It was *not* your tree, Jameel.' She let loose a wintry callousness disconnected from the warmth she had shown before, when I moved heavy things, right? Or when I helped an insane relative with a school essay? Well, the old lady, with a yard covered completely with fresh sod kept green with bags of poison, pissed some words to claim her turf. She pursed her lips again and was about to say something.

I backed away and turned to walk down the driveway. I heard her say, her voice raised and rushed: 'The hole in the garage, Jameel. Wait! When do you think we can fix it? It's above fifty!'

I kept walking.

'What did you say?' her words trailed. 'When we come back? OK?' My mind was violent with words. Was it because I had come too close, no longer the 'friend' at a satisfactory distance? My bearing was altered. Maybe the political scientists, the ugly-miners of my family, had the acumen they were denied of. This was not some random suburban pointlessness. It was about civilization. Vivian and James had no choice, you see. Imbibed by a severed, traditionless ethos that power was truth, they chopped for no reason other than sheer capacity, provoked by something as ordinary as my new proximity. It's about rootless living, in which riding a limo makes a person as animated as a Disney character. What's the use of power when you can't destroy something beautiful, like a tree or Jerusalem, Gaza, Beirut, or Baghdad?

I had never felt so angry and mentally exhausted at the same time. Beneath the thoughts about Vivian's civilisation and her 'Bahama' triangle, there was more streaming through my mind. It was complex. It wasn't merely the tree but everything. It was the backyard discussions, the metaphors, touching dead people you loved like crazy, and most of all sadness, not merely for their deaths but for their heirs made indifferent to transcendence, now partners in a grid of the profane, assuaged by property and wealth. Their parents left ancestral grounds for no promise higher than economics; pulled away by the lure of material success severed from any sacred narrative. The stranglehold of remote hegemony is tenacious, colonising a people by infusing your colonised desires with theirs; populations imbued with an alien sense of progress that requires some to migrate or that seduces a populace into deadlock purchasing agreements that fill their skies with diesel and with ugly scrapers and their ancient soil with toxins. But strangely, very odd, back home, as I reclined for rest, I felt what can only be described as relief. It was stimulating, almost fragrant, like musk; finally unhinged from scheming emotions. I took a death-level nap for about three hours. Awake again, I looked up toward the ceiling and waited. I read two pieces in an anthology of best essays, each piece on the loss of a pet; one a dog and the other a fish, with the authors thinking that they're grappling with the meaning of life and conscience, each of them gallantly trying to figure 'it' out, quoting European philosophers articulating well-phrased answers that ultimately peddled hopelessness, a horizontal existence that genuflects before the loins of agnostic science. I slept more. When it was dark, I headed back to the Mensons. I carefully opened the garage door. I took the weapon and held it in my hand. It felt right. I looked at the spade and knew it would do the work I now obliged it. I walked toward the stump. I bent over and started to pull clumps of new sod. It gave up easily. I dug in the soil, here and there, with the spade and then with my hands. The smell and the feel drew me back to my childhood, but I fought it off. I really didn't want to go anywhere. Every clump of soil I scooped I felt thoroughly, searching with my fingertips for any shape of a cherry seed, any sign of mercy. My back ached, but I remained stooped, not wanting to hit the thick bottom branch that does not exist: perhaps the blankness I first felt when I was eleven years old, that now made me smile. The heavy flesh of my thirty-five-year-old face pulled toward the earth. I sat down hard. A grown man in someone's yard in the middle of the night fighting tears: this wasn't the way I imagined my adulthood. A few deep and long breaths later, I got on my knees and pressed back in place the patch of sod.

Shovel hung back in place, I walked home, pockets lined with soil and, with luck, good seed. Determined to kill the meme, I thought about the men who spoke on our patio back then and their dented children with inherited damage. I walked in my house; my wife began to yawn but stopped halfway when she looked at me and wondered with her Brazilian eyebrows: What happened to you? With one finger and an edgy smile, I asked her to hold on. I moved swiftly to the bathroom as if I needed it really bad. There I emptied my pockets and separated cherry seeds from pebbles, mud, insect parts, and, oddly, an old infantryman. I wrapped the seeds in a moist paper towel so that the next day I could plant them in a small pot for future transfer to a land that surely will come back to me.

So, I leaned against the vanity top then looked up with eyes of a frescoed saint, gazing for help in some place unpainted and unseen, and begged as a beggar had never done before me: please don't let it be too late. My lips moved. I asked for everything, going through some accumulated list until finally I got to where I wanted to go from the beginning. I wanted to be unoccupied, released. And one more thing: Please, if ever I'm given issue, I'll help them with their minds and never make them feel split or foolish. Please, more than sweat on my forehead. Let them love life, empower them, no separated personas; that's right, make them powerful, really dangerous.

SHORT STORY

'I MARRY YOU MYSELF'

Hamida Riahi

He came quietly. Told the matchmaker he liked her profile. Took her number. Called. Introduced himself. Sent a photo – a bearded Arab Muslim man. The picture said it all. No flirtation like the others. She thought: this time, it's right. A religious man. A Muslim man.

She introduced herself. They agreed to meet for a sharia-compliant first look. It was Ramadan. Two days later, he sent his plane ticket. He was coming. He said he wanted to eat her food. From her hands. Taste Tunisian cooking.

She didn't know how to explain that a religious man shouldn't say such things. But being the generous soul she was – and not wanting to sound rude – she came up with a diplomatic solution: she'd cook the food at home, pack it up, and they'd eat it together in a restaurant, pretending it was freshly served. To keep things modest, she even floated the idea of a simple café meet-up after they each had Iftar separately – he at the hotel, she at her flat. And later, once they were properly married, she promised, he'd get the full home-cooked experience.

He insisted. He wanted to taste her food to make sure she was a good cook.

She thought: Why not have him over for Iftar? It was Ramadan. Nothing would happen. He was religious. She called him. Told him to come to her flat directly.

He came. Had Iftar. Was impressed – by her personality, neatness, beauty. She wore black trousers and a beige T-shirt, slightly form-fitting. She had makeup on. Hair done. She looked good. She liked him too – tall, dark-skinned, Arab. Her type.

They laughed. He prayed in her house. They talked. She explained she wanted marriage. A good Muslim man.

Then, suddenly, he said he was tired, and if she said 'I marry you myself,' they'd be married. Just like that.

She was shocked. Hurt. She asked: How? No contract? No family? No paperwork?

He said it was halal. A valid Islamic way. She said she didn't believe in that. She wanted a contract. Official. Legal.

Suddenly, she burst out, 'If you think I'm the kind of woman who says yes to anything just because I live alone – you're wrong.' Tears slipped down. 'I want a husband because I've been alone in this country for ten years. If I die, no one would know. Sometimes I leave the door unlocked – just so my body won't rot before someone finds me.'

He stood, walked over, and kissed her gently on the brow. 'I'm sorry,' he whispered.

Then she nearly asked him the burning question: What exactly is the difference between 'I marry you' and 'I marry you myself'? As if the 'I' and the 'self' were two separate entities – one making the proposal and the other officiating it. But she bit her tongue. He didn't seem like the type who'd appreciate grammatical nitpicking over sacred phrases, or her mild suspicion that he was improvising sharia on the fly. She figured if she started unpacking his syntax, he might accuse her of apostasy – or worse, of being a feminist with a sarcastic streak.

He promised to prepare documents. Said marriage would come.

She felt uneasy. But her face kept smiling. Joking. Hospitality, she thought. A culture of saying yes when she should say no. And these yeses – often led her into trouble. Financial. Emotional. Even danger. But this time, she said no. Still, she joked about it. This 'I-marry-you-myself' moment. She almost asked him: How many times had he pulled that trick? Lost count?

They went to a café. Talked more. Her field was English literature. He told her he was once married to a Moroccan woman – she had passed away. He wanted to read her a story – written with ChatGPT – about that Moroccan woman.

Then he said when they marry, he wanted to be spoiled. Skin care. Massages. Good sex.

She was shocked again by his bluntness. But she told herself: It's normal. That's marriage. That's life.

She kept silent. Didn't want to mock him. Didn't want him to flee. She knew she was critical by nature. Feminist. And she wondered: why was she here, vulnerable again? Why did she tolerate a man asking for sex in exchange for 'I marry you myself'? Why was she overlooking this behaviour? Wasn't he a religious man? A women-friendly one?

He left to pray *qiyam al-layl* at the mosque. She was amused. And confused. So devout. So direct. So contradictory.

He returned. They had suhoor together. Then he left to sleep at a hotel.

She was happy. Almost in love. This religious, devout, Muslim man. Without thinking, she texted, invited him again for Iftar the next day. Told him he was a good man. Let's meet again.

He came. The food was delicious. Then he said he had to catch his plane. Time to say goodbye.

He asked to hug her. Like earlier in the car, when he'd tried to hold her hand. She pulled away.

It was Ramadan. He was religious. Bearded. She didn't want him to think badly of her.

She refused to kiss him, despite his efforts.

He said he'd come back. Support her. Be there for her.

She keeps texting him, asking about the papers, waiting for something concrete – dates, signatures, proof of a path forward. Still, the contradictions circle in her mind. 'I marry you myself'. The words still echo. She laughs – half shock, half disgust. She doesn't know why the feelings stay, buried in her blood. She can feel them even now: shock, confusion, misunderstanding – laced with something else. A kind of humour she can't shake. His words confuse her. Shame her. Hurt. And still, she laughs.

FOUR POEMS

Wietske Merison

The stranger

We are taught to love the stranger
The needy and the poor
And O, that love is easy
Till they're knocking on our door

When they enter in our lives
Seeking shelter from the rain
We don't want our carpets tainted
By their muddy stains

We hide our diamonds in the safe
Carefully lock our hearts away
Reminding our guests
It's just a temporary stay

We keep the stranger at a distance
Behind a barrier of words
Between us and them a moat is formed
Only overcome by birds

For the hardest love of all
Is for the one that comes so close
That we ourselves become estranged
It's them we fear the most

For isn't it 'the other'
That allows for 'us' to be?
Isn't it their captivity
That allows us to be free?

Well yes, well no
Oh well, you see
In your language that's true
But not so for me

In my language 'us' is only 'us'
When it includes us all
Thus, we can only be free
When we tear down all the walls

To love the stranger as the other
Isn't written down as love
To love the stranger as yourself
Is what is spoken of

So find the stranger in yourself
Make his bed and pour her tea
For when you locked your heart away
You gave to them the key

And find yourself in the stranger
So you may truly get to know
That water is still water
Be it vapor, ice, or snow

Open your door
So you can enter in
So you can come home
In the arms of your kin

Embodied

Make my body like the *mushaf*
Embodying Your Word
Let upon my every breath
The *basmala* be heard

My eyes opening up
To receive the light
Like *Surah al-Fatiha*
Granting me sight

The seven layers of my skin
Like the *Al Ha-Mim*
My heart beating steadily
Like *Surah Ya-Sin*

Make of *al-Falaq* my left fist
And of *an-Nas* my right
Protecting me from harm
Even when it's out of sight

Let me smile with the grace
Of *Surah ar-Rahman*
Let me cry like the sky
And the earth in *ad-Dukhan*

Make my chest hold
The treasure of *Al Imran*
Make my scent
The fragrance of the *Zahrawan*

Let *Surah Qaf*
Be my jugular vein
Let *surah ash-Sharh*
Be my comfort in pain

Let *Surah Mariam*
Be my womb
So out of my suffering
New life may bloom

Let *ayah al-Kursi*
Be my crown
To keep my head up
When life pulls me down

Al-Balad my lips
My eyes, my tongue
Al-Furqan my conscience
To tell right from wrong

My body is the *mushaf*
My body is Your Word
Help me hold it with honor
So Truth may be heard

The poet's tree

Tonight I will not write another piece of poetry
Much rather I would sit in peace under the poet's tree

Much rather I would read the lines my loved one wrote for me
Much rather I would hear the lines the birds give out for free

The ballad of the rainfall or the sun's soliloquy
The meter of my heartbeat or the sonnet of a bee

The epic tale of love reaching beyond what eyes can see
All rooted in that single verse of be and it will be

Tonight I will not write another piece of poetry
Oh God forbid I ever dare to claim the poet's me

Tell me who I am

Can someone tell me who I am
I seem to have forgotten
I know the name you call me by
And the body I am caught in

Its sensations and its cravings
I know them all by heart
Its anger and its sadness
The way it has been scarred

Its joy and its pleasures
Are no strangers to me too
Its heartbreak and its longing
For something that is true

I know the colour of my skin
And the place from which I stem
But I would be a fool to claim
That that is who I am

I know my gender and my faith
And who my people are
But saying that is who I am
Is equally bizarre

So please just tell me who I am
I'm caught up in the play
All I see is gains and plots
And characters of clay

Call me by my name
Not the one I have begotten
The one that's truly mine
The one I have forgotten

Take me from the realms
Of ignorance to see
Who I truly am
The true meaning of me

Take me from the reams
Of loneliness to see
That maybe I am not
But we are
In unity

THREE POEMS

Saba Zahoor

Treasure chest of potsherds

I.

Drunk with Tethys, belly filled with her fishes,
she gave birth to the demon's child – Kashmir.

Until the gold diggers bored through their chests,
like sentinels they stood – the mountains of Kashmir.

The lamb was seized by civilised wolves;
fattened for sacrifice and fondly named Kashmir.

The ruler sold out to invaders for a treasure chest of potsherds:
statesman became the salesman, and the barter – Kashmir.

II.

I died the other day while crossing a dream
a street on the other side of which awaited Kashmir.

Urdu, Farsi failed me when I met you:
I could only describe you in the mother tongue of Kashmir.

I shun the world. I remain unaffected
for I've drunk my fill; I've known Kashmir.

Why do I fear losing you, you ask?
Because in you I've found Kashmir.

III.

The snow clad *moet* now imbued with red,
sits brooding on the history banks of Kashmir.

The fisherwomen have long since witnessed water
draining from their wickerbaskets and life from Kashmir.

The conquerors of yore still
exchange pleasantries over a cup of Kashmir.

The mystic returned by the same road home:
The house stood its ground, but not Kashmir.

*moet, a Kashmiri word meaning 'a fakir'. In folklore, he is a wanderer, has no real habitat or home, is oblivious to his self.

They call it the paradise on Earth

A land beneath which miseries flow,
abundantly so;
where trees are laden with guilt, and people
trail garments embellished with sins.

The sun shines splendidly
on this land of dismay –
of receding glaciers and fast clearing forests,
of people clinging on to their
firepots of decay.

How can we be prepared to die,
blindly so,
for anything other than the One
closer to us than our jugular vein?
This city is dying of strange diseases:

he died from rubber pellets;
his mother, of his death –
while the conscience was declared
brought dead.

I took to calling it 'Moej Kasheer',
ardently so,
without any likeness of the rights upon me
of my mother, three times over.

There is no moral of the story.
I have no morals; there is no story:
Kashmir once fell in love with futility
and bore children with limbs deformed
– their lives reduced to a footnote.

*Moej-a Kashmiri word meaning mother.

Inebriation

I have lifed a life of sobriety
in a drunken state;
clambering over one hill after another,
dazed yet focused on my Sisyphean task.
"What's wrong with me?"
I whisper to the draught
sneaking through my window;
I yelp at the gale
blowing away my roof;
I howl at the tempest
sinking my ship.
Then I turn to the intoxicants:
the books on the shelves
leaning wryly on each other;

the music pouring forth
into the wine glasses of my ears.
How they lay an ambush
and wreck havoc on my life
— as the locusts lay waste the crops!

REVIEWS

RECONSIDER, REEVALUATE, REIMAGINE *by Shamim Miah*
GOOD JOURNALISM *by Zain Sardar*
MORAL AMNESIA *by Leila Sansour*
SPIRITUAL JOURNALIST *by Yahia Lababidi*
DEMONISING MAMDANI *by Khuda Bushq*

RECONSIDER, REEVALUATE, REIMAGINE

Shamim Miah

Writing in the tenth century, the philosopher Al-Farabi identified wisdom and justice as fundamental qualities of political leadership, arguing that a ruler must combine intellectual insight with moral virtue to pursue the governance of the state. *The Virtuous City*, Al-Farabi's political treatise, includes many interesting insights into the use of theoretical wisdom and practical virtue. Perhaps what is not explicitly addressed by Al-Farabi is that the exercise of practical virtue may entail considerable personal sacrifice, including exposure to physical violence, imprisonment, or even character defamation. It is precisely for this reason that Anwar Ibrahim's *Rethinking Ourselves* assumes particular significance for our times, especially in understanding that the pursuit of the virtuous city constitutes a profoundly arduous endeavour.

Anwar Ibrahim is a household name within the Muslim activist circles and seasoned political readers throughout the world. To demonstrate the significance of Anwar for wider global readership, as early as October 1997, the *Times* Magazine had 'Anwar and the Future of Asia' on the front cover. He became an icon, particularly for the Muslim, during the financial boom of Asian tiger economies through his role as the Finance-Minister (1991) and Deputy Prime Minister (1993) which oversaw prosperity and high economic growth – thus earning Malysia the 'tiger club' status. But Anwar is not just a shrewd politician. He is also a public intellectual, who has contributed to numerous debates ranging from the 'Islamization of knowledge' discourse of the last quarter of the twentieth century to powerful interventions of how to understand and navigate change. He was a member of the 1980-1990 *ijamlis,* a group of intellectuals who championed reform in Islamic thought. And he is a literati in his own right: the book is full of literary references.

Rethinking Ourselves is an elegantly written, powerful treatise, that delves into the complexities of contemporary society, exploring how individuals and communities might navigate an era marked by uncertainty and rapid change. As the subtitle title suggests, the book critically examines 'Justice, Reform and Ignorance', as well the shifting sands of democracy and the notion of the ummah (the international Muslim community), and challenging readers to reconsider, reevaluated, and rethink them. By weaving together philosophical and literary insights and practical reflections, Anwar seeks to encourages a thoughtful reappraisal of values and attitudes necessary for fostering resilience and equity in a world undergoing profound transformation.

> Anwar Ibrahim, *Rethinking Ourselves: Justice, Reform and Ignorance in Postnormal Times*, Hurst, London, Penguin, Singapore, 2025.

I followed Anwar's political career, like so many other Muslim activists in the diaspora and the Muslim world, rather closely. Born in Malaysia in 1947, Anwar Ibrahim entered a world where the political landscape was still shaped by colonialism, with many Muslim countries yet to gain independence from European rule. The sociological understanding of groups of people by their social, historical context is a widely held practice – for example, in the West we regularly refer to the Baby Boomers to describe those experienced prosperity following the Second World War. In the context of Malaysia, Anwar is a member of what the local vernacular calls the 'Merdeka Generation'. *Merdeka* being the Malay word for independence. Anwar was ten years of age when Malaysia gained its independence from British colonial rule in 1957. He was seven years old when the meeting of newly independent countries from colonial rule met in the famous Bandung Conference held in neighbouring Indonesia in 1955. Whilst Malaysia gained its independence in 1957, it wasn't until 1963 when the British colonial administrators finally left Malaysia, following when the Federation of Malaysia was declared with Sabah, Sarawak, and Singapore joined the Federation. Singapore would later separate from Malaysia in 1965 due to racial tensions, between various ethnic groups, in part motivated by political and economic factors.

The Merdeka Generation had first-hand experience of colonial oppression, they recognised that both individual and collective experiences were not isolated but rather they were an outcome of power imbalances and chronic and systematic political structures. Rooted in active political struggle and activism, Anwar had a natural knack for direct political action. The Merdeka generation tackled very difficult questions, such as was colonialism made possible not *only* by superior military prowess but the socio-political and intellectual decline that allowed Muslim nations to be *colonisable*. But, Anwar notes, history reminds us that *colonialisability* was never an inherent destiny of colonial subjects; rather, colonial exploitation ignited conflict, provoked responses, and inspired resistance. It is within this spirit of resistance the Merdeka Generation came of age in a defining moment of history – an age marked by the violence of colonialism and the courageous assertion of agency against it. Among the many responses to colonial oppression was an intellectual one – seen in the profound and far-reaching works of the Franz Fanon on colonialism, race, identity, and liberation. The works of the Algerian writer and philosopher Malik Benabi, French poet and politician Aimé Césaire, the Filipino writer and polymath José Rizal, whose life was cruelly ended by Spanish colonialists at just thirty-five, together with the powerful voice of Syed Hussein Alatas through his *Myth of the Lazy Native* which explored how ideas of the lazy native was used to justify the colonial rule in Malaysia. Anwer grew up reading these works; and grappled with many deeper questions relating to colonialism, trying to connect theory to practice. How does colonialism shape the psychology and self-perception of the colonised individual? What happens to a person's sense of identity when they are forced to see themselves through the eyes of the coloniser? And given the colonial history of Malaysia, can a colonised person achieve self-acceptance in a society that privileges whiteness and European culture?

The concept of justice has continued as an integral feature in Anwar's political and theological worldview – this is not surprising considering that he was moved by the injustices inflicted on others. In his late twenties, as leader of the Muslim Youth Movement of Malaysia (ABIM), Anwar witnessed the severe rural poverty and hardship caused by the sudden drop in rubber prices in the Baling District, located in the southeast of Kedah. In response, he mobilised mass student protests. Under the Malaysian Internal Security Act (ISA), Anwar was subsequently detained for twenty months.

This will be his first and not the last time Anwar was to see the inside of prison. Despite global condemnation, Anwar was sentenced in 1999 during the peak of his career as the Deputy Prime Minister under politically motivated charges until 2004. After his release in 2004 he would be imprison again in 2015 until 2018. Many human rights groups, including Amnesty International and Human Rights Watch, raised very serious doubts about the due process of his trial and subsequent imprisonment. In total Anwar would spend well over a decade in prison. This symbiotic relationship between witnessing the injustices of others whilst simultaneously having injustice inflicted upon himself provided him with an awakened and enduring commitment to the concept of justice. Throughout his time in prison Anwar would immerse himself in reading and writing. He read every and anything that could be smuggled into his prison cell, ranging from the classical Islamic sciences, Russian, English and Malay classics, together with wider political history. From Aleksandr Solzhenistyn' *The Gulag Archipelago*, to *The Prison Note Diaries* of the renowned Italian Marxist, Antonio Gramsci, and the complete works of Shakespeare stand out.

Thus, it is not surprising to see each of the chapters of *Rethinking Ourselves* covering a broad survey and critical engagement of literature. The section on justice, the writings of John Rawls, Nobel laureate Amartya Sen, and Malaysian thinker Syed Muhammad Naquib al-Attas stand out. For Anwar, justice comprises of a journey *and* destination. Drawing upon the writings of Al-Attas especially his idea of *wusul* or arriving, Anwar sees justice as an active and an ongoing process. In other words, 'the pursuit of justice never ends.' Once people have a conscious ontological reading of justice, we can have the realisation that the project of justice 'will never be completed. In a sense, we will always be arriving from each subsequent analysis, from generation to generation, we will watch a rich tapestry weave itself in the work we do.' Furthermore, Anwar reminds us that we 'cannot remain ignorant of what has been left for us from history, be it wisdom or even a lesson we would be foolish not to take to heart from the past failures of others'.

The significant role philosophy can play in the ordering of political affairs is one of the critical features of *al-Madinah al-Fadilah* or the *Virtuous City*. We also learn the centrality of political leadership in shaping the city based upon Islamic virtues and principles. The development of such a metropole,

Anwar reminds us, requires more critical reflection and less political slogans, He argues that 'critical thought and contemplation must take places for all politicians and law practitioners. Otherwise, we are just applying the law, and this is insufficient fulfilments of the definition of justice.' The role of active and engaged political processes, of the various strands of the state, also requires much deeper questions, for example, to what extent can true justice be achieved by postcolonial states built on inherited colonial laws and power structures? Does the existing legal and judicial system perpetuate colonial power structures and injustices? Or what type of justice is enacted and how can this develop public trust and legitimacy. For too long we are reminded that the quick solutions to some of these questions have been to 'Islamise' key instruments used to deliver justice. For instance, in addressing the tension between administering justice and protecting human rights, the solutions has been to use 'Islamic human rights.' Or how can 'Islamic' Economics break free from structural dependence on the West or more fundamentally can the *Muslim Ummah* achieve sustainability without replicating western development models. Sadly, the quick solutions have paradoxically perpetuated injustices inherent in capitalist and neo-liberal judicial and economic models through the name of Islam. The lack of ontological critique has resulted in the Islamised ideas more 'subservient and subject to the same flaws as the Western paradigms'. Anwar, highlights the case of Islamic finance to demonstrate the lack of 'attention to the principles of *adl wal Ihsan* continues to be a point of contention on account of an overly strict, legalistic interpretation of Islamic rules'.

Anwar is and always has been a strong advocate of democracy. But he recognises that democracy is under pressure given the evolving relationship between the state and its citizens in the context of increasing global mobility, migration, and diversity. He argues that modern states are challenged by the complexities of a mobile, multicultural world, experiencing accelerating change. He thus urges democracies to embrace plurality in both ethics and representations, and emphasises the importance of inclusive discourse, robust education, and fair representation – while warning against the abuses of practices such as gerrymandering. He also addressed the dual challenges of technology and money: technology as both an enabler and a threat to democratic values, and money politics as a corrupting force that undermines equality and the rule of law. Ultimately, he calls for systemic reforms, ongoing watchfulness, and active participation by all citizens to safeguard democracy against fragility, historical decline, and contemporary threats, encouraging a collective effort to adapt and strengthen democratic systems for future generations.

When talking about Malaysia, described as a periphery state within the global capitalist system, he draws on Samir Amin's Dependency Theory to illustrate how wealthier core nations exploit the resources and labour of poorer states. He argues that policies intended to alleviate poverty, such as the (New Economic Policy (NEP)), have at times perpetuated cycles of debt and dependency, while also highlighting innovative solutions like Tabung Haji, which leveraged Islamic economic principles to support Malays in performing the hajj without subsequently falling into poverty. The postcolonial Malaysian experience, the nation's struggle to live authentically, is compared to the regrets of Tolstoy's Ivan Ilyich, and draws on the works of thinkers such as Franz Fanon and Ashis Nandy to underscore the psychological and societal impacts of colonialism. Anwar warns that colonialism is not only a historical and present affliction but also a looming threat to the future, manifesting in technological determinism and cultural homogenisation.

Anwar critically examines the concept of ummah, contrasting the inclusivity of the Medina model under the Prophet Muhammad with the exclusivist tendencies of contemporary Islamic fundamentalism. He argues that the true understanding of the ummah should embody pluralism, communal engagement, and respect for diversity, drawing upon historical examples of multicultural Islamic societies. Despite the current fragmentation and disunity within Muslim communities, he notes, the idea of ummah remains essential – a universal consciousness that transcends sect, ethnicity, and nationality. He wants both to open up the concept of the ummah to a broader, pluralistic perspective; and the Muslim world to embrace the differences and complexities of the contemporary world. Ummah is not something that is limited to Islam and Muslims; all communities have ummahs; and flora and fauna have ummahs too. Anwar wants to embrace all these ummahs – make nature, ecology and environment an integral part of the ummah, the oppressed and marginalised of the world an essential part of the ummah. So, the task before the 'Muslim ummah', as he sees it, is to build a shared ethical consciousness, which transcends geography, history, and nation-states. Its ethical manifestation can be found in the collective pursuit of justice, and its embodiment is based upon the pursuit of hadith of the Prophet Muhammad, which states that 'Muslims are like a human body, if one part hurts the whole-body suffers'. But 'the body' now includes climate change, the existential threats from AI, the rise of fascism, and even the possibility of nuclear war. Similar to the concept of justice, the consciousness of the ummah is not a destination rather it's a constant, ongoing and individual and collective struggle. The ummah must continue to cultivate an inclusive consciousness – one that balances ecological concerns and human diversity.

Injustice, inequality, and social marginalisation have become a ubiquitous feature of the Muslim world. Anwar contends that these phenomena should be fully understood through the Arc of Ignorance. This concept suggests that present-day injustices are not random nor isolated; rather, they emerge out of a historical process, constructed through centuries of limited access to knowledge, uncritical thinking, and social stagnation. By tracing the historical origins of this hatred against Muslims, the 'Arc of Ignorance' provides a framework for understanding how past patterns of intellectual, social, and political neglect continue to influence contemporary conditions. For Anwar, confronting this arc requires a renewed and genuine commitment to critical inquiry, and informed civic engagement to break the cycle of ignorance and foster a more just and harmonious society. Ignorance, he argues, now goes hand in hand with progress in knowledge. And, as such, we need to pay as much attention to our ignorance as we give to knowledge creation. It is now pervasive both at the personal level – as fake news and deep fakes, as xenophobia and Islamophobia, as the politics of far right, as economics of neo-liberalism – as well as the collective levels where it has a direct impact on decision-making, social cohesion, and policy formation.

Rethinking Ourselves is an intellectually dazzling book. The various themes of the book are knitted together as a multicoloured tapestry, with strings from Islamic philosophy and patches from the great literature of the world. But it is also a deeply humane and passionate text. When Anwer came out of prison in 2018, he forgave all his political foes who imprisoned and tortured him. (They went on to stab him in the back, yet again!). So it is not a surprise to see him discuss the themes of human fallibility, forgiveness, and the redemptive power of mercy. He argues that even when one's efforts seem destined to fail, hope for relief and pardon remains possible through sincere appeals and acts of compassion. Ultimately, he suggests that persistence and understanding can bring about justice and freedom, urging readers to extend the same generosity to others as they would wish for themselves. Throughout the book, Anwar urges both personal and collective action to dismantle ongoing systems of oppression and to foster genuine equality and authenticity, in hopes of creating a freer and more equitable future for all. This combination of intellectual virtuosity and humanitarian outlook makes *Rethinking Ourselves* an enduring and pivotal book of our times.

The task that we are set by *Rethinking Ourselves* is far from easy. It entails addressing multilayered and complex issues, especially given the political and intellectual challenges faced by the postnormal condition marked by complexity, chaos, and contradictions. Overcoming these obstacles requires strategic thinking, long-term vision, and a willingness to critically engage in difficult but necessary transformations. We live in unprecedented times; where our futures are trapped and locked into an endless cycle of attempting to resolve crisis through existing paradigms that produced these crises in the first place. The way out of the permacrisis – whether of climate change, capitalism's structural inequalities, or the escalating risks of artificial intelligence – demands a critical rethinking of human identity, values, and purpose. Going forward 'rethinking ourselves' requires viable and plural futures argues Anwar. It requires critical revaluation of the received wisdoms passed on through academic disciplines, secular ideologies, national politics, and religious obscurantism. Instead, a matrix of virtues, both old and new, is needed to navigate our current and perilous condition. These virtues, Anwar concludes, must function as a three-dimensional lens, 'our basic navigational tool – a new-age sextant and compass – that helps us negotiate accelerating change, transcend contradictions, orient complexity through profound simplicity, and survive chaos'.

I will follow where Anwar leads. I recommend you do the same!

GOOD JOURNALISM

Zain Sardar

We have arrived at a post-truth world in which 'polycrises', from intensifying climate catastrophe to retrograde wars perpetuated by autocrats, are enveloping many traditional societal institutions, exacerbating the trust deficit between the public and the establishment. To add to all this, the ongoing AI revolution threatens to reconstruct self and society in ways that we have not fully grasped.

It has been stated ad nauseum that the narratives that we are told in the West by politicians and cultural elites to help us make sense of the world are breaking apart. The 'rules-based world order' has evaporated and has been replaced with 'might is right' directives. Western liberalism, as argued in the previous issue of *Critical Muslim*, has all but collapsed. The resulting vacuum has been filled by malicious actors taking advantage of these vertiginous circumstances to further the post-truth agenda. In his 2016 documentary, *Hypernormalisation,* Adam Curtis, discusses the influence of the relatively obscure Russian political strategist Vladislav Surkov. The politician and businessman, a Kremlin insider, drew on subversive public relations tactics to sustain Putin's hold on power. These resembled a form of Jackson Pollock inspired conceptual cum-avant-garde high artistry, curating and propagating multiple conflicting political and media messages. The effect was to generate a perpetual 'fog of war' that shrouds everything. The goal was to lessen the hold, or even the desirability, of discovering the truth behind any official media and government narratives. The tactics of diminishing the truth behind tissues of fabrications to make the truth appear like another consumer simulacrum was subsequently mastered by the US President, Donald Trump and his MAGA movement.

Eric Wishart, *Journalism Ethics: 21 Essentials from Wars to Artificial Intelligence*, Hong Kong University Press, 2024.

No professions or industries have been immune to these disorientating developments. None more so than journalism and, by extension, the mainstream media industry. A number of interesting questions arise. What are the responsibilities of journalists in the post-truth age? Are the rise of social media influencers and citizenship journalism presents an acute challenge to, what is often referred to as, the 'legacy media'? Or, is it perhaps a democratic challenge, as many human rights organisations support networks of citizenship journalists in war zones? Are there any professional standards still operating in an industry that is supposed to be underpinned and checked by certain ethical principles? Does generative AI make the journalist's lot easier? Or does it only serve to reinforce deeply held biases and drown us in an endless plethora of pernicious deepfakes, clickbait, and fake news?

Eric Wishart, Ethics Editor of Agence France-Presse (AFP, the international news agency) sets out to answer these questions. His guide for early career journalists with a concern for adhering to ethical principles is one of the very few recent books written on the ethics of journalism. One of the pressing reasons for Wishart's publication — which draws on a collation of ethical frameworks and guides produced by different media agencies — is to reestablish the integrity of a profession that has come under sustained attack from all sides: the public that has lost almost all trust, authoritarian regimes, Left and Right of the political spectrum, forcing it to become their PR outlets.

Many of the values that he is keen to uphold in the profession are, of course, decent and necessary. But they may appear somewhat quaint and old-fashioned in a world in which the constant onslaught of misinformation is very real. Perhaps, more than anything, this reflects the road we have travelled down to get to this point. The untruths or 'fake news' is exactly what sound journalism is supposed to expose. Investigative and news journalism ought to present well-researched and evidenced, corroborated details, and leaves them hanging in the court of public opinion for well-informed citizens to make the final judgement. That is, the ultimate judgement should be left to a Habermas public sphere, where individuals come to have a rational and critical debates about important issues of our time.

The path to rebuilding trust between the press and the *demos* must go through the deontological – duty based – ethics that Wishart professes. Unsurprisingly, his writing is replete with the language of duty, care, responsibility, integrity, and neutrality. There is a sense that young journalists wishing to gain a foothold in the industry need to practice this responsible stewardship of the profession, to revolutionise it — in the conventional sense of revisiting the original principles that constitute the foundations of good journalism.

Much of the tenor also implicitly evokes the Brazilian educator and philosopher Paulo Freire's notion of teaching as an 'ontological vocation'. In his original rendering, this meant that pedagogy could assist in supporting others to reimagine their own social reality. In other words, teaching can upend uncontested assumptions about how the world operates, allowing us to see a new world of present and future possibilities. Good journalism can undertake a similar task, Wishart suggest, penetrating into the darkness of corruption, falsehoods, scandal, and the definitive issues of our time in order to empower and inform a media hungry public. The investigative journalists Carl Burnstein and Bob Woodward's uncovering of the Watergate scandal for the *Washington Post* can be considered the textbook example of this. The profession's tussle with misinformation and conspiracy theories (and not merely acting as a means to amplify them) is of the utmost importance as a vocational mission.

One of the principles Wishart advances, alongside ensuring accurate and fairness in reporting, and balance in coverage, is the imperative for journalists to seek the truth in the story that they are covering. The seemingly Platonic language here invokes a very traditional view of journalism as the profession that works in the public interest to hold those in power to account. It does seem as though Wishart is stating the obvious. But given the media control of vested interests, as well as unscrupulous upstarts wearing the garbs of anti-establishment insurgency, emphasizing that the function of journalism is to speak truth to power is an imperative. In the tumultuous aftermath of the UK phone hacking scandal and the 2012 Leveson Inquiry into the culture, practices, and ethics of the press, the sad necessity to repeat this again and again is all too evident. Yet, the message has not been received. The unabated streams of Islamophobia and unbalanced reporting on Palestine-Israel not just from right-wing broadcasters such as GB News but also from mainstream outlets like the BBC, in addition to the right-wing print press, from the *Daily Telegraph* to *The Express*, clearly suggests that ethics has all but vaporized. The chasm in confidence is particularly deep amongst minority communities; Muslims being the favoured targets of misreporting and demonisation in the British press. This may be business as usual in a context in which the business model itself is increasingly under threat of becoming bust.

Conversely, Wishart is content just to push the stance that all journalists should stop to carefully consider whether they have the public interest at heart in pursuing a story. Reflexivity is paramount. Not simply reflecting on the story being covered but the impact that the reporting makes on the story itself. A corollary of this is the salience of going out of your way to follow all stories to their natural conclusion and not being tempted into dropping it once the sensationalism has evaporated. Humane and empathetic reporting, Wishart argues, minimises the harm to the public (echoing the UN principle of 'do no harm'), including victims of crime and vulnerable people. Thus, the obligation to bring marginalised communities into the stories in ways that enhance their agency and enables them to comment as spokespeople of various issues and not only on the topics that directly affect them. Needless to say, this also touches on the lack of diversity in the industry as a whole; something that crucially shapes editorial decision making.

What complicates the picture of reinstituting good journalism is the multiplicity and radical heterogeneity of publics that exist in the contemporary times. There has been fracture and fragmentation in the media landscape. The lines have been blurred between journalism and simple documentation of and commentary on events through modern communications technology, such as through smart phones. This speaks of a profession very much in flux. The spate of well know print newspapers, such as the UK's *The Independent*, going under and resurfacing as online shadows of their former selves is a case in point. It is something that Wishart is all too aware of. He constantly suggests the need for standards in print and online journalism to be mirrored in the realm of social media.

In distinguishing the practices of excellence within journalism, the epistemology — in philosophical parlance — behind journalist practice is of key concern. Or, to put it in a more anodyne manner, what is strongly advocated is adherence to procedures for verifying knowledge behind reporting. The usual method of doing this, seeking several sources and reliable witnesses, constitutes the basics of professional practice. Nonetheless, where generative AI poses a risk by generating précis with questionable attributions is when every journalist shows their true worth by conducting diligent fact checking and effective background research. Alongside this, and more interestingly, Wishart argues for framing and tonality that deploy the American linguistic and philosopher George Lakoff's 'truth sandwich'. It is a technique that circumvents the simple echoing or reproduction of falsehoods. The idea is to surround an outrageous statement designed to grab headlines from a prominent public figure with the facts of the matter. It is a cognitive frame that disarms the rhetorical potency of the original statement to fan the flames of disinformation, safely ensconcing it in the evidence. Techniques such as this should be standard practice. But these constructions appear for the most part in the guise of firefighting. Typically, in response to controversial statements directly broadcast to followers. For instance, via platforms that circumnavigate the mainstream media, such as Elon Musk's 'X' and Donald Trump's preferred channel, the crudely and very ironically named, Truth Social.

The sections of the book that overlap with some very raw, live events, concern reporting during conflicts and war, and balance, impartiality and fairness. Wishart reiterates the importance of avoiding double standards, although stays clear of mentioning Palestine-Israel. His basic principle stresses the importance of reporting overseas events in the same manner as domestic ones, not diminishing the dignity of people overseas in a way that would not occur in the national context. This applies in cases of war and conflict, as well as instances where there is coverage of vulnerable communities.

However, when speaking of instances of war and conflict, one cannot, as Wishart does, gloss over Israel's actions in Palestine. How media outlets have covered the horrifying events unfolding in the Middle East has much to tell us about the ethics of journalism. In the climate of ever rampant Islamophobia in the West, civil society organisations like the Centre for Media Monitoring (CfMM) have been instrumental in documenting media misrepresentation of Muslims in the British Press.

CfMM exposes media biases in a bid to both educate and hold guilty parties accountable, with the aim of raising editorial standards. The Centre's report, *BBC on Gaza-Israel: One Story, Double Standards* is an absolute *tour de force* of meticulous analysis and sustained scrutiny of news coverage across a period of year in the aftermath of 7 October 2023. Within it, the UN Special Rapporteur Francesca Albanese — who has been particularly outspoken on the treatment the Palestinians at the hands of the Israeli state — provides a sobering endorsement: 'most mainstream media have failed in their basic duty: they have largely manufactured consent, enabling Genocide in real time'.

The BBC's lack of impartiality, the role it has played in 'manufacturing consent' through the creation of a lopsided 'moral universe', comes under the spotlight. The disposability of Palestinian lives — invoking Stalin's chilling remark that one death is a tragedy while a million deaths are a mere statistic — and the 'marginalisation of their suffering' underscores the grotesque lack of impartiality and balance. To add to this grim predicament, international journalists have been barred by the Israeli regime from entering Gaza; Palestinian reporters have had to carry out live reporting, documenting their own demise for the world to see. One tragic case comes to mind. The Palestinian, Al-Jazeera journalist Hossam Shabat poignantly left a letter to be published in the event of his death (he was killed by an Israeli airstrike). His remarkable testament can be read as a vindication of Wishart's argument that good journalism is ultimately at its heart an uncovering of the truth despite many who conspire to hide it. In the letter, Shabat reflects on his dedication to reporting the 'horrors in northern Gaza minute by minute, determined to show the world the truth they tried to bury.' Shabat was killed by an Israeli airstrike, and his death was widely reported by the press in the Middle East. But CfMM has shown that the death of less than a fifth of journalists killed in Gaza have been covered by the BBC. This is a significant failure to represent the full extent of the sacrifices made to capture gross violations of human rights.

The varying standards in reporting across different conflict zones sharply accentuates the point on BBC impartiality. The Ukraine-Russia war has received fuller reporting with discussion of the broad range of facts, in contrast to the decontextualisation that suffuses coverage of Palestine. The history of the Palestinian people, their cause and struggles, is very rarely done any justice by news agencies. In this flow of ahistorical content from media broadcasts, Palestine-Israel is presented as a conflict of equivalence, which does nothing to inform the public's views on such issues.

With this entrenchment of double standards as seemingly intentional policy, we see reporting techniques such as the 'truth sandwich' have been wholly cast aside. Wishart makes the argument that fair balance in journalism does not crudely mean giving the oxygen of publicity to a preposterous, discredited opposing view, what he labels it 'false balance'. For example, scientifically evidenced facts on climate change cannot be balanced by absurdities of climate deniers, or giving a platform to bigoted views that are designed to cause harm rather than further the debate. However, the purported balance and neutrality observed by the mainstream media, as pointed out by the Palestine Ambassador to the UK, Husam Zomlot, has only served as a means to conceal oppression and injustice.

The imbalance is striking. On the BBC alone, Israelis are more than twice as likely to be interviewed compared to their Palestinian counterparts. One daresay that the BBC's editorial standards fall far short of honouring Wishart's ethical principles. Extreme commentators that routinely spout dehumanising rhetoric in relation to Palestinians are given plenty of airtime. The *Times* columnist Melanie Philips has been a regular feature of political panel shows such as *BBC Question Time*. She has gleefully seized on such opportunities to deny the existence of the Palestinian people and to circulate tired and tawdry Islamophobic tropes. Other polemicists such as the neoconservative Douglas Murray have been given prominent platforms on news programmes such as *Newsnight*. He has mused openly, in his usual egregious manner, that Israel, 'will finally put an end to this insoluble nightmare, raze Hamas to the ground, or clear all the Palestinians from that benighted strip...It could be a good time to do it.'

This in turn raises another contentious issue. The terminology and language deployed in BBC reports on Palestine have sought to limit the responsibility behind Israeli actions that have resulted in Palestinian deaths. Palestinians killed by Israeli military operations are cast as passive victims of an anonymous force. Inversely, the episodes of Palestinian attacks have been described more readily as 'barbaric', as 'massacres', acts of terrorism, or with a similarly charged rubric. The attribution of malign intent is unmistakable. The death of Israelis at the hands of Palestinians have been accompanied with predictably emotive verbiage. There has been a 'one-sided humanisation' in operation here, whereby editorial decisions have only reinforced the lack of dignity granted to Palestinian victims of Israeli state aggression and violence.

The ethical journalist, of the variety that Wishart would approve, ought to fairly record the extent of the harm that conflict causes. In the cases of those people and communities who are already greatly marginalised in political discourse, this becomes even more of a duty. Both the magnitude of harm meted out to the Palestinian people, and the unspeakable order of the destruction of the Gaza Strip, has tested the inclinations of the mainstream media and journalists as a class. Whether journalists aspire to an ontological vocation, to liberate us from preconceptions and the worst of our prejudices, is the fundamental question that follows from this.

Wishart's answer to the question of the liberatory power of journalism is to foreground the strong relational ethics inherent to good journalism. It is praiseworthy that the journalistic practices he advances puts concern for people before, for instance, satisfying editorial teams' obsession with being the first to break a story, or prioritise commercial purposes. This is notable in his chapter on climate change, where journalism can play a critical role in cutting through the lazy narratives; the 'war on woke' rhetoric being a prime target. The ethical journalist is obliged to convey the scale of the challenge but also centre positive stories and initiatives that break up the gloom that can induce severe anxiety or indifference in the public. An interesting point to note is that Wishart wants ordinary citizens to be able to differentiate between a good ethical and a bad morally dubious journalist. So he provide study exercises at the end of each section, designed to getting the reader to consciously think about people-centred journalism. The scenarios that he sets up very effectively stimulates the reader into actively ruminating on who may be harmed by a news report, what may undermine credibility in reporting, and what responsibilities need to be discharged in fulfilment of ethical obligations.

Overall, what stays with you after reading *Journalism Ethics* is how integral and essential good journalism is for preventing society's slide into authoritarianism and autocracy. This is sometimes taken for granted or said somewhat glibly, but the seriousness of this sentiment cannot be made understated. Even so, we, somewhat despairingly, get a sense of how far away the current journalism of 'legacy media' is from embedding Wishart's ethical principles. This, after all, is a time in which traditional forms of media are being vigorously contested or coopted for political agendas. Undoubtedly, the mainstream media has been complicit in amplifying harm to already marginalised communities. It has hidden itself behind so-called balance and neutrality to aid and abet injustice, enabling it to thrive unchecked. Now it is in danger, once the corporations and 'tech bros' take over completely, of becoming the soapboxes and megaphones of oligarchs to vent their deranged worldviews. Thus, the enormous and very necessary task — the ontological vocation undertaken by Wishart — of strengthening and developing ethical frameworks in journalism. It is the return to ethics as first principles that will in the end save the profession; and, with it, society itself.

MORAL AMNESIA

Leila Sansour

There are books that read you first – they articulate the disquiet that has long been wordless in you. You close them feeling that the air around you has grown more voluminous, that something within you has shifted to accommodate the change. *One Day, Everyone Will Have Always Been Against This* is one such book. Omar El Akkad writes from the conviction that the true work of a writer happens long before the first line is written – in the arduous journey inward, to the borderlands of self and conscience. Reading him, one feels the strain of that descent: his excavation of the mind's terrain stretches your own until the familiar grows foreign and the foreign feels intimate. It is a reminder that understanding the fabric of reality must begin with examining the lens through which we see it. In the collective discourse surrounding Gaza, that lens has never been more violently contested.

Already a *New York Times* bestseller and winner of the National Book Award, *One Day, Everyone Will Have Always Been Against This* is a landmark. It carries the rare distinction of being both urgent and enduring. It appears at a moment when perception itself feels besieged, when language buckles under the weight of manipulation, euphemism, and moral fatigue. In this context, the book feels like a rare intervention – a restoration of lucidity amid moral vertigo. In a culture saturated with managed speech, where distortion wears on the nervous system, I found El Akkad's voice almost medicinal: a kind of moral and linguistic therapy, recalibrating one's sense of what words are for.

Omar El Akkad, *One Day, Everyone Will Have Always Been Against This*, Canongate Books, Edinburgh, 2025.

And when I say this book will last, it is because I believe it will join – unmistakably and on its own terms – the long human conversation that stretches from Primo Levi to Hannah Arendt: the lineage of those who wrote to confront the cruel grammar of history itself, to trace the anatomy of horror, to ask, from the depths of lived anguish, why 'never again' is always spoken in the future tense – and why, each time, it must return.

The book is structured as a constellation of essays, memoir fragments, reportage, and moral argument. Each chapter has a prologue that disconcerts and disallows you to read quietly; there is a sequence of memories – about his family fleeing Egypt in the wake of Sadat's assassination, growing up in a caged culture in Qatar, going to Western schools, believing, at the worst of times, that the West was still salvageable – and there are the harder chapters, which lean heavily into Gaza, into complicity, into the daily witness of images that break you open.

Threaded through these fragments is the quiet drama of disillusionment: a boy who once believed in the promise of the 'free world' – its books, its laws, its reason – slowly realising that the cracks run through its very foundations. He writes of how he once thought the West could be repaired, that the core was still sound, 'until the fall of 2023, until Gaza'. It is this moral unmasking – rendered with calm precision, without bitterness – that gives the book its strange blend of moral ferocity at the same time as unassuming grace.

By the time you close it, you have travelled, in 187 pages, through a landscape that feels immeasurably large: the inner geography of conscience, the habits and failures of western liberalism, the anaesthetic techniques of euphemism, and the small muscles of resistance that might yet jam the machinery of power.

It is not quite a memoir, but a slow act of excavation – a tracing of fractures, Gaza being the last and deepest fissure. The journalist in him is always present, visible in the clean precision of his prose, in the decisions of what to recount and what to let stand. There is discipline in this writing – a deliberate, almost ascetic kind of austerity. Voltaire once remarked that 'everything too stupid to be said is sung'. The line came to mind, though the comparison is imperfect. Songs live in what they do not say, forcing the imagination to do the work. El Akkad's utterances, by contrast, are never foolish – on the contrary – yet his prose moves with the quiet inevitability of song. Its leanness gives thought the space to reverberate. Each sentence feels weighed against silence, tuned to let imagination complete what it begins. Stripped to its essence, the writing acquires resonance; it is in the pauses between his lines that the reader begins not only to think, but to feel.

Though composed of fragments that loosely chart the writer's own biography, the book's true architecture is conceptual: an inquiry into language and its complicity with power. El Akkad is acutely attuned to the politics of naming, to the quiet violence encoded in words. In a passage about his childhood in Qatar, he observes how survival depends on the swift mastery of the right label – 'expat' for some, 'migrant' or 'illegal' for others. It is a small moment, yet a revelation in political linguistics. Language, in his telling, becomes the battlefield where power and resistance meet. That single, measured observation exposes an entire moral architecture: vocabulary is never neutral; it is the first line of defence for hierarchy. Where language is weaponised, the poor, the brown, the unwanted – the surplus communities of empire – appear only as administrative problems to be contained.

The heart of El Akkad's work is this vigilance about words. He is interested in the moral ecology of language: how phrases can anaesthetise, how euphemisms can hide the machinery of harm. It is useful here to be explicit about what this euphemistic fog does to a person. When the vocabulary that shapes public life is systematically dishonest, the effect is not rhetorical but existential. Eyes report horror; tongues are told to call it something else. The consequence is moral paralysis: language ceases to perform its human work – to make pain shareable, to build communal response. George Orwell wrote, in the plainest of terms, that political language aims to make lies sound truthful and murder respectable. El Akkad carries these lessons forward into our mercurial present. His sentences resist the lullaby of consensus. He calls out the polite syntax of power – a state that can call killing 'statecraft,' while a citizen, refusing to buy products complicit in the killing, is accused of 'economic terrorism.' That inverted grammar is a technique of domination; El Akkad names it with the quiet authority of someone who has looked too long to be deceived. It is difficult to imagine a reader whose moral radar could resist, even briefly, being resuscitated.

I write this as someone who, like El Akkad, has also grown up between worlds — fluent in dislocation and the strange lucidity it brings. Those of us who live in transit, the quiet nomads of culture, develop a natural allergy to easy sentiment; we learn that words are more often camouflage than revelation. I too once believed in the West's promise — its books, its open speech, its shimmering idea of freedom — in the faith that knowledge might refine conscience. But reason, it turns out, is an obedient servant: it can polish cruelty until it shines.

El Akkad's title was born from a tweet he posted on 25 October 2023: 'One day, when it's safe, when there's no personal downside to calling a thing what it is, when it's too late to hold anyone accountable, everyone will have always been against this'. That single sentence seeded the book. It captures, with unbearable simplicity, the moral choreography of our age — how outrage always arrives too late, how the arc of opinion bends not toward justice but toward safety. One of the ways El Akkad captures this pattern is through what he calls 'modular opinion': the kind of moral posture that appears responsive to fact and experience yet is, in truth, engineered for survival within the frameworks of acceptability. Its allegiance is not to truth but to belonging. It keeps one foot in every future, ready to pivot when the tide of consensus turns.

We like to imagine our convictions are shaped by evidence, witness, empathy — but more often they are tuned to the frequencies of our tribe. We hold the belief that we are guided by the rational mind, but our true guiding star always navigates back to comfort. We learn, almost instinctively, to phrase outrage in ways that will not cost us, to express compassion only once it is socially inexpensive. And so, by the time a moral position becomes broadly acceptable, the catastrophe it names has already run its course. The framework shifts, the conscience cleanses itself, and history rehearses its ritual of absolution once there is nothing left to save.

If Nietzsche was right that only the slave truly sees the master, it is because survival sharpens perception. Only the dispossessed can map the subtle machinery of domination. The vantage point on the human condition does not belong to the powerful; it belongs to those who must study power in order to live beneath it. Illusion about the law is a privilege of those who do not live under its weight. It is those on the receiving end of empire who must read reality in its raw form. This double consciousness – the capacity to see both through one's own eyes and through the eyes of authority – is the inheritance of the colonised, the exiled, the unwanted. It breeds a kind of moral and cognitive precision that those at ease in the world will never know.

The powerful can afford a counterfeit language – words that decorate rather than reveal – but the powerless must become anatomists of truth. They learn to read omission, to detect hypocrisy, to decipher the syntax of evasion. Their knowledge is forensic: a study of systems beneath the skin. There is an important corollary here about culture-making. Those on the receiving end of injustice often end up inventing the idioms that wake us up. When the official language abandons you, you must make one that will not. El Akkad is alert to this – he listens to poets, to small acts, to marginal narratives.

And this is the bitter paradox of civilisation – that while the powerful claim the right to interpret, the most enduring human commentary has always belonged to those denied that privilege. El Akkad understands this perfectly. In writing this book, he quietly reclaims the sovereign right to interpret the world – a gesture more radical than any overt declaration. The coloniser may own the archive, but the colonised hold the commentary. They see not only the edifice of power but the scaffolding that sustains it; they dwell in the space where language meets its limits. Theirs is the clarity of those who have seen the world unmasked – and who know that to restore meaning to words is to push against the grip of power.

El Akkad writes from this terrain. His gaze does not avert itself, does not soften for civility's sake. It is the gaze of one who has lived long enough on the underside of power to know that moral vision begins where comfort ends.

If there is a grief threaded through this work, it is the grief of unflinching clarity – the pain of seeing through every veil and knowing that such vision offers no comfort. El Akkad writes from the understanding that our institutions have perfected a choreography of blindness: they can name atrocity only once it has become history. What he calls the 'moral arithmetic' of the West is precisely this – its talent for compassion in hindsight, its need to convert the suffering it ignored into moral capital. 'One of the hallmarks of Western liberalism,' he notes, 'is an assumption, in hindsight, of virtuous resistance as the only polite expectation of people on the receiving end of colonialism.' The powerful, he implies, do not simply inherit the spoils of empire; they inherit its narrative voice. The victor's language inhabits the mythology of triumph, while the victims inherit only experience.

You feel the effect of El Akkad's economy the way one feels the knock of a bell: it draws you, briefly, out of the habitual. He writes as if language itself were wounded, and each sentence an attempt at healing. In interviews, El Akkad has said that during Gaza he could not write 'as though language were neutral.' To write, he decided, was not to explain the senseless but to refuse the pretence of sense altogether. This refusal – to normalise, to aestheticise, to find moral consolation – is the book's most radical discipline.

He asks, again and again, what kind of resistance remains possible in a system that has learned to monetise everything – even dissent. Is it even possible to speak of tampering with the calculus of power? His answer is not a program but a posture: the practice of refusal, the refusal to let power script our speech. To cast off euphemism is a quiet revolt; it reopens the circuit between language and reality. When words find their measure, we may yet stand a little taller. In fact, every small act counts. He quotes the Palestinian poet Rasha Abdulhadi, who urges: 'wherever you are, whatever sand you can throw at the gears of genocide, do it. If it's a handful, throw it'. El Akkad's book is full of such handfuls – small disruptions that slow the machinery of moral anaesthesia.

If the political imagination today feels exhausted, this book quietly proposes another way of conceiving power: not through spectacle or certainty, but through attention, through small acts of refusal, through disciplined hope – the kind that endures without the comfort of answers or the promise of arrival. 'Giving up hope,' El Akkad writes, 'is a surrender to the very machine one must resist.'

There is a rare solace in reading a writer who reminds us that language still matters, that small acts still matter. For those of us who, like him, have kept a billion tabs open to Gaza, helpless before the flood of images, the act of reading this work feels like an act of resuscitation: a slow restoration of the capacity to feel, to name, to mean. It is a book for those who have run out of words, it offers companionship in the search for meaning.

One Day, Everyone Will Have Always Been Against This feels like both an autopsy and a manual: an anatomy of how conscience fails, and a quiet rehearsal in how it might gain power. It teaches us to resist skimming over the surface of language, to look longer, to reclaim words from the machinery of gaslight.

If you recognise what I am describing – if you have struggled, as many have, to endure the public language of our time, the news, the statements, the endless commentary that numbs and infuriates more than it illuminates – or if you are simply curious to hear how the world sounds from the other side of your argument – then this is the book I most sincerely recommend. For some, it will feel like therapy; for others, like a challenge. Whoever you are, read it slowly, as you would a letter from someone who refuses to lie to you. Let it test your endurance, the measure of what you can bear to know, and your capacity to look without flinching.

And when you close this book, you may feel, as I did, that the borders of your inner world have quietly expanded, that a new equilibrium has formed between your mind and the world, not through any softening of reality, but through the enlargement of the self that has to face it.

SPIRITUAL JOURNALIST

Yahia Lababidi

In these days of unfortunate polarisation, religious and political, it seems we cannot hear one another without suspicion or recrimination. An answer to this impasse may be found in Carla Power's powerful record of friendship built on sacred encounter. When it was originally published, it was on the non-fiction finalist list of the 2016 Pulitzer Prize. Her humble and uplifting book, a meditation on the possibility of reverent curiosity even in a time of profound estrangement, has now been republished as a paperback.

The premise is simple. A Western journalist, raised in a secular Jewish-Quaker household, spends a year studying the Qur'an with Sheikh Muhammad Akram Nadwi, a classically trained Islamic scholar living and teaching in Oxford. Their meetings are modest in setting, held in libraries lit by slanting afternoon light, or over tea grown cold in quiet cafés, but rich in their unfolding. Texts are read aloud. Silences are allowed their full length. Questions rise slowly and are not rushed toward conclusion.

Sheikh Akram is more than a scholar. He is a vessel of tradition, formed by years of study in the Indian madrasa system and refined by the demands of modern scholarship. When Power first meets him, she encounters a man who can recite Qur'anic commentary from memory while offering incisive views on current global affairs. His bearing is learned yet unassuming. There is no academic bravado, only a steady light drawn from long devotion.

Carla Power, *If the Oceans Were Ink: An Unlikely Friendship and a Journey to the Heart of the Quran*, Henry Holt, 2015; Holt paperback, 2024.

His most monumental achievement, a forty-volume biographical dictionary of female hadith scholars, emerges as a needed corrective to historical forgetfulness. As Power writes, 'by digging up the buried tradition of women scholars, Akram has prepared the ground for radical social change'. This labour of remembrance reveals a spiritual and intellectual heritage obscured by time and opens a doorway into Islam's plural past. In its scope and moral purpose, the work refutes the notion that women have stood at the periphery of Islamic knowledge. Power is stunned, and rightly so. Here is a tradition misrepresented by its loudest critics and, at times, misunderstood even by those within it.

That Sheikh Akram's *Al-Muhaddithat* contains more than 9,000 entries on women scholars of hadith speaks to the depth and endurance of this forgotten lineage. Some taught in the Prophet's Mosque in Medina. Others granted *ijazat* to male scholars whose names would later eclipse theirs. These women were also transmitters of sacred text, participants in a living tradition, traveling great distances to seek knowledge and embody it. Their recovery serves as historical correction as well as an act of spiritual resistance: a reclamation of the right to interpret, teach, and lead.

To study this tradition is to discover how historical amnesia often serves contemporary power. The silencing of these women was not an accident. Rather, it reflects broader tendencies in religious institutions, across faiths, to sanctify structures of authority by pruning their histories. In this light, Sheikh Akram's scholarship moves beyond mere academic labour. It is a moral act. As Power notes, 'he's not writing them back into history. He's revealing that they were always there.'

The portrait that emerges of these two unlikely companions is endearing. Power brings to the text the questions of her time and temperament. She asks about gender, law, violence, modesty, and marriage. Her inquiries arise from concern and a genuine longing to understand. One such exchange centres on the Qur'anic verse describing wives as obedient. Rather than deflecting, Sheikh Akram guides her through neighbouring verses: those that speak of mutual consultation, spiritual striving, and the delicate balances of marital responsibility. He draws upon classical interpretations while remaining attuned to contemporary sensibilities. He listens, then responds from within the heart of the tradition.

That passage, Surah An-Nisa (4:34), has been a focal point of modern debates on gender in Islam. The verse is often misused, both by critics outside the tradition and by rigid literalists within it. Sheikh Akram offers a method of interpretation that is both rooted and responsive, beginning with the ethical imperative to understand the Qur'an in its holistic context. As Power learns, interpretation in the Islamic tradition is a centuries-long conversation, with voices that challenge, refine, and deepen one another.

Here, the study of Qur'an becomes an exercise in moral imagination. Sheikh Akram demonstrates how the text is not a static code, while honouring its legal and theological gravity. He exemplifies what the tradition calls *tafsir bi'l-ma'thur*, exegesis grounded in transmission, doing so in a spirit that honours *tafsir bi'l-ra'y* as well: interpretation shaped by sound judgment and lived conscience. What renders this method persuasive is its integrity. As he tells Power, 'purity of the heart' is the key to understanding. In this, his method insists that clarity in reading requires clarity of perception in the reader.

The question of women's roles, too often flattened into symbols, receives fresh consideration. As Power reflects, 'too often the meaning of the hijab is taken as clear and unequivocal, like an on-off switch, a neat binary code.' By unsettling these assumptions, the book restores dimension to lived faith, where personal conviction resists cultural shorthand and practice returns to inner intention.

Each session unfolds like a spiritual exercise. There is repetition, variation, and return. The Qur'an, in these moments, lives in recitation and reflection, through the humility of the student and the responsibility of the teacher. Power's presence is more like that of a guest at a sacred meal: grateful, observant, still learning the manners of the house. She allows herself to remain uncertain. This is one of her subtle strengths. Her awakening arrives as an accumulation of small recognitions. She becomes porous to another way of seeing. Power understands that spiritual growth rarely announces itself. It arrives, rather, like light shifting across a room already occupied.

During one such lesson, Sheikh Akram sketches a line and a circle on the whiteboard. The line, he explains, represents our external conditions, whether we live in a prison or palace, under tyranny or freedom. The circle stands for our cycle of days, the steady passage of time gifted by God. 'Your circumstances were given to you by Allah,' he says. 'Using the cycle of your days to practice *taqwa*, or love and awe of God, is your job.' The clarity of this teaching, so simple yet meaningful, echoes long after the page is turned.

This pedagogical style, repetitive, oral, dialogical, is itself a sacred technology. The madrasa model Power encounters prioritises oral transmission, embodied learning, and spiritual accountability. One studies such matters of the heart in hopes, one day, for transformation. The granting of an *ijaza*, or teaching license, is a spiritual trust, passed from soul to soul across generations. In contrast with the Western academic model, which prizes originality, this form of learning honours transmission as a mode of intimacy. Knowledge is inherited, and its faithful bearing is a form of gratitude.

Power's secular Jewish-Quaker upbringing gives her a unique vantage. Though she begins as a journalist, her method becomes something closer to *lectio divina*, that ancient Christian form of spiritual reading. The book records how she is read by the experience. She listens to Sheikh Akram's words as well as to his silences, hesitations, and refusals. His pauses speak volumes. And in those subtle intervals, she begins to discern that learning in this tradition is inseparable from being.

This ethos of instruction, so central to Sheikh Akram's method, recalls the classical Islamic principle of *ta'lim wa ta'allum*: teaching and being taught as reciprocal spiritual acts. Power enters this sacred circle as one who learns through listening, the cultivation of receptivity. The madrasa, considered this way, becomes a sanctuary for *adab*, those forms of courtesy, comportment, and ethical elegance within the Muslim tradition that must accompany the transmission of sacred knowledge. Learning, here, is a refinement of the soul.

One of the book's deeper offerings is its meditation on sacred text as living tradition. The Qur'an, we come to see, breathes through commentary, legal reasoning, mystical reflection, and communal memory. Meaning is cultivated. Interpretation becomes a form of love, tethered to lineage. Power enters this ecology of meaning with care, aware that her questions, however earnest, must pass through a different register of time. As Sheikh Akram gently reminds her, 'you must be willing to become part of the tradition in order to understand it'.

This is also a work that confronts the responsibility of representation. Power writes across difference, yet she resists the temptation to explain Islam to outsiders or to resolve her inner contradictions. What she respectfully and humbly offers is a form of bearing witness. What moves her is the integrity of a tradition willing to be itself in her company.

In this way, *If the Oceans Were Ink* becomes a meditation on friendship as another form of faithfulness. There is genuine affection between Power and Sheikh Akram, and a polite distance that is honoured. And through that honouring, we glimpse a model for something deeper than tolerance, something like spiritual hospitality. 'Our friendship wasn't forged through agreement,' Power writes, 'but through trust, that we were trying to reach toward each other.' It is this effort, sincere and sustained, that gives the book its lasting radiance.

In an age when religion is often reduced to caricature or wielded as cultural ammunition, this book offers a different possibility: the slow, unglamorous work of learning across perceived fault lines. Power's encounters allow differences to breathe. Her approach challenges the prevailing rhythms of media discourse, which too often reward outrage in place of understanding. Seen this way, *If the Oceans Were Ink* underscores the need for new forms of journalism, ones rooted in modesty, patience, and deep listening.

Trust is earned. Power does not ignore the asymmetry of their positions; she, as a journalist with a platform, he, as a scholar shaped by a different moral economy. She recognises that understanding takes time and does not rush the process. Her book is a reminder of the importance of choosing to linger in the discomfort of unknowing, to let profound relationships remain incomplete, faithful to the mystery that true encounter preserves.

In their friendship is a model of what the Islamic tradition calls *husn al-zann*, thinking well of others, approaching differences with generous assumptions. This ethical principle, which Sheikh Akram embodies in his patient responses to Power's questions, beginning with the assumption that the other person's questions arise from sincere seeking. This stance transforms potential confrontation into collaborative inquiry. Power learns that to study Islam authentically, one must first cultivate the inner posture that makes learning possible: a willingness to be changed by what one encounters.

During these unfortunate days when our religious traditions are often mined for controversy or reduced to political shorthand, Power's account restores nuance. She brings to her reporting a form of spiritual journalism, one that withholds premature conclusions, honours ambiguity, and insists on ethical proximity. The stakes are more than academic. In an age of cultural suspicion, her approach offers a blueprint for how one might study without dishonouring, and witness without distortion. It is a reminder that the contemplative mode is a necessity if understanding is to outlast opinion.

The book also illuminates how Power's background as a journalist shaped by both Jewish and Quaker traditions uniquely prepares her for this encounter. The Quaker emphasis on silent waiting and inner light resonates with the contemplative dimensions of Islamic spirituality, while her Jewish heritage offers familiarity with textual interpretation and the sacred weight of commentary. These convergences are providential, suggesting that interfaith understanding often requires the deepening of one's own tradition. Paradoxically, Power discovers that her secular upbringing has cultivated in her the very qualities—doubt, wonder, ethical urgency—that make sacred study possible.

Through Power's careful narration emerges the subtle miracle of transformation that sustained attention enables. Her writing reflects the same virtues she admires in her teacher: steadiness, patience, and an aversion to spectacle. She listens more than she asserts. She waits where others might summarise. In doing so, she reveals that listening can be a sacred act.

In her exemplary book of spiritual journalism, Power has created a space where reverence and inquiry are permitted to coexist. Hers is a book about interfaith dialogue as a record of shared labour: two souls holding space for one another beneath the canopy of a tradition older than either. What renders this book timely and timeless is its emphasis on openness and healing. It illustrates that the most valuable conversations must begin with trust: with one person willing to ask, and another willing to answer with the fullness of their being.

DEMONISING MAMDANI

Khuda Bushq

One of the foundational myths of 1990s America was that the nation had not only defeated racism but attained that most coveted status of being 'post-race'. The two presidential elections where the Democratic Party sported one Barack Hussein Obama as their candidate and the eight years he was in power, so beautifully documented by the American journalist Ta-Nehisi Coates through his articles written for *The Atlantic* that eventually became the book *We Were Eight Years in Power*, served as a rude wake up call to all who had believed the US had reached that mountain top. What happened in New York City in November of 2025 with Zohran Mamdani only reaffirms the point for those who haven't been paying attention.

For those who follow American politics, an odd numbered year's election day is hardly worthy of headlines barring an exceptionally slow news day. Even though the first Tuesday of every November is the ritualistic 'election day', most Americans do not even cast a ballot on a so-called 'off year', even when it has become exceptionally easy to vote without even leaving the comfort of your own home. If you're lucky, your state's Governor is up for election, otherwise, unless you are a zealous citizen with an axe to grind with your mayor or city council, or a senior citizen with nothing better to do, the polling stations remain without queues. Few bother if it's not the big presidential race or a chance-to-send-a-message mid-term election. That was the norm. Of course, nothing much has been normal since the 2016 election of Donald J Trump to the highest office in the land, and even more so in his equally, if not more, divisive victory in 2024. Now, with a much more polarised political arena, every chance to vote is a chance to sway, a chance to protest, or a chance to send a message. Nowadays, even those odd, springtime elections for local members of the School Board have come to mean more than they have in history. Just one year of another Trump presidency has his opposition exploring every political avenue and grasping for every outlet of power. This of course makes sense when American democracy is in the greatest danger it has ever faced is the zeitgeist. However, the spirited opposition to Trumpism has garnered a backlash that along with destroying American democracy as we know it, threatens the very soul and humanity of the US and beyond.

> Equality Labs, *Tracing the Online Hate Against Zohran Mamdani*, November 2025. Available to download from equalitylabs.org

The epicentre of the most historically important, off-year election in American history was the mayoral race in New York City. It was a race that had next to zero bearing on the lives of 97.3 percent of Americans, yet it had the nation, and the world, watching with desperate anticipation. Despite it being one of the US's largest and most recognisable cities, I would wager that few could think of any of the other 110 people who have held the office of the Mayor of New York City. As one who has never lived in New York City, yet who is an avid watcher of *Saturday Night Live*, a comedy sketch show that often features famous faces of New York, I struggle to pull from memory one of its mayors. There is Michael

Bloomberg, but do I remember what he did as mayor or only that he has unfathomable wealth and a media empire behind his name? Of course, there is Rudolph Giuliani who took advantage of the 11 September 2001 attacks to earn himself the title of 'America's Mayor' but even more noteworthy is how far one can fall, and he certainly did, into the absurdity of Republican political incoherence and truth not being truth.

The mayoral election begins with a primary election, where each party choices their candidate for the real race to come. Common sense dictates that in New York City, someone more to the left, and someone with large sums of money, is likely to win any races in that city. Therefore, the democratic primary is likely to give a good idea of who will win the overall race. And the casual political junky would have taken one look at the context, seen Andrew Cuomo's name and thought it's probably in the bag, feelings be damned. It is New York after all. Sure, he left office in disgrace after being #MeTooed. Despite how uncomfortably common it has been for New York politicians to become embroiled in sexual scandals dating all the way back to the nation's founding, it has been a few years, and we are only human, right? But when the ricer man, who was also former governor of the state, Cuomo lost, those in opposition to Trump had a new face to embody the classic underdog trope. Zohran Mamdani, a Muslim of South

Asian descent, born in Uganda, raised in the Bronx, a product of interfaith and multiculturalism, a champion of the working class and diverse communities, stood three months from becoming the 111th Mayor of New York City. While the three-month walk may not be considered a long walk, it was certainly a difficult walk and not just for Mamdani.

Electoral politics is politics at its ugliest. Nothing is sacred and all's fair. And while the affairs of New York City may not have bearing on most Americans, one American in particular could not afford to sit by idly as his home turf was taken over by one of the Others, Donald Trump. As Trump exudes with every breath the greed, opulence, arrogance, and self-righteousness stereotypical of the New Yorker, in a way, Zohran Mamdani is the perfect foil to Trump and thus it makes sense that he became the poster boy of whatever was to go down in November 2025. Yet, it also made him a lightning rod for one of the greatest coordinated hate-campaigns the world has ever seen. While Trumpians might see the nuance of how Adolf Hitler loved his mother and Joseph Stalin loved his daughter, they could think of no redeeming qualities for Zohran Mamdani. While this should surprise no one, the scale of hatred levied against Mamdani speaks to the shifting terrain of democracy and politics in our digital, post-truth age fuelled by the flames of anger, hatred, fearmongering, conspiracy theories, and the perpetuation of ideological divisions.

This hate is given a critical analysis and necessary exposure through the latest report from Equality Labs. Born out of a group of Dalit feminists organising against the horrors of caste in 2015, Equality Labs has become a transnational organisation of South Asian feminist activists working to 'end caste apartheid, gender-based violence, Islamophobia, and religious intolerance'. Their report, *Tracing the Online Hate Against Zohran Mamdani*, may seem an odd subject for such a global organisation taking on global problems, but it does show that Mamdani's campaign represents a microcosm of a new degree of hatred and politics that has ramifications not only for New Yorkers or Americans, but for all democratic states and the future of social cohesion. Through this report, Equality Labs has also provided a new way to make hate demonstrable, an object of study and critique. They have pioneered new ways of analysing social media, an often treacherous, endless sea of data without end or beginning. Thanks to their work, we not only see where the Mamdani hatred came from, who was able to see it, but also tease out the impacts at the root of certain post-truth phenomena.

Equality Labs began by looking at the various categories by which Mamdani hatred was stirred, finding significant clustering around sentiments that were Islamophobic, Anti-Immigration, what they called 'red-baiting' – a slightly dated term for people with 'socialist' or 'communist' leanings in the shallow Cold-War sense of these ideologies. Then they also focussed on a few areas that clearly contradicted his views such as his pro-LGBT stance, which doesn't square with the Trumpian stereotype of the 'Islamist'. We may or may not be multitudes, but surely Mamdani is a two-dimensional cartoon stand-in for the embodiment of an evil, apocalyptic harbinger. What sets this report apart from other analyses of social media is that their use of a metric known as 'total reach', which helps appreciate the complexity of social media while allowing analysis of social media to not undermine that complexity or become reductive. One revelation that comes out of this analysis is the rich incoherence behind the logic of hate as the subject becomes ensnared in irreconcilable contradictions. Mamdani is a violent Islamist, jihadist, yet also a card-carrying communist. He must also be an immigrant who hates the Statue of Liberty, the ultimate symbol of the old myth that the US was supposed to be a land of opportunity for the oppressed masses from around the world. He must be a self-hating immigrant. Much of the hatred traced revolves around fears directed at New Yorkers – for instance that the election of a Muslim as the Mayor of New York is the coming full circle of the World Trade Center Attacks; or those of MAGA American voters – turning Mamdani into the worst of immigrant-terrorist-anti-American caricatures. The ignorance behind these posts, which are steeped in conspiracy theories, that are impossible to confirm, and straight up lies, makes for an intersection point of other forms of hatred. Equality Labs strikingly found that not only were there the overt attacks from Trumpian and Republicans within and across the United States, but also numerous attacks from international politicians and diplomats of the Far Right and Alt Right and even other White Supremacists and Hindu Supremacists, who see Mamdani as, at least by looks, the ultimate enemy of Hindutva and other international fascists projects. Mamdani is not only the enemy of Trump, but of all fragile and oppressed majority ideologies. Truly a global pariah.

Although Mamdani succeeded in being elected the first Muslim Mayor of New York City, this happy ending comes with an unsettling air. In the smear campaign of disinformation, conspiracy mongering, and unabashed hate against Mamdani, we see the danger post-truth and ignorance present to democracy and the future. Islamophobia finds its apotheosis in the Mamdani experience. Not only is racism alive and well in the US and beyond, so too is Islamophobia, now easier than ever to utilise with the aims of sowing hate and nurturing fear. The same party that, admittedly clumsily, attempted to not generalise all Muslims as the perpetrators behind religious extremism and the 11 September attacks two decades ago, now wields Islamophobia like the bicycle one never really forgets how to ride without batting an eye or giving it a second thought. And to underline the impact the tactics used by the Hate Mamdani camp was significant. Cuomo, who had to run as an independent on his own dime, still managed to rack up 41.6 percent of the vote. Mamdani won significantly but only received 50.4 percent of the vote.

Mamdani's campaign was a master class in campaigning. This should not be forgotten, and its significance should not be understated. From the design of his campaign imagery to his self-deprecating humour and clear and effective rhetoric, Zohran Mamdani's campaign has been hailed as the new textbook case for running an election in our contemporary world. His patience and care were top notch as he refused to be baited into speaking poorly about Israel directly, as getting anything remotely perceived as Antisemitic out of his mouth would be seriously detrimental in a city with a large and diverse Jewish community. He was also clever in pointing out the ridiculousness of the contradictions that arose out of the Mamdani hatred campaigns through effective use of social media to communicate to the people. While he perhaps had to dedicate too much time on such matters, he eloquently ridiculed those ignorant of the debates around hijab and other Muslim and South Asian cultural concepts. Perhaps thanks to Trump and his followers, now it is not such a bad thing to hold radically progressive ideas. Mamdani was able to throw his more progressive views back at his opponents through such quotes as 'they spent more money on his campaign than I would tax them' in reference to Cuomo and the billionaires behind the Political Action Committees (PACs) that raised obscene quantities to fund the campaign of hate. His doubling down on

New Yorker attitude and the city's diversity and tireless effort to keep his campaign local as his opponents tried to drag him into the mud of international issues, resulted in New York, indeed, not being for sale, as Mamdani declared in his final rally the weekend before the election.

Regardless of the difference it will have on all of our lives who reigns as mayor in New York, Zohran Mamdani's campaign and the uphill battle he will face with a hostile federal government and political climate exemplifies the issue ahead of us in our post-truth, polarised political future. We indeed have a long way to go in combating racist and other xenophobic sentiments, especially when Islamophobic rhetoric has been made norm by Trumpism. Equality Labs nicely lays out its recommendations for those campaigning, reporting on, and living in this frenzied climate, yet these recommendations ring of a profound simplicity. At the end of the day, effective communication is the name of the game. Of course, now, social media monitoring is a must, and further research into combating the touch and impact of ignorance and lies is always in need of expanding and refining. Yet, it is up to all of us to stand against the perpetuation of divisions within such minority communities as the South Asian communities of the US and beyond, and not allow stereotypes and vitriol to cloud our political opinions.

I must admit that in the days that followed Mamdani's victory I enjoyed the memes that followed. One showed a guy wearing a hat that read 'I Heart New York', holding in one hand the Holy Qur'an and in the other hand, *The Communist Manifesto*. The title of this meme was: Day 1 in Mamdani's New York. Another one had Mamdani superimposed in the likeness of Mao Zedong standing over the burrows of New York as Cuomo takes on the militarised likeness of Chiang Kai-shek over Staton Island, the only burrow he won in an allusion to the famous division between the Communists and Nationalists during China's twentieth-century civil war. They not only made me laugh, but tickled my penchant for a nice referential humour. While we can celebrate victories in many different ways, it is important that we work continuously to debunk and cast off the pernicious questions of contemporary democracy – such as government defined as 'rule by the people' – but who are 'the people'? And in those democracies equipped with diverse and multicultural populations – people – in our extreme times, the result appears to be one of two options. Either tyranny by the majority or tyranny by the minority – but his actually gives us one real option. Tyranny. This is the narrative of fear. It is up to us to deny this supposed destiny and seek out more inclusive and diverse approaches to the real problems before us as people and not let ignorant hate and blatant lies steer our duty to choose at the ballot box.

ET CETERA

LAST WORD: ON HALAL INVESTING *by M Yaqub Mirza*
OBITUARY: ROBERT IRWIN *by Barnaby Rogerson*
THE LIST: TEN OUTLETS TO CHECK OUT (DAILY)
CITATIONS
CONTRIBUTORS

LAST WORD

ON HALAL INVESTING

M. Yaqub Mirza

When I first arrived in America in 1970, the question of how to build financial security while staying true to Islamic principles seemed nearly impossible to answer. Like many Muslim immigrants, I found myself navigating an unfamiliar financial landscape that was not designed with Islamic values in mind. How could we save for marriage, our children's education, plan for retirement, help others, or purchase a home without compromising our beliefs?

This journey—finding the delicate balance between worldly success and spiritual integrity—has shaped my personal life and professional path for nearly five decades. I've seen firsthand how the seeds planted by early pioneers in Islamic finance have blossomed into viable options for families like yours and mine. What began as a deeply personal quest has evolved into something more significant: a movement transforming how Muslims and people of all faiths think about the relationship between their values and finances.

I share these reflections with you not as abstract theory but as lived experience—as someone who has wrestled with these questions alongside my family at our dinner table. I hope that by sharing what I've learned, your path will be easier than mine and perhaps inspire you to see your financial decisions as meaningful expressions of your faith.

The beauty of Islamic teachings about wealth lies in their profound balance. Unlike some spiritual traditions that view material prosperity with suspicion, our faith recognises wealth as a blessing from Allah – but one that comes with significant responsibility. The Prophet Muhammad was a successful businessman before receiving divine revelation, and he continued to promote ethical commerce throughout his life.

When we align our financial choices with our spiritual values, something remarkable happens – our investing becomes an act of worship, our wealth becomes a vehicle for good, and the artificial boundary between 'worldly' and 'spiritual' concerns begins to dissolve. This is the essence of halal investing: recognizing that our financial decisions are inherently spiritual. As the Qur'an reminds us: 'And when the prayer has been concluded, disperse within the land and seek from the bounty of Allah' (62:10). This beautiful verse captures the Islamic understanding that properly conducted business and investment are not distractions from spiritual life but extensions of it.

In my conversations with Muslim families all over the world, I have found that many Muslims intuitively understand these principles but struggle with their practical application. How do we translate these timeless values into today's complex financial reality? Rather than seeing Islamic financial guidelines as restrictions, I've come to view them as a compass – pointing us toward investments that are not only permissible but beneficial, not just for ourselves but for society as a whole. These principles aren't arbitrary rules but wisdom that protects us and others from harm.

The most distinctive aspect of Islamic finance is the prohibition of *riba* (interest). The Qur'an clearly states: 'Allah has permitted trade and forbidden *riba*' (2:275). While this immediately rules out conventional bonds and interest-bearing accounts, it helps to focus on what this principle encourages rather than what it forbids. By steering us away from interest, our faith guides us toward investments with real-world impact – businesses creating actual products and services, properties providing needed housing, or ventures solving genuine problems. When our investments are tied to actual economic activity rather than abstract financial engineering, we participate more directly in building the world around us.

I remember sitting with a group of young Muslim professionals who felt discouraged by what they could not invest in. When we shifted the conversation to what they could support with their investment dollars – innovative technologies, healthcare advances, sustainable infrastructure – their perspectives transformed completely. They began to see halal investing not as a limitation but as an opportunity to direct capital toward what matters most.

Islamic finance also avoids excessive uncertainty (*gharar*) or ambiguity in transactions. Contracts should specify what is being exchanged, in what quantity, and when the exchange will occur. This principle naturally steers us away from highly speculative investments, where outcomes depend primarily on chance rather than productive activity. In today's financial markets, this principle helps us avoid derivatives with excessive leverage, many forms of speculation, and financial products so complex that their risks cannot be reasonably assessed. There is profound wisdom here – focusing our resources on ventures we can reasonably understand and evaluate.

Our faith asks us to avoid investments in businesses primarily engaged in activities considered harmful – alcohol, gambling, conventional interest-based financial services, adult entertainment, tobacco, and weapons designed mainly to harm rather than protect. Some may see these screens as limitations, but I've always viewed them as aligning our financial decisions with our broader values. After all, would any of us knowingly encourage our children or loved ones to consume these products? If we wouldn't want them in our homes, why would we want them in our investment portfolios? By directing our capital elsewhere, we help nurture industries and innovations that contribute positively to society.

Islamic finance emphasises sharing risks and rewards rather than guaranteed returns regardless of outcomes. This principle has profound implications, pushing us toward partnership models, profit-sharing arrangements (*musharakah* or *mudarabah*), buy-sell agreements (*murabahah*), and lease-to-own (*ijara*) rather than pure debt. I have noticed that this focus on shared outcomes frequently fosters healthier relationships between capital providers and entrepreneurs. When investors succeed only if the underlying business thrives, interests naturally align toward sustainable, long-term growth, rather than short-term value extraction.

In today's interconnected economy, even companies whose primary business is permissible might derive some portion of their income from non-compliant activities. Islamic scholars have developed the concept of 'purification' – calculating the proportion of returns from non-compliant sources and donating it to charity. This practice acknowledges the practical realities of modern investing while maintaining our commitment to ensuring that what we ultimately benefit from is halal. It's another example of how Islamic financial principles balance idealism with pragmatism, providing workable solutions rather than impossible standards.

My own family's path to halal investing began with simple steps. Like many of you, we started by focusing on the most accessible options – avoiding interest-bearing accounts and being mindful about which companies we owned through stocks. The availability of specialised Shari'ah-compliant funds was almost non-existent when we began. Still, even these modest steps helped us feel that our financial choices were becoming more aligned with our values.

I encourage families beginning this journey today to be gentle with themselves. Perfect alignment might not be immediately possible, but each step brings you closer. Start where you are, with what you have, and know that even minor adjustments matter. Our family's most essential first step was beginning the conversation – talking openly about how our faith should shape our financial decisions. These discussions, sometimes around the dinner table, helped us clarify priorities and determine where to make changes.

The landscape for Muslim investors has transformed dramatically since those early days. If you're beginning to explore halal investing, you'll find more options than ever before. Let me guide you through a progressive approach to building your halal investment portfolio—from simple starting points to more advanced strategies.

STEP 1. Start with Shari'ah-compliant mutual funds and ETFs (Exchange-Traded Funds). They offer most families the most straightforward starting point. These professionally managed portfolios provide instant diversification across many companies, all screened to ensure alignment with Islamic principles. I've been a founder, trustee, and chairman of Amana Mutual Funds Trust since its early days, watching it grow from pioneering to managing billions in assets. Similar options now include ETFs like the SP Funds S&P 500 Sharia Industry Exclusions ETF (SPUS) and the Wahed FTSE USA Shariah ETF (HLAL) and mutual funds Azzad Ethical Fund, and HSBC Islamic Global Equity Index Fund. What matters most isn't which specific fund you choose but that you begin the journey. Each fund has its approach and personality – some focus on income generation through dividends, others on growth companies, and others on international markets. Take time to understand these differences and how they align with your family's needs and timeline.

As you explore different funds, you will notice they may use slightly different approaches to determine Shari'ah compliance. Most apply business activity screens (excluding prohibited industries) and financial ratio screens that examine a company's debt levels, interest income, and cash positions. Standard financial ratio screens include:

1. Debt ratio: Total interest-bearing debt divided by market capitalization must be less than 33 percent.
2. Cash and interest-bearing securities ratio: Cash plus interest-bearing securities divided by market capitalisation must be less than 33 percent.
3. Accounts receivable ratio: Accounts receivable divided by market capitalisation must be less than 33 percent.
4. Impure income ratio: Non-permissible income divided by total revenue must be less than 5 percent.

These screening methodologies help ensure that even when investing in publicly traded companies, your investments remain predominantly aligned with Islamic principles. Different scholarly interpretations may result in slight variations across funds, but the core principles remain consistent.

STEP 2. Real estate has traditionally been a cornerstone for many Muslim investors. It offers the tangible security of physical property and the potential for income and value appreciation. When properly structured, real estate investments can fully comply with Shari'ah principles without relying on conventional mortgages. Many families begin with their homes, using Islamic home financing through providers, in the US, like Guidance Residential, UIF, or Ijara CDC. Others gradually expand to rental properties or real estate investment partnerships with family members or friends. I particularly appreciate how real estate investing connects financial activity to community well-being. When you provide quality housing or commercial space, your investment benefits others while generating returns for your family – a beautiful alignment of interests.

Real estate investments can take several forms. Direct ownership: purchasing properties outright with available capital. Partnerships: pooling resources with family members or friends to acquire properties together. REITs: Some regions offer Shari'ah-compliant Real Estate Investment Trusts, though these require careful evaluation of their debt structures. Private equity real estate funds: specialised investment vehicles focused on property acquisition and management according to Islamic principles. Each approach has advantages and considerations regarding management responsibilities, liquidity, and potential returns. The right choice depends on your circumstances, knowledge, and comfort with direct property management.

But we need to be careful. Fluctuating market conditions warrant extreme caution for real estate investors. The real estate cycles can be precarious, with elevated prices in many markets, rising interest rates affecting affordability, and uncertain economic indicators. Even Shari'ah-compliant investments are not immune to market downturns. Before committing capital to real estate ventures, thoroughly analyse local market fundamentals, rental demand, and potential economic headwinds. Consider maintaining higher cash reserves than usual, focusing on properties with strong cash flow rather than speculative appreciation, and scaling back investment plans until market stability improves. Remember that patience is not just virtuous but often financially rewarding when navigating volatile market conditions.

STEP 3. As your knowledge grows, consider building your collection of individual stocks that meet Shari'ah requirements. This approach requires more time and attention but offers greater control and potential tax advantages. Several resources, including IdealRatings, Zoya, Saturna Brokerage, and various Islamic market indices, can help identify compliant companies. What I find most beautiful about this approach is how it transforms the act of researching investments—you begin to look beyond just financial metrics to consider how a company treats its employees, impacts communities, and contributes to society. Parents who take this approach often tell me it creates wonderful teaching moments with their children. Researching companies together becomes an opportunity to discuss financial concepts and ethical considerations, helping young people develop a more holistic understanding of economics. For those building their portfolios, I recommend a disciplined strategy, investing a fixed amount regularly regardless of market conditions. This approach naturally leads to purchasing more shares when prices are lower and fewer when prices are higher, potentially lowering your average cost over time while removing emotion from the investment process.

STEP 4. For investors seeking income-generating alternatives to conventional bonds, sukuk (commonly referred to as 'Islamic bonds') provides an interesting option. Unlike traditional bonds, which represent interest-bearing debt, sukuk represents ownership shares in tangible assets, projects, services, or ventures. The global sukuk market has grown substantially recently, with issuances from Muslim-majority countries and Western corporations and governments. For retail investors in Western markets, access to sukuk investments has historically been limited, but this is gradually changing as financial institutions develop more accessible products. While typically less volatile than stocks, sukuk still carries risks that should be understood, including credit risk, liquidity risk, and rate-of-return risk. As with any investment, diversification, and due diligence remain essential.

STEP 5. For those with entrepreneurial inclinations, starting or investing in small businesses offers the purest expression of Islamic financial principles. Partnership structures like musharakah naturally align with how small businesses typically operate, sharing risks and rewards among participants. I've witnessed impressive instances of Muslim families collaborating to support relatives or community members in launching businesses, generating opportunities while reinforcing community ties. These arrangements, frequently formalised through straightforward agreements, can offer financial returns and the deep fulfilment of aiding others in attaining independence. Owning a business through a Limited Liability Company (LLC) or investing in one offers unique tax benefits and wealth-building opportunities that passive investments typically lack. For those equipped with the right knowledge or skills, direct investment in a business can significantly enhance a diversified wealth-building strategy.

Few financial decisions carry as much emotional and practical weight as purchasing a home. For Muslim families in Western countries, this decision has long presented particular challenges, given the prohibition of interest in Islamic finance. I still remember many families' creative approaches in earlier decades – saving for years to purchase outright, borrowing interest-free from family members, or creating informal partnerships where one or several parties provided capital and the other gradually bought ownership shares over time.

Today, structured Islamic home financing options make this journey more accessible. These typically follow one of several models.

Diminishing Musharakah (Declining Partnership). In this model, the financial institution and the homebuyer jointly purchase the property. The buyer makes payments that serve two purposes: (1) rent for the portion owned by the financial institution and (2) purchase additional ownership shares over time. As the buyer's ownership share increases, the rent portion decreases proportionally until the buyer owns 100 per cent of the property. This approach explicitly reflects the reality of shared ownership gradually transitioning to full ownership, with the payment structure adjusted as ownership percentages change.

Ijarah wa Iqtina (Lease-to-Own). Under this arrangement, the financial institution purchases and leases the property to the buyer for a specified period. The lease payments include rent and a contribution toward the purchase price; at the end of the lease term, with the last payment, the ownership transfers to the buyer. The structure is transparent about the leasing relationship during the payment period, with a clear path to eventual ownership.

Murabaha (Cost-Plus Financing). In a Murabaha arrangement, the financial institution buys the property at market price and promptly resells it to the buyer at a higher price, to be paid in instalments. This structure frontloads the financial institution's profit received over time.

What matters most isn't the specific structure but that the arrangement respects the letter and spirit of Islamic principles while making homeownership accessible. Each family must make their own decision about which approach best fits their circumstances and understanding of Shari'ah requirements.

Our most important investment is preparing our children to navigate financial decisions with wisdom and faith. In my family, involving children in age-appropriate financial discussions helped them develop healthy relationships with money from an early age. Consider creating opportunities to discuss financial concepts within a faith framework. When giving children allowances, encourage them to divide their money between immediate spending, saving for future goals, and charitable giving (*sadaqah*). As they grow older, involve them in family discussions about major financial decisions, explaining how Islamic principles guide these choices. Consider opening custodial investment accounts for teenagers. This way, they can experience firsthand how investments grow over time while learning about Shari'ah screening. Share stories of the business ethics of the Prophet and how he approached commercial transactions honestly and fairly. These conversations lay the groundwork for financial literacy infused with ethical awareness – a precious gift in today's complex world.

The landscape of halal investing continues to evolve in exciting ways. Several noteworthy trends are expanding opportunities for faith-conscious investors. The rise of financial technology, for example, has dramatically democratised access to halal investment options. Mobile apps and digital platforms now allow Muslims to invest in Shari'ah-compliant options more efficiently than ever. Companies like Wahed Invest, Azzad Investments, and Sarwa have leveraged technology to lower barriers to entry, bringing Halal investing to younger and less affluent Muslims who might previously have found such options inaccessible. These platforms typically offer automatic Zakat calculation, purification tracking, and simplified portfolio management tailored to Muslim investors' needs. The democratisation of Islamic finance represents one of the most significant developments in recent decades.

One of the most encouraging developments is the increasing convergence between Islamic finance and other ethical finance movements, such as Environmental, Social, and Governance (ESG) and socially responsible investing (SRI). Although these approaches arise from different philosophical traditions, they share numerous practical concerns, including: avoidance of harmful industries; emphasis on positive social impact; concern for environmental sustainability; and focus on good governance and ethical business practices. This convergence has created opportunities for collaboration and cross-pollination of ideas, expanding the potential market for halal investments beyond the Muslim community. Funds that combine Islamic screening with ESG considerations are increasingly common, appealing to a broader spectrum of ethically conscious investors.

Efforts toward greater standardisation of Shari'ah screening methodologies and contractual structures are gaining momentum. This could reduce confusion and increase confidence among investors. Organisations like the Accounting and Auditing Organisation for Islamic Financial Institutions (AAOIFI) and the Islamic Financial Services Board (IFSB) continue to develop and refine industry standards. These standardization efforts help create greater clarity for providers and consumers of Islamic financial services, making it easier for families to understand and compare different options.

The journey of faith-aligned investing is not intended to be taken alone. Engaging with others on similar paths offers both practical insights and spiritual support. Saturna Capital provides valuable podcasts on a range of topics related to halal investing. You might also consider joining or forming an investment circle with friends or community members who share your values, or attending, or even organising, workshops at your local mosque or Islamic centre on financial planning. Participating in online forums where Muslims discuss financial questions can also be worthwhile. And, I would argue, that seeking out financial advisors knowledgeable about both conventional financial planning and Islamic principles is essential nowadays. My conversations with scholars, financial professionals, and ordinary families grappling with these questions have enormously enriched my understanding. Each perspective adds another dimension to our collective wisdom.

Despite significant progress, halal investing still presents challenges that require patience and wisdom to navigate. While the range of halal investment options has expanded dramatically, it remains more limited than the conventional universe of investment products. This limitation is particularly noticeable in asset classes like fixed income, where Shari'ah-compliant alternatives to traditional bonds remain relatively scarce in Western markets. The exclusion of specific sectors (mainly conventional financial services, which constitute a significant portion of major indices) can create diversification challenges for halal portfolios. Careful asset allocation becomes especially important to mitigate these potential concentration risks. Moreover, differences in interpretation among Islamic scholars regarding specific financial structures or screening criteria can create uncertainty for investors. While standardisation efforts progress, investors should understand the particular scholarly perspectives underlying their chosen investment vehicles. These challenges are real, but they need not be discouraging. Each represents an opportunity for further growth and innovation in Islamic finance. As more Muslims seek alignment between their finances and faith, the market will continue responding with expanded options and solutions.

So, wherever you find yourself on this journey, I encourage you to take the next step forward. Whether you are just beginning to explore halal investing or looking to deepen your existing practice, each thoughtful decision brings your financial life into greater alignment with your spiritual values. Start where you are. Learn continuously. Adjust gradually. And take comfort in knowing that your sincere intention to honour divine guidance and family needs is an act of worship.

OBITUARY

ROBERT IRWIN

Barnaby Rogerson

Photo: Rehan Jamil

Robert Irwin was my role model of a free scholar and a creative writer. There was also something timeless about the way he lived his life. I could so easily imagine him slipping into the streets of Abbasid Baghdad, or the Athens of Demosthenes, or Mameluke Cairo – just as easily as he moved around his twentieth century London homeland.

Robert mostly wrote at home, but like the pinball machines that he loved to play, there were a number of fixed points in London which he bounced off from, and where you might come across him. He worked for decades as the Middle East editor at the *TLS* (The Times Literary Supplement) both commissioning reviews and writing them himself. I remember his early advice which was to react passionately about a book one-way or the other. Your task was to engage with, not to solemnly salute this new arrival with a precis of its contents. The stream of books to the TLS kept him in touch with every scholarly feud, which he would observe with amused detachment at book launches, leaning against the bookshelves glass in hand, which made him a familiar face at such London bookshops as Hatchards, Daunts, and Waterstones.

He was also a regular face at any interesting lectures in the Royal Asiatic Society or School of African and Oriental Studies (SOAS), and liked to use the desks in the London Library or the London College of Printing, or within the rarefied world of the Warburg Institute and Alastair Hamilton's once secretive Arcadian library. But throughout his academic life, there was an invisible moat of brimstone, that divided any gathering of Middle Eastern academics into two adversarial camps. This division originated with Edward Said's *Orientalism* (published in 1978) which looked at how the western intellectual tradition had worked to diminish the societies it had studied, and in the process weaken and subordinate them. It is a very interesting thesis, albeit almost buried in academic jargon, and was a liberating concept that kick-started post-colonial studies. But it had the unfortunate bi-product of nationalising scholarship, of unintentionally upholding the ethnic right to record your own history, and casting suspicion on the work of outsiders. Robert knew just how much work yet needed to be done (most especially in the editing and transcription of medieval manuscripts, as well as their translation and publication) and was infuriated by how Orientalism was used to negate and delay and dismiss.

There was, I believe, another, almost personal agenda behind Edward Said's book. Edward Said was Palestinian by blood but in every other way was a highly cultured, and privileged Levantine intellectual who had been educated in an Egyptian boarding school directly modelled on the English system. But *Orientalism* was a weapon which he forged to assist his Palestinian homeland resist the erosion of their identity by the incredible energy of the many pro-Zionist western intellectuals, exemplified by Bernard Lewis. Robert Irwin had studied under Lewis at SOAS, alongside such brilliant writers as John Wansbrough, Michael Cook, and Patricia Crone whose work (sometimes collectively known as the Revisionists) seemed to be dismantling the foundations of Islamic culture. It was not true of course, but it added further fuel to the fire of factionalism.

Just when things were calming down a little between the two rival camps of scholars, Robert published (in 2006), *For Lust of Knowing: The Orientalists and Their Enemies* – an accurate and relentless assault on Edward Said's many errors of fact, as well as an explanation of how the vast range of European scholarship stood outside the narrow imperialist machinations of France and Britain. Robert's book might have punctured hundreds of holes into Edward Said's thesis but the Neocon-supported invasion of Iraq in 2003 by the US (publicly acclaimed by the ninety-year-old Bernard Lewis) also showed the world how much we needed Edward Said. In my review, I likened *For Lust of Knowing* to a petrol bomb casually lobbed into the dying embers of a communal bonfire.

Robert was also an active member of the editorial board of the *Critical Muslim*. He never failed to turn up to editorial board meetings, even when he was quite seriously ill, always brimming with ideas. He wanted to work on an issue on 'Fake Sheikhs'. But unfortunately, it did not materialise during his rather busy life. He was also one of the three co-founders and directors of Dedalus Books. This publishing house, founded in 1983 had literary ambition, but was not afraid to also champion the Bizarre, Grotesque, Surreal, and Gothic. I also ran a small publishing company, so we would try to keep ourselves cheerful in the great book fairs dominated by four giant international corporations.

He haunted antiquarian bookshops (enjoying the quixotic search for a rare work of French scholarship, by Claude Cahen on northern Syria). Typically for a man so fascinated by the bizarre coincidences, when he at last found himself a copy, he also found out from the crossed out institutional label, that it was the same one he had read in the medieval department library of St Andrews all those years ago! He also adored the October Gallery, which was at one and the same time a temple to outsider art, but also an open house to dance, storytelling, scientific self-sufficiency, and the shared strands of world mythology.

For many years, he co-hosted a gathering of creative writers in the upstairs room of the Blue Post pub in Fitzrovia, so that we could steal each other's plots and swap gossip about publishers and agents. Poets were theoretically banned, but in practice there was no membership policy behind this fascinating gallery of faces and sharply held opinions, all buying their own drinks. He also chaired a group which had been formed out of the creative courses run by Morley College – an amazingly progressive and active late nineteenth century London institution founded to make all forms of education open to workers.

As an academic, Robert had a lifelong passion for the late medieval world of the central Middle East. The Mameluke Sultanate, ruling from the two great cities of Damascus and Cairo, was at the heart of his historical area of interest, which naturally embraced the historian Ibn Khaldoun and the street story-telling tradition embodied within the tales of the *Thousand and One Nights*. He wrote histories, biographies, commentaries, and undertook original translations that expanded our knowledge of this fascinating era. On behalf of the interested, general reader, ignorant of both Arabic, Persian, and Turkish, I can attest that he always succeeded in making things accessible without ever dumbing down.

The Arabian Nights: A Companion (1994) was the first book of his that I read and remains one of my favourites, as he takes his scholarship onto the road, trying to track down the last of the public storytellers. It was followed by a fluent, illustrated survey of *Islamic Art* (1997) and then by *Night Horses and the Desert*, an inspiring anthology of classical Arabic literature (1999), well published by Penguin. His *The Alhambra* (2004) was succeeded by, *Mamluks and Crusaders* (2010) and *Ibn Khaldoun: an Intellectual Biography* (2018). There was also a book on camels published by Reaktion, in their series on literary animals. These books were in fact just surface smoke for the great work on Mameluke history, sourced from original documents, which he had first started upon as a callow student, but had never completed, either as a thesis or a doctorate, let alone a finished book. Somehow it is entirely appropriate that this hefty academic volume, larded with footnotes and bibliography was completed before Robert died, and will be published by the Princeton University Press some fifty years after it was began and when he is dead.

I have listened to Robert speak at a number of learned societies and academic conferences, and began to realise that although he was relaxed and wacky and amused in conversation, this ease disappeared in direct relationship to the size of his audience. I began to notice that he needed to grip the lectern to keep his hands from shaking, and sometimes beads of sweat would appear on his forehead by the time he had finished his paper. And although I have always found him inspiring as a writer he was not a gifted lecturer, preferring (or perhaps needing) to read out from a typescript, with little eye to eye engagement with his listeners. I never asked him about this, but talking in public clearly looked an ordeal, and probably helped necessitate his choice to become a freelance writer rather than remain a university lecturer. He loathed and would not easily speak about his schooldays; and I imagined that this nervous twitch might have been acquired at his English boarding schools. His younger brother found the experience of their schools so depressing that he came close to taking his life. He showed me the scars on his wrist, many decades after he had inflicted them on himself. He was fortunately saved by working in the theatre and the love of a good woman, and is now a remarkably busy and happy and honest and open man.

Robert and his younger brother, Ted, were first educated at Dane Court, in Surrey, a brand-new day school that had branched off from a traditional preparatory boarding school. Robert was one of the first batch of a dozen schoolboys taught by the headmaster Robin Pooley. He was a major and positive influence on both boys. 'Mr Robin' would arrive in class waving a copy of the *Manchester Guardian* declaring it to be the only newspaper worth reading. He force-fed the children under his care with literature (especially Conrad) and regaled them with tales of his life in the wartime Merchant Navy which included being torpedoed off West Africa and surviving on a lifeboat. Ted Irwin wrote, 'this school was a joyous experience unlike the Gulag-on-the-Downs that was to follow'.

Aged thirteen they were packed to the English boarding school of Epsom College. Epsom was then locked into the traditional spartan attitudes of elite education in England which circled around excellence at sport or the classics, and very minimal standards of privacy or comfort. It had been founded as a school for the medical profession, in much the same way that Marlborough was associated with the Church of England. He made a few lifelong friends there, such as the maverick genius art-historian Peter Fuller (born in Damascus) as well as Robert Chenciner, an orphan from Canada who would become an expert on Daghestan culture in the Caucasus. Robert was hopeless at Maths, but exceptionally talented in the humanities. He read modern history at Merton College, then worked on a thesis on Mameluke documentation of the Crusades at SOAS under the supervision of Bernard Lewis. It was at this period that he met his wife, Helen, who was studying Russian in the nearby School of Slavonic Studies. Although he never actually finished his thesis, he was talent spotted for the medieval history department of St Andrews by Professor Lionel Butler to replace Jonathan Riley-Smith, who taught the Crusades (but from western historical documents). It would enrich the course to strengthen the Arabic perspective. By chance, Hugh Kennedy had also been recruited as an Arabic scholar to the same department, but rather than become rivals they became lifelong friends. Robert spent five years teaching in St Andrews, living in three different flats on the grand medieval avenue of South Street. In their third year, Helen gave birth to their daughter, but two more Scottish winters (and the remorseless sound of dripping taps in a cold flat) were enough, especially as her old employers in London had generously given Helen the opportunity to return.

Robert was given the task of finding a house in London. All their friends laughed at their impossible list of requirements: for they had no inherited money but wanted a Georgian terraced house of old London-stock yellow brick, within walking distance of the House of Parliament and it had to have its own garden and space to house a library. Robert picked up one of those free-trade newspapers made up entirely of classified ads (there was a famous one called *Exchange and Mart*) in Waterloo station. It was the sole issue published, but by the end of that day Robert had found an affordable home (albeit on a busy road).

If you have read any of Robert's novels, you will not be surprised by the bizarre confluence of neighbours that he had chanced upon his lifelong home. Nearby was the British Interplanetary Society, the remnants of Vauxhall Gardens (a licensed place of entertainment and debauch throughout the eighteenth century), a Catholic mission (St Anne's) to minister to the slums of south London, the headquarters of Mi6 and the Royal Vauxhall Tavern, one of London's oldest and loudest drag bars. On the other side of the Thames stood Tate Britain (England's leading art gallery) built over the vaults of a vast penitentiary – shaped like a vast, six petalled geometric flower, from where convicts were shipped off to Australia.

His wife now took over as the bread winner. Robert became a writer in residence at home, and picked up their daughter from school in the afternoon. Helen had read History at King's College, and had toyed with also becoming an academic (albeit in modern Russian history) but had also, in a belts and braces manner, filled out an application to join the civil service. It transpired that she was what they were looking for, proven in her first placement among the bewigged clerks who ran Parliament in the Palace of Westminster.

Robert's first (and his most successful) novel was *The Arabian Nightmare (1983)*. This novel was also embedded in this world he knew so well through his academic studies. Robert created a naive young Western traveller, Balian of Norwich (both a Christian pilgrim and a French spy) who gets caught up, and drawn into a world full of charismatic sheikhs within Mameluke Cairo, followed closely by the reader who gets drawn into a labyrinth of stories within the story. It did not do well, until AnneMarie Schimmel, the brilliant German Oriental scholar, fell in love with it, translated it and got it published in Germany. It was very well received in Europe (twenty different translations would be made) which helped it get the attention it deserved in England, and would eventually be published by Penguin. But this was the first and last cross-over between his non-fiction and his fictional identities.

Robert's second published novel was *The Limits of Vision*. This was the highly imagined world of an obsessive housewife in South London, framed by her paranoia and aggressive neighbours expanded by her imagined allies amongst the great scientists. It must have been at least partly fed by his own experience of being a male house husband, and failing to bond with the mothers as the lone dad at the one o'clock club. *The Mysteries of Algiers* (1988) is an extraordinarily page-turning and violent chronicle of a French double agent, working for revolution within the Algerian War for Independence. Of all his works this would be the easiest to turn into a film. *Exquisite Corpse (*1995) manages to be both mockingly absurd, funny, and sinister as we follow the painter Caspar immersing himself into the pre-war Surrealist quarters of London, Paris, and Munich leaching into cult sex and dark neo-Nazi mythology. *Prayer Cushions of the Flesh* is a novella set in seventeenth century Istanbul, that playfully romps around the language and conventions of classic erotica, without of course getting a single historical detail wrong. It was made into a very low budget puppet film.

Satan Wants Me (1999) is a farcical but accurate portrait of the sixties; with its drugs and sexual liberation, its manipulative but mean hippies, proto-paganism, and failed academics. Arguably it is part of a trilogy that maps out some of Robert's own experience. *Wonders Will Never Cease* (2016) is a fabulous compilation of gangster violence with a detective-like quest that immerses the reader in Arthurian mythology set amongst one of the bloodiest episodes of the Wars of the Roses, so that we explore the language and belief systems of England in the Mameluke period. There is a bit part for a nasty sidekick called Barnaby. *My Life is like a Fairy Tale* (2019) is bewilderingly different, for it takes the reader on a dance through the Nazi film industry trailing behind the fabulous self-obsession, and criminal naivety of a film star. Robert claimed that this anti-hero was the closest that he came to creating a fictional self-portrait. This claim may have been based on his technical knowledge behind the dance scenes, for *The Runes Have Been Cast* comes much closer to home with its imagined world of academics from the Universities of St Andrews and Oxford immersed in Tolkien-like medievalism and M R James ghost stories. *Tom's Version* continues to play around with the inverted imagination of the modern male mind; tied in with systems, collectors, control, and deviant sexuality to arguably conclude the trilogy begun with *Satan Wants Me.*

And Robert died while still writing. *The Madman's Guide to Stamp Collecting* was already in the hands of Pushkin Press and ready to be printed. *Rapture of the Deep* was nearly ready to be sent to the publishers with yet another work three-quarters written (which might be finished by a friend).

I was always amazed and impressed by his astonishing diversity, both of period, language, character, and theme. Especially when you compare his work to other contemporary novelists, who in mood and theme and drawn characters seem drawn to just one invented world. But now I look back, I can see that there are certain things common to many of Robert's novels. He respected the craft of the storyteller, so there is some sharp-paced plotting and lots of salacious details which allow for a galloping narrative. The central character tends to be an innocent plunged into a dark, complex, malevolent world, but we also begin to wonder as we progress into an Irwin book, how much is true, and how much is fearful imagination or delusional fantasy. A second, slower reading, will unearth an extraordinary playful delight in his accumulated literary sources, and the themes and attitudes of each chosen period displayed for our amusement, a sort of library echo box of the vast amount of reading that went into each apparently fictional work. I have been allowed to wander around his house, where there were six rooms filled with books (the shelves hugging the corners) while also serving as bedrooms, studies and sitting rooms. But within these rooms you could recognise great concentrations of books that had eventually been boiled down into a novel.

I remember him explaining the process at a mischievous speech he gave at a book launch one evening amongst the bookshelves of John Sandoe (a beloved Tardis of literature surviving against all the odds in the centre of fashionable Chelsea). He claimed that he never advance planned a book, but slowly became aware of one becoming incubated as he realised that he was becoming ever more obsessive, and immersed and particular in his reading. Once he had dug a historical hole for himself, he knew he could best escape by adding something new, spinning like a spider, a fictional ladder to escape his own web.

Robert had a trusted relationship with his lifelong literary agent, Juri Gabriel as well as Eric Lane, with whom he set up Dedalus Press, and who published most of his fiction. Robert first met Juri by attending his creative writing course at Morley college when they came back to London from teaching at St Andrews. The story I was told, which I only partly believe, is that Robert wanted to learn to become a bookbinder, but that course was full up, but there was space on the creative writing course.

I am a publisher, so have met more than my fair share of live writers. Robert was exceptional in not being interested in expensive restaurants, fashionable clothes, front row seats (be it on the aeroplane or the concert hall), boutique hotels or becoming a member of one of London's establishment Clubs. He owned no car, no boat, no country cottage and never even bothered to learn how to drive. He adored books, but the other objects that decorated his home, were not designed to enhance his status as an aesthete or to demonstrate his clever eye. The wooden sculpture of a writer carved in Sierre Leone was a gift, the Venetian carnival mask that sat above the fireplace in the upstairs study (had been bought in a street market) and the Qur'an stand came from a rough and ready auction house in St Andrews.

Robert was interested in a life of learning, in reading, listening, dreaming, and expanding the already vast internal theatre of his knowledge. He was never in any danger of becoming a curmudgeonly bachelor scholar alone in his tower, or embedded in the well-salaried quad of an institute. He was a family man, a devoted husband and father and a climbed all-over grandfather. He could juggle, play with cards, and conjure up some magic. He lived in a terraced house on a very busy London street, where the bus stop was visible from his front door. He could be (and often delighted) in being controversial in print, but was entirely affable in the conduct of his personal life, going out of his way to encourage and counsel young writers and to quietly open doors, or recommend new lines of reading. Although he must qualify, on at least half a dozen categories, for his seat amongst the intellectual elite of this kingdom, there was something refreshingly, innately democratic about his soul.

One of his favourite activities, which he wrote of as being almost as sublime as sex, was roller-blading through the parks and streets of London. By some happy, neighbourly coincidence, he and his close friend Robert Chenciner (who was, like myself, the father of two daughters) would take my youngest daughter off for long roller-blading sessions on a Sunday morning, when all the parks in the centre of London (such as St James's and Green Park) are closed to traffic and become a roller blader's safe paradise. But in his younger days, Robert (the revered intellectual with an international scholarly reputation) would be part of that fast-moving column of highly animated life – the LFNS (the London Friday Night Skate) which used to start off at 8pm from Hyde Park corner.

I don't know what it is like now, but on a summer evening, this column of skaters was a wonderful caravan of energy. A totally safe and free urban happening, often moving in time to some hidden rhythm, working to the beat of music on their headphones. Part Carnival-Part Sports Club, they made up their own rules. Fit outriders, would act as volunteer marshals, briefly stopping motorised traffic with no more than an outstretched arm, so that hundreds, if not a thousand skaters (often dressed in bright, fluorescent colours) would sweep through the narrow streets of central London.

Robert also loved wasting time on pinball machines, and as a young man, would invest hours on these games in the companiable squalor of the basement common room of SOAS. There was a young Yemeni poet who was his most determined partner. SOAS had initially been established in the middle of the First World War as a semi-independent department of state. It's principle aim being to teach diplomats and imperial administrators about the languages and culture they would have to work with. But England being England, it both did this, but also became an almost comical reversal of itself. I remember following Robert down for a cup of tea, before some lecture, to this hive of student militancy. Every conceivable revolutionary and insurrectionary movement in our world was represented by posters on the walls, and stacks of pamphlets on the tables, flyers on the floor and stapled to the doors, with at least half the tables being actively used for some loud, impassioned impromptu political meetings.

Robert never sold himself to a big corporation but always preferred to work with small businesses and self-governing charities. He loved a glass of red rioja, almost as much as me, but despite sharing many bottles together, he would never be drawn into any vintage chateau chatter. I can remember how that topic was decisively dismissed, 'I select my wine from whatever is stacked up on the discount shelf in the supermarket'. Robert as a young man had experimented with every mind-altering, mood enhancing drug in existence, but had come to the sage decision in the middle of his life that wine gave the most reliable and controllable lift.

The daily tenor of his life was otherwise remarkably calm and self-sufficient. Breakfast of brown toast with honey and coffee with milk, led to a round or two of solitaire (a solo card game which he in later life would play on the computer screen) followed by the *Times* crossword. He was then ready to write, fiction in the morning, a twenty-minute nap after lunch, then non-fiction in the afternoon, all to the background hum of music. He had an eclectic library of hundreds of CD's, old tapes and records – and much preferred to experience his music this way, rather than attend a live concert.

I once tried to talk to Robert about the influence of his father on his work, and whether his fictional interest with powerful sheikhs and the recording of dreams and fantasies, did not lead in some way back to his relationship with this man. I can remember the snort of derision with which he greeted this polite speculation, so what I now write, has been officially denied at its source.

As well as hating his school days, Robert retained a powerful loathing for his father's father, a dentist who practiced in Workington in Cumberland. Ted Irwin confirmed this, 'our English grandfather, known as "Pop" by us, was a truly awful man. He treated his wife "Nana" like dirt and made a habit of seducing neighbour's wives, resulting in frequent house moves. He also had the appalling habit of kicking any dog that came within range of his feet.' Their mother was devoted to their father, yet she promised 'that if he let that man (Pop) anywhere near her children's teeth she would leave him'.

Robert's own father, (Joseph) Alan Irwin was of a completely different temperament, and as a young man training to be a doctor was called up to serve in the Royal Army Medical Corps during the last war. He never spoke so much as a word about his experiences at that time. Although a peaceable man, he clearly knew how to use his fists, especially when he saw a Canadian soldier pushing his luck too forcefully on a Dutch girl at a rowdy barn dance. He knocked the man down and rescued Wilhemina Cornelia Drapers. That impulsive action began a love affair that lasted all their lives, and Robert was born soon after their post-war marriage. His mother's father was an established figure in Dutch society, the Royal Notary or some such thing, and presided every year over his three daughters and their extended families who were summoned to spend three weeks in the Grand beach Hotel (in Schevening) on the Dutch coast where he took over a whole floor.

After the war, Alan Irwin continued his medical training but got drawn towards psychology and eventually rose to become Superintendent of the

Holloway Sanitorium, near Virginia Water. It was a vast Victorian complex, spread over 22 acres, with around 380 patients and 230 staff. Robert, his mother, and younger brother knew this Asylum well, helping his father humanise the place by playing there in the summer as well as attending Christmas Day celebrations. Ted Irwin wrote to me, 'he was a good psychiatrist and beloved by those that worked with him. This I know because I once did a holiday job in the records office at Holloway. He could be "on call" a couple of nights a week and summoned to local police stations to "section" disturbed offenders.' He also sat on tribunals at Broadmoor.

My suggestion to Robert that he had witnessed his father rule over this palace of madmen, like an enlightened Sultan, eavesdropping on their dreams whilst administering drugs, might have influenced some of his own work was once again roundly dismissed. Instead I was informed how his mother and father had very bland contemporary taste (completely anti-gothic tendencies), building a light-filled suburban house outside Farnham, surrounded by fir trees and whose only ornament was a swimming pool. Far from being a Sultan his father switched off from his professional responsibilities by such simple and repetitive tasks as swimming, gardening, and sunbathing. This was confirmed by his brother Ted who wrote, 'he was handsome, a Ronald Colman lookalike, a good tennis player, swimmer, and diver. I think that he was disappointed that neither Robert nor I showed any sporting talent. The most surprising thing about Dad was that he wrote the script for the annual Hospital Sports & Social Club Panto, "Sisterella", "Babes on the Ward", hit after hit.'

Years later, Robert did tell me what had affected him most deeply about his father, and it was a tale of everyday domestic terror that had stuck into him like a knife, and could and will probably happen in some shape or form to us all. It began with his beloved five-year-old daughter being rushed into hospital with a mastoid bone infection, the stress of which brought on Robert's first attack of neuralgia. His medically trained father sprang into immediate action, and quickly came up to give sympathy at St Thomas's hospital. That evening Alan was floored by a massive stroke, and a failed rescue operation left him unconscious for thirteen years, the rest of his life. All that knowledge and experience lost and turned into a drooling half animated doll, albeit one lovingly cared-for by his wife. Then to cap it all, Robert's mother (who had bought her own ambulance, so that she could take her husband home for the weekends from the hospital) was undermined by dementia which deteriorated into a paranoia that made her distrust her own children. This was his acknowledged burden.

I was fascinated to hear a slightly different perception of these events from his younger brother Ted. 'Dad, as I remember it, suffered a sub-arachnoid haemorrhage and collapsed in the bathroom smashing his head on the corner of the bath as he fell. The failed operation that caused his final paralysis was to tie off the blood vessel that originally caused his collapse. His final words to me as they wheeled him into theatre were: "Listen if this operation doesn't work, no switching me off. I will take whatever life there is". He was effectively "locked in" unable to communicate by any of the many means we tried. However, he undoubtedly enjoyed watching football on telly with me.'

In later life, Robert was immensely proud of his daughter who worked at the Oxford Refugee Study centre. He also liked and admired his Irish son-in-law, whose first book had been on the troubled border of Northern Ireland. But he had gained even greater status by abandoning the academic gravy train in order to dedicate himself to the organisation of the Palestine Solidarity Campaign. I murmured something about secular saints which was politely ignored. For his wife Helen was another source of immense pride. On retiring from running the British parliament, in black robes and a hair whig, she was invited to visit other elected chambers and share her knowledge about the pragmatic details, such as: how to set up select committees, how to take evidence and how to write it up in reports. And Robert was allowed to come along on some of these travels with a sense of purpose, as her plus one. And he had learned something very important from his father, which was to enjoy swimming and to enjoy lying completely idle beside a swimming pool. I agreed that was a useful skill to inherit.

Does this all add up? Not quite yet.

Robert only wrote one factual memoir, which avoids any mention of his boarding schools or his time at Merton College Oxford or his family but chronicles his years as a highly impressionable student between 1964 and 1967. In this period he travelled across Europe every summer for three years to Mostaganem, on the northern coast of Algeria (just east of Oran) to attend a residential *zaouia*. At this place he formally converted to Islam. He learned to recite the Arabic of the Qur'an as a living revelation, not as a dry manuscript to be annotated. He learned to dance, or circle for the love of God, like St Francis of Assissi, and the Mevlevi dervishes. It is the period before he met and fell in love with his wife Helen, and before he met his lifelong friend Hugh Kennedy (who would rise to become Professor of Arabic at SOAS), so neither of these two intimates, feel able to comment on these years, or the how and the why he identified as a Muslim for the rest of his life. I can remember hearing the intensity of this belief on just one occasion, which left me in no doubt that he believed in free will, and that his actions on this earth were vital choices, and that at some stage he would be called to account for them. Maybe a neo-Platonist could have said much the same thing in ancient Athens, the vital need to strive for knowledge in this life as the truest act of worship that an intelligent man can express from his gifts.

Memoirs of a Dervish is a fascinating and revealing, but also confusing book. It is a personal map of youthful experience, with no space for the historian. So there is no mention of the complexities of Algerian history, which had in 1962 emerged from an intense and savage War of National Liberation that in eight years had killed at least 400,000 Algerians to the loss of 26,000 French servicemen. The existence of this *zaouia*, freely welcoming naïve inquiring westerners to its assemblies, after such a brutal national experience, is therefore even more extraordinary. Esther Freud's novel, *Hideous Kinky*, observes this same community, albeit through the eyes of a young daughter, accompanying her mother across Morocco in order to reach the *zaouia* at Mostaganem. The Alawiyya brotherhood was founded during the strongest and most intense period of French rule in Algeria by Ahmed Al Alawi (1869-1934), who combined an easy-going tolerance of his Christian neighbours ('if only they would abandon the concept of the trinity and the incarnation there would be no difference between us') with suspicion of what the slow creeping spread of western secularism would do to the strengths of traditional society. So he was both easy going with European languages and its peoples, but intensely proud of his North African heritage: his clothing, his poverty, his virtual illiteracy and the fifteen-year traditional apprenticeship in learning that he received from his teacher, a sheikh of the Darkawi. As part of this confident yet tolerant heritage, the brotherhood opened branches in France for Algerians working in France, and tried to support the last Caliph-Sultan of the Ottoman Empire.

Roberrt Irwin at the *Critical Muslim* editorial board meeting, 12 March 2014. Photo: Rehan Jamil

Robert Irwin has written elsewhere on all these historical matters, which left him free in his own youthful memoir, to quote from my own published review,

> to dwell on a lifetime of reading, selective drug-taking, chanting, eastern travel and dancing, all undertaken in the search for God. Or at least the God within us, for Irwin is both sincere in his quest and like all true searchers also terrified of the final encounter. At one moment he reflects that 'believing one is in love with the Invisible…was perhaps, like falling in love with a girl whom one has never seen' and yet two sentences later he speculates that 'the mystic union between man and God was horrific and obscene, like copulation between a man and a shark'.

Yet when Irwin was a disciple of the dervish community at Mostaganem he soon got used to everyday visions, but as his teacher warns him 'if you see a miracle, let it pass like a train before you…and continue on the Road'. Similarly, Irwin would later learn that the physical ecstasy of the mystical circular dances of the brotherhood (the Imara) was not an end in itself but a door opening in the search for purity and peace. The process could be likened to both a war dance and an instance of possession – where 'it was as if something vast, alien and dispassionate was reaching into the heart of me to take me over'.

Irwin was a welcome guest at Mostaganem, though he makes it clear that he was never completely trusted by the Shaykh. This is in refreshing contrast to the vast majority of spiritual memoirs that I have worked my way through, whose overriding purpose is to raise the spiritual authority of the author.

Another surprising element of *Memoirs of a Dervish* is that it is consistently funny about the mystical search by westerners. The text bristles with brilliantly re-imagined comic scenes: the whispered aside that punctuates the theatrical but false solemnity of a pagan ritual, the horrors of being appraised during a naked encounter group or the babble of seasonal nonsense at a hippy poetry convention. He is also cruelly accurate with self-mockery, be it the opening line:

'It was in my first year at Oxford that I decided I wanted to be a Muslim saint'

or in depicting himself:

'I was pale and thin and my hands shook from unfocused intensity.'

Irwin is also receptively alive to the other world outside the closed meeting halls of the gurus. The impact of the Velvet Underground, the merits of Donovan versus Dylan, the Sufi origins of Eric Clapton's 'Layla', or the redemptive power of the film 'If', are all treated not as the disposable scum of pop culture, but important enough to be put beside such key influences as John Fowles's *The Magus* or J.D. Salinger's *Franny and Zooey*. But in the process, he also introduces you to more gurus, sheikhs, spiritual movements, and masters than is good for either your sanity or chequebook. Most are revealed to be exploitative charlatans, on the Scientology scale of worthlessness. Others, such as R.D. Laing and the School of Economic Science, are given savagely short shrift. The claims of the latter to teach philosophy are described as 'sub-occult tripe from Ouspensky'. P.J. Bennet and (Frithjof) Schuon are also dissected ruthlessly but you are at least left with some respect for their original integrity, even if it was later occluded by egocentric madness. Others, like an old lecturer at Oxford, John Aiken, is affectionately assessed as 'a walking encyclopaedia of dodgy knowledge'. Fortunately there are a few magnificent, if deeply flawed, characters amongst this circus of intellects and Islamic-inclined God searchers whose work remains useful: Bernard Lewis before his Neo-Con apotheosis, his successor at SOAS, the American-born John Wansbrough (judged 'one of the most remarkable men I have ever met') and the Ottoman emigre and scholar of Ibn Arabi, Ali Bulent, and a reticent scholar of manuscripts at the British Library, Martin Lings.

Irwin never turns his potent invective on his teachers back at Mostaganem. Indeed, if there is a single heroic figure in *Memoirs of a Dervish*, it is Abdullah Faid, a Breton sailor long converted to Islam, a long-term resident of the Sufi *zaouia* in Mostagenam, who acts as a sort of spiritual assistant to the ruling Shaykh – especially when it comes to greeting and instructing visiting westerners. The sad tale of how he and his master would be treated, first as dissidents, then as potential traitors, by the Algerian Ministry of the Interior is like a dark shadow that grows into a true horror story.

The importance of this period on the lifelong creative imagination of Robert Irwin is clear, even if the details are opaque. As we are often warned, 'be careful what you show an eighteen-year-old mind'. Or let us be grateful, that the summer holidays from Cambridge tramping across central Asia helped inspire William Dalrymple, as it did Patrick Leigh Fermor charming his way across pre-war Middle Europe, or Robert Irwin dedicating his student summer holidays to a Sufi confraternity in western Algeria.

Robert Graham Irwin, Muslim scholar, historian, novelist, polymath
23 August 1946–28 June 2024

THE LIST

A DOZEN MEDIA OUTLETS TO CHECK OUT (DAILY)

Stuff the BBC. Forget Sky News, CNN, and the rest of the so-called legacy media. Quit Facebook, shun TikTok, and the rest of the pestiferous social media. The Gaza genocide has exposed the true façade of conventional, mainstream media in the West; and the toxic nature of western dominated online platforms. So, enough said about their bias, the western establishment propaganda they espouses, and how they subtly and not so subtly dehumanises non-western cultures. Be reasonable; spurn the bastards! Instead, here is our list of a dozen media outlets you ought to be watching, reading, streaming, and supporting.

1. Al-Jazeera (English)

We take our hats off to al-Jazeera. There is no television news channel that comes close to the breath of its coverage, from Tierra del Fuego to the Arctic Circle, the Far East to the far West, and all-around Africa. In its coverage of Gaza, Al-Jazeera not only excelled but put every western channel to shame. While BBC, CNN, and other reporters were riding with the Israeli army, or conducting interviews from the comfortable safety of Tel Aviv or Jerusalem, Al-Jazeera journalists were reporting from Gaza with bombs and artillery dropping around and on them. It is mostly due to Al-Jazeera that the world saw the true horror of the genocide of Gaza. Some of its journalists were deliberately targeted and killed by the IDF. It also has some of the best documentaries anywhere on topics as wide ranging as global warming, Germany's Israel obsession, Burkina Faso's agricultural development, and, of course, the war on Gaza.

2. Al Araby

Arabic speaking folks tend to turn to Al Araby Television Network, which is also based in Qatar and has acquired a reputation for objectivity and journalistic professionalism. It began life in London in 2015, but moved to Quatar in 2022 to focus more on the region where its core Arab audience are concentrated. Al Araby is not so much concerned with some fake notion neutrality but strongly supports and promoted the right of Arabs to freedom of expression, integrity, and political participation – a brave stance in a region dominated by dictators and monarchs. Al Araby is in fact three outlets: Al Araby TV which is a news and current affairs channel, Al Araby 2 devoted to cultural entertainment, and Al Araby al-Jadeed, which is a pan Arab news website and daily newspaper. The pages of Al Araby al-Jadeed are full of columns and op-ed opinion pieces from the Arab world's most prominent authors. We have counted over a hundred. So all the diversity of opinion of the Arab world, with all its contradictions, is to be found at Al Araby al-Jadeed.

3. TRT World TV

The Turkish global channel, TRT World TV, started shakily in 2015. Its earlier news presentations were a bit amateurish and production values left something to be desired. But it transformed beyond recognition within a few years. It's a slick operation with truly global coverage and solid reporting from the ground. Its coverage of the Gaza genocide was second only to al-Jazeera, and its reportage of Muslim issues is next to none. TRT has also become a gathering place for Western dissidents, like Avi Shlaim and Richard Folk, and diaspora Muslims like Ebrahim Moosa. And the channel is the only place where you are likely to see the adventures of Oruc Reis, the Ottoman Sultan of Algiers, and witness the greatness of Mevlana Jalaluddin al-Rumi. But, in all honesty, the Turkish government PR needs to be toned down – seriously.

4. The Guardian / Observer

The Guardian is, and remains, the only truly independent newspaper in the UK; and it should be read and supported by all fair-minded folks on this best of all possible planets – the Earth. It is the only media outlet that called what happened in Gaza with the correct word: genocide. And, it has reported, the death and destruction perpetuated by Isreal with proper context, unflinching honesty, and in appropriate horrific details. It is the kind of paper where you will find investigations such as 'Isreal demanded Google and Amazon use secret "wink" to sidestep legal orders'. And 'long reads' such as 'A "magic pill" make Israeli violence invisible, we need to stop swallowing it'. It has some truly superb commentators – including the fearless and perceptive Nesrine Malik, the consistently magnificent Aditya Chakrabortty, Owen Jones, George Monbiot, and Jonathan Freedland (who always manages to suppress his love for Zionism and come out on the side of justice, Bravo!). Even though the sister paper, the *Observer*, which comes out on Sundays, has been carted off and sold to someone called Tortoise media, it still retains much of its original concerns for social justice, fair play, and fair reporting. And, to top it all, it is freely available to all, everywhere – not behind some ridiculous paywall. But we recommend, you subscribe, if you can.

4. The National

Across the border in Scotland, there is *The National*, which only emerged in 2014. It is somehow connected to the Scottish National Party, and thus, not surprisingly, champions independence for Scotland. But apart from that, it is a cracking good read, with a very strong sense of social justice. Recent front pages such as 'How Genocide Happened' (13 October 2015), listing the 'damning words – from the country's own prime minister, press and more', and 'What are you hiding Labour' (19 October 2025), on secret meetings between UK and Israeli ministers, clearly show where *The National* stands. It is also lovely to have someone on the up and up who fearlessly puts down the UK government at every misstep!

THE LIST: A DOZEN MEDIA OUTLETS TO CHECK OUT (DAILY)

6. Zateo

When the exceptional, sharp-witted, Mehdi Hasan, was fired from MSNBC for his stand on Palestine, he brushed his shoulders, and launched Zeteo. For the uninitiated, Zeteo is an ancient Greek word meaning 'seeking out' and striving'. That's about the only opaque thing about Zeteo. The rest is as clear as micellar water; Zeteo cuts through lies, propaganda, and disinformation with hard evidence, strong arguments and with some panache. It is an astonishing success story that took the Substack world by storm. It is where you should go for real in-depth analysis, and really hard-hitting interviews with the likes of Zohran Mamdani, the Mayoral candidate for New York, Mohammad Yonus the interim Prime Minister of Bangladesh, and Eylon Levy, the British Israeli who serves as Israeli government spokesman. Splendid, gasping stuff. Zeteo declared it is not just a media company but a movement for media accountability. God speed, we say!

7. Middle East Eye

Co-founded by David Hearst, former foreign correspondent of the *Guardian*, *Middle East Eye* has become an indispensable source on the Muslim world since its launch in 2014. Its coverage of the Gaza genocide and Israel has been an exhausting regime of exposé after exposé. And it has a string of great regular contributors and commentors, including the Canadian journalist and lawyer Faisal Kutty, the former Israeli negotiator Danial Levy, the former Prime Minister of Türkiye Ahmet Davutoglu, and British journalists Peter Oborne and Jonathan Cook. Not surprisingly, it has been banned and blocked in Egypt, Jordan, and Saudi Arabia.

8. New Lines Magazine

It describes itself as 'a local magazine for the world'. *New Lines* is devoted largely to long form essays and reportage, it has carried reports about influencers in Syria, Poland's Bisons, to Argentina's textile industry. There is also plenty of good pieces on Gaza, Palestine, and Isreal, including first person account. It has some very good journalists, including Hassan

Hassan, who covered the Iraq war for the *Guardian*, Faisal al Yafai, the former investigative reporter for the *Guardian*, and Danny Postel, formerly of openDemocracy. Most of its writers are from the area they are writing about and thus have a grasp of the local culture. When it first started some seven, eight years ago, *New Lines* had a great deal of fire and anger. It has become somewhat subdued since; and lost a bit of its initial edge. However, certainly worth a regular read.

9. Haaretz

Diamonds are sometimes found in coal mines. And *Haaretz* is a polished diamond. It is one of the oldest – founded in 1918 – daily newspaper and the only thing coming out of Israel that suggests that there is a modicum of human life still untouched by supremacy, fascism, and pathological paranoia in, what its detractors call, the 'Zionist entity'. *Haaretz* not only opposes the occupation of the Palestinian territories but actively supports Israeli Arabs as well other marginalised communities. It coverage of the genocide in Gaza was both honest and eye popping. It columnists and opinion contributors are outspoken and seldom mince their words; Gideon Levy, the Palestinian affairs columnist, alone is worth his weight in gold! If the majority of the Israelis read *Haaretz*, peace will prevail all over the world. If only!

10. Wired

It may be a technology magazine, but *Wired* has a long history of investigating journalism, and strong sense of objectivity. Its analysis of cybersecurity, privacy and hacks is unmatched. Once you have flipped through coverage of technology (and some science) stories, you will come across 'The Big Story' about killer chatbots, the darker side of AI, Peter Thiel's Antichrist obsession, the madness of rich white guys who want to live forever, and how tech billionaires captured the White House. Its Spring 2025 'Money Issue' – who has the money, how they wield it, and what it means for the rest of us – is a superb expose of an industry awash with trillions. It should also be noted that *Wired* was the first to begin reporting on the dubious links between Trump's administration and various tech bros and billionaires hungry for influence at the beginning of his second presidency. Bravery remains a virtue in these postnormal times!

11. The Atlantic

In its heyday, *The Atlantic Monthly*, campaigned to abolish slavery, published slave narratives, championed educational reform, and exposed racism. While the magazine printed stories by Ernest Hemingway and the letters of Martin Luther King Jr, the Atlantic Monthly press published groundbreaking fiction such as Walter Edmond's *Drums Along the Mohawk*. But all that is history. The press has ceased to exist. The magazine became *The Atlantic*, shedding its month moniker and appearing ten times a year. (But it may yet go back to being monthly!). It does, however, its tradition of publishing detailed investigations, lengthy essays, and feisty opinion pieces. It is strongly anti-Trump; but a not-so-critical supporter of the Democrats. It championed the Christian Zionist Joe Biden and the Wall Street loving Hilary Clinton. And it has fallen as low as to promote the cult of scientology. Still, it is probably the only American magazine worth reading nowadays.

12. Daily Maverick

The only criticism we have of the *Daily Maverick* is that it is not a daily but a weekly newspaper. Since its launch in 2009, the South African paper has lived up to its motto to 'Defend Truth'. It is a forceful defender of democracy in South Africa and quite objective and balanced in its coverage. We have enjoyed some refreshing South African voices here. By necessity, we suppose, it focuses on local stories but it manages to show how Africa is changing with a style of its own. It is also nice to see a periodical that is sharp in its criticism and striking in its layouts.

13. Declassified UK

Ok. We lied! Actually, its baker's dozen, which as we all know is 13: in the good old days, when empathy and generosity were real values, bakers used to add an extra one when packing orders of twelve loafs. Hoping that genuine virtues may return to this age of post truth, we offer a bomber bonus. Focused on the nasty side of Great Britain, Declassified UK (DCUK) investigates how the British government, military, media, corporations as well as colonial legacy and empire undermine human rights and the environment not just in the UK but all over the world. It is the sort of place you go to find how many British MPs are filling their pockets with Israeli lobby funds, where in the world British troops are illegally operating, how the likes of the BBC try to fool their audience with claims to neutrality, and the pro-Israeli bias of newswire. You will also find historical analysis of colonial crimes from Ireland to Indonesia. DCUK is totally independent and its journalists *really* know how to investigate. So it naturally puts conventional British media to shame.

We also recommend that you read, devour, and follow: Chris Hodges, Caitlin Johnstone, Owen Jones, Carole Cadwalladr, Shaun King, Andrew Brown, Antony Loewenstein (watch his film on Germany), and Craig Murray, former British ambassador to Uzbekistan, on Substack. Look for the English version of Egyptian publication *Mada Masr*, which is often under pressure from the authorities (but then who isn't, it's Egypt,); the independent *Enab Baladi*, which was originally started by women in revolutionary Daraya, Syria, and handed out in the street, but is now online and much bigger; and Byline News, Media Lens, and Novara Media, whose reporters and commentators know how to call a spade a spade (unlike BBC journalists).

CITATIONS

Introduction: This *is* the BBC by Ziauddin Sardar

Peter Oborne's *Complicit: Britain's Role in the Destruction of Gaza* is published by OR Books (2025); *Bad News from Israel* and *More Bad News from Israel* by Greg Philo and Mike Berry are both published by Pluto Press (2004 and 2007); *Dianarama: The shocking true story of deception, cover-ups and the Panorama scandal that betrayed Princess Diana* by Andy Webb is published by Michael Joseph (2025); *Strange Places, Questionable People* by John Simpson is published by Pan (1999); and a new edition of *Why is this lying bastard lying to me?* by Rob Burley is published by Mulark (2024).

'BBC on Gaza-Israel' and other reports from the Centre for Media Monitoring can be accessed from: cfmm.org.uk. Francesca Albanese's report, 'Gaza Genocide: a collective crime' can be accessed at: https://www.ohchr.org/en/documents/country-reports/a80492-gaza-genocide-collective-crime-report-special-rapporteur-situation

David Aaronovitch's article, 'The Prescott memo flunks the impartiality test' can be found at: https://observer.co.uk/news/opinion-and-ideas/article/the-prescott-memo-flunks-the-impartiality-test

Peter Johnston's Report of the Editorial Review into Gaza: How to Survive a Warzone' can be accessed at: https://www.bbc.co.uk/aboutthebbc/documents/report-peter-johnston-review-gaza-how-to-survive-a-warzone.pdf

See also the excellent articles by Alan Rusbridger, 'The real threat to BBC impartiality', *Prospect*, https://www.prospectmagazine.co.uk/ideas/media/bbc-news/71592/the-real-threat-to-bbc-impartiality and 'An inside job? Robbie Gibb's campaign to rewire the BBC' in the *Observer*, https://observer.co.uk/news/national/article/an-inside-job-robbie-gibbs-campaign-to-rewire-the-bbc; and Daniel Trilling, 'Inside the BBC's Gaza Fiasco', Equator.org

See Media Lens, 'Burying Genocide – The BBC, Gaza And The Role Of The UK', and 'Media silent over the 'Hannibal Directive on 7 October 2023', on https://medialens.substack.com

On the 40 'beheaded babies' story, see, in chronological order:

The Israeli news channel i24NEWS on 10 October 2023: (https://uni.oslomet.no/dscguide/case-study-2-hamas-beheadings/?) and https://x.com/i24NEWS_EN/status/1711697093151056355?s=20

The UK tabloid *Daily Mail* front-page "Hamas cut the throats of babies". https://www.dailymail.co.uk/news/article-12615031/Hamas-terrorists-beheaded-babies-kibbutz-slaughter-IDF-soldiers-reveal-horrific-scenes-carnage-discovered-site-scores-people-massacred.html and cover story "Holocaust Pure and Simple" https://x.com/hendopolis/status/1711858912217928095?s=61

The Times story citing beheadings of babies on 10 October 2023. "Hamas cut the throats of babies in massacre." https://x.com/hendopolis/status/1711857913604538858?s=20

President Biden statement on 12 October: https://x.com/dpatrikarakos/status/1712219633594376581?s=20 and tracking back: https://www.aljazeera.com/news/2023/10/12/white-house-walks-back-bidens-claim-he-saw-children-beheaded-by-hamas?utm_source=chatgpt.com

The *New York Times* 28 December 2023, 'Screams Without Words: How Hamas Weaponized Sexual Violence on Oct. 7': https://www.nytimes.com/2023/12/28/world/middleeast/oct-7-attacks-hamas-israel-sexual-violence.html

January 2024, Declassified UK report: https://www.declassifieduk.org/beheaded-babies-how-uk-media-reported-israels-fake-news-as-fact/?

The Intercept Debunking the NYT article: 'Between the Hammer and the Anvil" The Story Behind the New York Times October 7 Exposé' https://theintercept.com/2024/02/28/new-york-times-anat-schwartz-october-7/

and

New York Times Puts "Daily" Episode On Ice Amid Internal Firestorm Over Hamas Sexual Violence Article: https://web.archive.org/web/20240903020524/https://theintercept.com/2024/01/28/new-york-times-daily-podcast-camera/

2 March 2024 Al Jazeera examination of NYT article: https://www.aljazeera.com/video/the-listening-post/2024/3/2/the-unraveling-of-the-new-york-times-hamas-rape-story?utm_source=chatgpt.com

Le Monde debunking, '40 beheaded babies: deconstructing the rumor…' in April 2024 https://archive.ph/20250122231930/https://www.lemonde.fr/en/les-decodeurs/article/2024/04/03/40-beheaded-babies-the-itinerary-of-a-rumor-at-the-heart-of-the-information-battle-between-israel-and-hamas_6667274_8.html

And an article by Associated Press (May 22 2024) 'How 2 debunked accounts of sexual violence on Oct. 7 fuelled a global dispute over Israel-Hamas war". https://apnews.com/article/israel-hamas-war-sexual-violence-zaka-ca7905bf9520b1e646f86d72cdf03244

Jonathan Cook's journalism and podcast are available at Substack. 'Israel Exposed Archives' of literary millions of documents, 'Witnesses of Atrocities and Genocide' are available at: watermeloncrimes.com

Everything else mention in the article can be easily found on the web or social media.

Return to Cockburn by Andrew Brown

For Cockburn's memoires, see Claude Cockburn, I, Claude...The Autobiography of Claude Cockburn, Penguin, 1967. And for his outlook on journalism, see Patrick Cockburn, Believe Nothing Until It is Officially Denied: Claude Cockburn and the Invention of Guerrilla Journalism, Verso, 2025. Michael Frayn's, The Tin Men, is published by Faber and Faber, 2015. The Nelk Boys can be found on the YouTube.

Democracy and Indian Journalism by Shiv Visvanathan

On Indian emergency, see Gemma Scott, Gender, Women and the Indian Emergency 1975-1977, Routledge, 2025. On Amarnath, see Rajender Amernath's biography, Lala Amernath: Life and Times – The Making of a Legend, SportsBooks, 2007. There is also a biography of Chandrasekhara Venkata Raman by P R Pisharot, published by Indian Ministry of Information and Broadcasting, 2015.

A fiftieth edition of C L R James, Beyond the Boundary (1963), was published by Duke University Press in 2013. Jack Fingleton, Batting From Memory:An Autobiography was published by Collings in 1981. And Ashis Nandy's The Tao of Cricket came out in 1989 as OUP, India, paperback.
See also: Shiv Visvanathan, Theatres of Democracy: Between the Epic and Everyday, HarperCollings India, 2016, and A Carnival for Science, OUP, India, 2007.

My Digital Media Life by Eric Walberg

Books mention in this article, include: Douglas Rushkoff, Program or be Programmed, Soft Skull Press, 2011; Marshall McLuhan's The Medium is the

Massage, Penguin Classic, 1967; Malcolm Thomas, *The Luddites: Machine Breaking in Regency England,* David and Charles, London, 1970; and Herbert Schiller, *Mass Communication and American Empire*, A M Kelley, London, 1969.

See also: Eric Walberg, *Postmodern Imperialism*, Clarity Press, 2011; and E J Hobsbawm, E. J. (1952). 'The Machine Breakers'. *Past & Present* (1): 57–70. 1952; and Robert Wright's NonZero Newsletter.

Asad's *The Unromantic Orient* by Josef Linnhoff

The quotes are from: Muhammad Asad, *Islam at the Crossroads* (Gibraltar: Dar al-Andalus, 1982); Leopold Weiss, *Unromantisches Morgenland: Aus dem Tagebuch einer Reise* (Frankfurt am Main, 1924), with translations taken from Muhammad Asad, *The Unromantic Orient*, trans. Elma Ruth Harder (Kuala Lumpur: Islamic Book Trust, 2004); Muhammad Asad, *The Road to Mecca* (London: Max Reinhardt, 1954); Muhammad Arshad, ed. 'Muhammad Asad: Twenty-Six Unpublished Letters,' *Islamic Sciences* 14 (Summer 2016); Muhammad Asad and Pola Hamida Asad, *The Unpublished Letters of Muhammad Asad* (Kuala Lumpur: Islamic Book Trust, 2024); Asad's *Jerusalem: The Open City* and *A Vision of Jerusalem* can be found in Muhammad Asad, *This Law of Ours and Other Essays* (Kuala Lumpur: Islamic Book Trust, 2001); Asad's *Jerusalem: A City for All People* is found in Volume II of M. Ikram Chagatai, ed. *Europe's Gift to Islam: Muhammad Asad (Leopold Weiss) Volumes I and II* (Lahore: Sang-e-Meel Publications, 2006).

For studies on Asad's life and thought see Gunter Windhager, *Leopold Weiss alias Muhamm ad Asad - Von Galizien bis Arabien 1900-1927* (Vienna: Bohlau, 2008); Dominik Schlosser, *Lebensgesetz und Vergemeinschaftungsform: Muhammad Asad (1900-1992) und sein Islamverständnis* (Berlin:E-B Verlag, 2015). The most useful articles in English include Martin Kramer. 'The Roads from Mecca: Muhammad Asad' in *idem*, ed. *The Jewish Discovery of Islam: Studies in Honor of Bernard Lewis* (Tel Aviv: The Mosche Dayan Center for Middle Eastern and African Studies, 1999); 225-247; Josef Linnhoff, 'Asad: The Neglected Thinker' in *Critical Muslim 40: Biography,* ed. Zia Sardar (London: Hurst, 2021); 89-102; Furzana Bayri. 'Li-qawmin yatafakkarūn (Q. 30:21): Muhammad Asad's Qur'anic Translatorial *Habitus'*, *Journal of Qur'anic Studies* 21:2 (2019); 1- 38; Abraham Rubin. 'Muhammad Asad's Conversion to Islam as a Case Study in Jewish Self-Orientalization', *Jewish Social Studies: History, Culture and Society* 22:1 (Fall 2016); 1-28; Shalom Goldman, *From Jews to Muslims: Twentieth-Century Converts to Islam* (London: Lexington Books, 2024); 19-51.

The Suwayda Massacres by Robin Yassin-Kassab

The Prisons Museum that I, Nour and Omar work with has two websites: https://prisons.museum/en/isis , which documents ISIS prisons, and https://prisons.museum/en/syria, which documents the Assad regime's prisons.

Mazen al-Ezzi's investigation can be found here: https://daraj.media/en/the-hidden-pathways-to-breach-suwayda/

The Peoples Want manifesto can be read here: https://thepeopleswant.org/en/manifesto

Al-Jumhuriya, the publication that Nour Abo Farraj writes for, was founded by Syrians in 2012. It offers nuanced, intelligent writing from a progressive perspective. Some of the articles are in English as well as Arabic. See https://aljumhuriya.net

Hrant Dink- The Journalist as Martyr by Boyd Tonkin

The '23.5 Hrant Dink Site of Memory' is at Halaskargazi Cad. Sebat Apt. 74/1, Osmanbey 34371, Şişli, Istanbul: hrantdinksiteofmemory.org. Quotations from Dink's writing come from the materials available there. On modern Turkish-Armenian relations, see Ece Temelkuran, *Deep Mountain* (translated by Kenneth Dakar; Verso, 2010). Fethiye Çetin's *My Grandmother* illuminates the "crypto-Armenian" presence in Turkish life through memoir (trans. Maureen Freely; Verso, 2012); Elif Shafak's *The Bastard of Istanbul* explores the theme in fiction (Viking, 2006). On the killings of 1915 and their aftermath see Taner Akçam, *A Shameful Act: the Armenian Genocide and Question of Turkish Responsibility* (trans. Paul Bessemer; Constable, 2007), Ronald Grigor Suny, *"They can live in the desert but nowhere else": a History of the Armenian Genocide* (Princeton University Press, 2015), and Thomas de Waal, *Great Catastrophe: Armenians and Turks in the Shadow of Genocide* (Oxford University Press, 2015). On the end of the Sultans' Turkey see Ryan Gingeras, *The Last Days of the Ottoman Empire* (Allen Lane, 2022). Erik J Zürcher's *Turkey: a Modern History* (IB Tauris, 2017) surveys the 20th century and Hannah Lucinda Smith's *Erdogan Rising: the Battle for the Soul of Turkey* (William Collins, 2019) the first decisive events of the 21st. Maureen Freely's "Why they killed Hrant Dink" (*Index on Censorship*, 36(2), 2007) lucidly presents the background to the assassination. Mohammed Alrmizan's study of "The historical development of the Turkish Press" appears in the *Dirasat* series (no. 46, 2019) of the King Faisal Centre for Research and Islamic Studies (kfcris.com). Orhan Pamuk's *Istanbul: Memories and City*, translated by Maureen Freely, was published by Faber & Faber (2005), as were his novels *The Museum of Innocence* (trans. Maureen Freely, 2009) and *The Black Book* (trans. Maureen Freely, 2006). Ahmet Hamdi Tanpinar's *The Time Regulation Institute* is published by Penguin Modern Classics (trans. Alexander Dawe and Maureen Freely, 2014). I have benefited from interviews, both formal and informal, with Orhan Pamuk and Elif Shafak (see for instance, Boyd Tonkin, *The Faber Interview: Orhan Pamuk* (October 2022; faber.co.uk), and from Maureen Freely's profound knowledge and understanding of Hrant Dink's Istanbul.

System Failure by James Brooks

Roger Hallam's *HardTalk* interview is available at https://tinyurl.com/4b8djann. 'What could happen if we just stopped oil? Six billion might die', Neil Record, *The Telegraph*, 19 December 2023 is available at https://tinyurl.com/ycy8k636. 'Prediction by Extinction Rebellion's Roger Hallam that climate change will kill 6 billion people by 2100 is unsupported', Scott Johnson (ed.), Science Feedback, 22 August 2019 can be found at https://tinyurl.com/r6whbyfw. Clip of BBC Radio 4 *More or*

Less discussion on climate change deaths is at https://tinyurl.com/2sns26px.

'Just Stop Foiled: Mastermind of eco mob Just Stop Oil nicked after The Sun blew whistle on plot to block motorway network', Scarlett Howes, *The Sun*, 6 November 2022 is at https://tinyurl.com/bddrfky7 and 'Just Appalling: I went undercover to smash Just Stop Oil's plot to halt M25 and was shocked by sinister boasts of sneering ringleaders', Scarlett Howes, *The Sun*, 19 July 2024 is at https://tinyurl.com/eyecu889. 'Global economy could face 50% loss in GDP between 2070 and 2090 from climate shocks, say actuaries', Sandra Laville, The Guardian, 16 January 2025, is available at https://tinyurl.com/bu777atr. Roger Hallam's social media comment on the report is at https://tinyurl.com/2s425s79.

'It is worse…' quote from *The Uninhabitable Earth: Life After Warming*, David Wallace-Wells (Tim Duggan Books, 2019). António Guterres quotes from speech published on United Nations website as 'Secretary-General warns of climate emergency, calling Intergovernmental Panel's report "a file of shame", while saying leaders "are lying", fuelling flames' at https://tinyurl.com/2vpxj9dr.

'Ocean Acidification: Another Planetary Boundary Crossed', Helen S. Findlay et al, *Global Change Biology*, 9 June 2025 is at https://doi.org/10.1111/gcb.70238. Coral tipping point study from Planetary Health Check 2025: https://www.planetaryhealthcheck.org/. Thermal satellite image of East China Sea heatwave: https://tinyurl.com/3pe4hr2t.
Jennifer Lawrence *Don't Look Up* clip can be viewed at https://tinyurl.com/rsj279dv. John Schellnhuber clip is at https://tinyurl.com/47wuh246.

PMC definition from 'The Professional-Managerial Class', Barbara and John Ehrenreich, Radical America volume 11, number 2 (March-April 1977), available in PDF format at https://tinyurl.com/2u5twjn3. Andrew Marr / Naom Chomsky interview is available at https://tinyurl.com/2kcytd62.

Journalism Has Futures by C Scott Jordan

The following were referenced or utilised in the writing of this piece, Steven Cushion's *Beyond Mainstream Media: Alternative Media and the Future of Journalism*, (London & New York, Routledge, 2024); Edward S. Herman and Noam Chomsky's *Manufacturing Consent: The Political Economy of the Mass Media*, (New York, Pantehon Books, 2002); Anand Giridharadas's *The Persuaders: Winning Hearts and Minds in a Divided Age*, (London, Allen Lane, 2022); and Werner Herzog's *The Future of Truth*, (New York, Penguin Press, 2025).

For more recent instances of futures challenges in the world of journalism see Mark Sweney's '"Existential crisis": how Google's shift to AI has upended the online news model,' *The Guardian*, 6 September 2025; and Ann Kennedy Smith's 'Two voices: On writing fiction and journalism and how they intertwine,' *Times Literary Supplement*, 22 August 2025.

For more on postnormal times theory, see Ziauddin Sardar and John Sweeney's 'The Three Tomorrows of Postnormal Times' in *The Postnormal Times Reader* (London, IIIT & CPPFS, 2017 or visit the website postnormaltim.es

CONTRIBUTORS

● **Ibrahim N Abusharif** is Associate Professor, Journalism and Strategic Communication Programme, Northwestern University in Qatar ● **Andrew Brown**, veteran journalist, worked on the *Independent* and the *Guardian* for decades before his intellectual rigour proved too much for his employers ● **James Brooks** is a science journalist ● **Khuda Bushq** is travelling around the world cheering for Zohran Mamdani after receiving his doctorate ● **Saoussen Ben Cheikh** is a researcher and the founder of MENA-can, an initiative that supports changemakers in fragile contexts across the MENA region ● **Abdullah Geelah** has been on a research trip to Canada, the US, and South Africa, to explore best practice in mosque architecture ● **C Scott Jordan** has been recently appointed Deputy Director, International Institute of Futures Studies, at the International Islamic University Malaysia ● **Yahia Lababidi**, an Egyptian- American thinker and poet, is the author of eleven collections of poetry and prose ● **Josef Linnhoff** is Editor-in-Chief, The Institute for Advanced Usuli Studies ● **Wietske Merison** is a poet, musician, Muslim chaplain, and doctoral candidate in Islamic law at UCLA ● **Shamim Miah**, Senior Lecturer in Education at Huddersfield University, is Senior Fellow of the Centre for Postnormal Policy and Futures Studies ● **M Yaqub Mirza**, a pioneering figure in Islamic finance, is the co-founder and Chairman of the Board of Trustees of Amana Mutual Funds Trust, which he helped develop from concept to managing billions in assets ● **Hamida Riahi** is a Tunisian academic and author of *A Study of Intertextuality in Mohja Kahf's E-Mails from Scheherazad* ● **Barnaby Rogerson** is a British author and founder of Eland Books ● **Muhammad Saad** is lead script writer for Eon Podcast, a digital media organisation based in Lahore with over a million subscribers across various social media platforms ● **Leila Sansour**, a Palestinian British filmmaker, is best known for her feature documentaries *Jeremy Hardy v. The Israeli Army* and *Open Bethlehem*, both released in UK cinemas and screened at the British Parliament and the US Congress ● **Zain Sardar**, a philosopher, is programme manager at the Aziz Foundation, London ● **Boyd Tonkin**, literary critic and internationally renowned journalist, won the Benson Medal of the Royal Society of Literature ● **Shiv Visvanathan**, Professor at the O P Jindal Global University, Sonepat, is a well-known Indian intellectual and political commentator ● **Eric Walberg**, Canadian Muslim journalist, specialises on the Middle East, Central Asia and Russia ● **Robin Yassin-Kassab**'s book about the post-Assad transition in Syria, *The Blood Between Us*, will be published in June 2026 ● **Saba Zahoor** is an engineer from Kashmir who turns to poetry as a way of tracing memory, longing, and the quiet, fleeting moments of everyday life.